Praise for

Autism Spectrum Disorders

"This is the book we've all been waiting for. It is an essential source of information and advice in plain everyday language that can help anyone who is affected by autism today, from the parent of a newly diagnosed child, to someone who has been in the trenches for years. Kudos to Chantal for providing us with this long overdue, user-friendly, how-to guide for dealing with autism."

—Portia Iversen,
  cofounder and scientific liaison, Cure Autism Now Foundation (CAN)

"Both parents and professionals will find a wealth of useful information in this user-friendly book written by a parent who really knows about living with a child on the autistic spectrum."

—Cathy Mercer,
  The National Autistic Society (UK)

"Chantal Sicile-Kira has written an encyclopedic book with care and concern for those persons who must deal with autism. It reads clearly and provides answers to the important questions. I recommend it most highly."

—Joseph E. Morrow, Ph.D.,
  professor of psychology, California State University, Sacramento,
  and president, Applied Behavior Consultants

"The essential book that parents, health professionals, and a wide readership will reach for in order to fathom this confounding condition."

—Douglas Kennedy,
  author of *The Big Picture, The Job,* and *The Pursuit of Happiness*

Autism Spectrum Disorders

*The Complete Guide to Understanding
Autism, Asperger's Syndrome,
Pervasive Developmental Disorder,
and Other ASDs*

CHANTAL SICILE-KIRA

A PERIGEE BOOK

A Perigee Book
Published by The Berkley Publishing Group
A division of Penguin Group (USA) Inc.
375 Hudson Street
New York, New York 10014

Perigee trade paperback edition: September 2004

Perigee trade paperback ISBN: 978-0-399-53047-0

Visit our website at www.penguin.com

Library of Congress Cataloging-in-Publication Data

Sicile-Kira, Chantal.
    Autism spectrum disorders : the complete guide to understanding autism, Asperger's syndrome, pervasive developmental disorder, and other ASDs / Chantal Sicile-Kira.— 1st Perigee pbk. ed.
    p. cm.
    ISBN 0-399-53047-9
    1. Autism—Popular works.   2. Autism in children—Popular works.   3. Asperger's syndrome—Popular works.   4. Developmental disabilities—Popular works.   I. Title.

RC553.A88S566 2004
616.85'882—dc22

                                                                        2004052935

Printed in the United States of America

15 17 19 20 18 16 14

For Jeremy, Rebecca, and Daniel,
the stars of my universe.

I know of nobody who is purely autistic or purely neurotypical. Even God had some autistic moments, which is why the planets all spin.

—Jerry Newport, Your Life Is Not a Label

The history of man's progress is a chronicle of authority refuted.

—Author unknown

CONTENTS

ACKNOWLEDGMENTS

MANY people have contributed in different ways to this book. However, if it were not for two people in particular, the thought of writing a sort of "guide for dummies" about autism would never have occurred to me. First of all, my son Jeremy is the reason this book exists at all. His attempts to understand our world, coupled with his extraordinary (if a bit obsessive) attachment to simple objects, never ceases to amaze me.

Second, my friend Debra Ginsberg (*Waiting, Raising Blaze, About My Sisters*) convinced me that I could—and should—write the book I always wished I could find in a bookstore. For this, and her constant support and pearls of wisdom, I am ever grateful. If it were not for Douglas Kennedy (*The Big Picture, The Job, The Pursuit of Happiness, A Special Relationship*), Charlie Viney, James Levine, and Sheila Curry Oakes, this book might still be a manuscript. Many thanks to them for sharing my vision.

This book would not have seen the light of day without the encouragement and support of some experts who gave generously of their time to read parts of the manuscript and give me input: Bernard Rimland, Ph.D. (director, Autism Research Institute); Portia Iversen (cofounder, the Cure Autism Now Foundation); Joseph Morrow, Ph.D. (founder,

Applied Behavior Consultants); Linda Lange (cofounder, Helping Autism through Learning and Outreach); Patricia E. Cromer, attorney at law; and last, but not least, Temple Grandin, Ph.D. (Colorado State University). These amazing, driven people have given selflessly of their time and effort over the years to advance the cause of people with ASDs. They, and any nonprofit organization they may be affiliated with, deserve our support.

The first time I encountered autism spectrum disorders was at Fairview State Hospital many years ago, and I am forever indebted to Shane Berli for being the best guide anyone could wish for in the interesting world of developmental disabilities. Shane's respect for and treatment of those severely affected individuals is the foundation on which my attitude towards people on (and off) the spectrum is built.

Thank you to Lenny Schafer for keeping us all posted with the daily Schafer Autism Report. Thanks to all those at the Berkshire Autism Society, UK, and the local chapters of the Autism Society of America in San Diego and in North County, as well as Merryn Affleck and Shirley Fett for their information-sharing and support. The activism of these individuals and groups is to be admired and is a constant reminder that the power of an individual or a group of parents should never be underestimated.

Tito Rajarshi Mukhopadhyay (*The Mind Tree*) and others like him are to be thanked for giving generously of their time so that more may be known about ASDs. Thanks to Soma Mukhopadhyay (educational director of Helping Autism through Learning and Outreach) for sharing her teaching method with the rest of us.

For their constant support and the creative brainstorming sessions, thanks go to the other members of the Spinning Planets—Ellen LeGare and Marsha Markle.

The acknowledgments would not be complete without a heartfelt thank you to all those who "get it" and who have strived to understand and teach my son, or provided respite and companionship to him over the years. He wouldn't be who he is today if it weren't for your expertise, patience, and friendship.

Thanks to the San Diego Regional Center for providing us with services that have helped Jeremy and the family, and Phylinda Clark Graham for her knowledge and expertise.

Special thanks go to Monique Smith (the Afternoon Angel) for holding the fort so I could meet my deadlines, and teaching Jeremy while I was writing. And to Maureen Shull, special thanks as well.

Thanks to all my family and good friends on both sides of the Atlantic (you know who you are).

Special thanks to my parents, Andre and Mathe Sicile, because if it weren't for them I wouldn't be here.

For providing relief from the night demons, Stephen King deserves a mention. His novels are excellent distractions from the stark reality of life, and reminders that what may feel like hell really isn't. Thanks go to Dave Matthews and his band, wonderful acoustic companions in my tiny office. At times I may think I live on Grey Street, but I guess that's better than being a character in one of Stephen King's books.

To Rebecca and Jeremy, thank you for understanding that you are more important than the book, but that I still needed the time to write it. Your patience (and snacks delivered with a hug) were much appreciated.

And lastly, to my husband Daniel, thank you for your unwavering loyalty and constant support on this strange journey called life.

FOREWORD

THE autism/Asperger spectrum is very broad, ranging from a brilliant scientist to a person who remains nonverbal with a severe disability. There are many characteristics that are the same along the entire continuum. Two of the most important are problems with social situations and sensory sensitivities. Sensory problems are often overlooked. When I was a child, a loud school bell was like a dentist drill hitting a nerve. It hurt my ears.

Chantal Sicile-Kira originally contacted me to discuss sensory processing issues. She told me she was writing a general reference guide to autism spectrum disorders. This led to a series of phone calls and faxes. Finally, we met at an autism conference in San Diego, where I had been asked to speak, and Chantal handed me her manuscript, asking me if I would read it and tell her what I thought.

I read her book on my plane trip back home, calling Chantal from two different airports to tell her how impressed I was with the thoroughness of her manuscript, as well as her ability to take complex information and simplify it, rendering it understandable to everyone. This book gives the general public, professionals, and parents a better understanding of the autism/Asperger spectrum, as well as providing lists of resources useful to those who are on the spectrum, and those who work and care for them.

I would like to give a word of advice to all people who work with children or adults on the spectrum: develop talents that can be turned into job skills or hobbies. Social interaction will develop through an interest that can be shared with other people. Special education teachers often put too much emphasis on deficits and not enough on building on areas of strength. As a visual thinker I was good at drawing, and my visual and drawing skills became the basis for my career as a designer of livestock facilities.

Skills tend to be uneven; an individual may be good at one thing and not another. I was good at drawing and building things, but algebra was incomprehensible because I could not visualize it. The minds of people on the spectrum are usually specialized. I have observed that there are three basic types of specialized minds: the visual thinking mind; the music and mathematical mind; and the nonvisual numbers and language translator mind. Teachers and parents should work on utilizing these strengths.

Individuals with autism often become fixated on a single thing, such as trains or airplanes. Use the strong motivation of the fixation to encourage activities. If a child likes trains, use trains in mathematical problems, read a train book to teach literacy, or invent a game involving trains that can be played with other children. A good teacher takes the fixation and broadens it out. Many great scientists pursued a childhood interest.

The autism/Asperger spectrum is a continuum from normal to abnormal. In my book *Thinking in Pictures*, I profiled former scientists such as Einstein who had childhood autistic traits. The British researcher Simon Baron-Cohen has also written on the appearance of autistic traits in scientists and physicists. When does "computer nerd" become Asperger's? There is no black-and-white dividing line.

Individuals who remain nonverbal will often have something they are good at. Many of them have fantastic memories. They may be good at jobs such as reshelving books in the library or taking inventory of the stock at a shop. They would be good at a job that most people would find boring. Develop these skills so they can be useful.

People on the spectrum who have a fulfilling life now often had four important assets earlier in their life: early education and treatment; medication or other treatment for severe anxiety, depression, or sensory sensitivities; development of their talents; and mentors and teachers to help them.

What I really like about Chantal's book are the many references to and quotes from people on the autism/Asperger spectrum. This information from personal experiences will give both parents and professionals much-needed insight into how autistic people perceive the world.

—Temple Grandin, Ph.D.
Author, *Thinking in Pictures*
Associate professor of animal science at Colorado State University
Founder and president of Grandin Livestock Handling Systems, Inc.

PREFACE

TWENTY-FIVE years ago, in need of a full-time job to sustain me through college, I applied for a position at Fairview State Hospital for the Developmentally Disabled in Orange County, California, and was hired to teach adolescents self-help and social skills in preparation for community living. This was my first contact with the intriguing world of autism and some wonderfully unusual people (including the staff). I then worked for a short while as a case manager at Orange County Regional Center for the Developmentally Disabled, providing information and resources to families and their children.

Little did I know that my professional introduction and hands-on experience would serve me well when, twelve years later in France, I had my son, Jeremy, who was eventually diagnosed with autism. The only course of treatment offered there at the time was psychoanalysis. I was strongly reprimanded for using behavioral techniques in an attempt to teach my four-year-old son. Eventually, we moved to England before making our way back to California, where Jeremy is now a client of the same agencies I used to deal with on a professional level.

Today Jeremy is fifteen, and I have this sense of déjà vu, just like Bill Murray's character in the movie *Groundhog Day* who wakes up every morning and lives the same day over and over again. For twenty-five years I've been getting up and researching for resources and new information in different countries, creating solutions "outside the box," advocating, going on community outings, and trying to teach appropriate behavior in public, only now it's to and for my own son.

Living in three different countries and challenging the status quo in each one has developed my resourcefulness, creative thinking, and negotiating skills to a level I never dreamed possible. Having a child with autism is challenging, but building all the family, educational, medical, and community support systems needed is the real challenge. And everyone has a responsible part in this, not just the parents.

Thankfully, attitudes toward autism have changed over the past decade and people in general appear to be more tolerant, which is a good thing considering that autism spectrum disorders (ASDs) have risen to epidemic proportions in many parts of the world. Another positive change is that people with differences such as ASDs are equal citizens and take part in everyday life, in community and recreational programs; they work and live in the community and attend college.

Yet in spite of the rise in ASDs and the integration of people with this "invisible disability" in all aspects of our society, there still seems to be a lack of basic knowledge available on the subject. Everyday people with everyday lives need to know a minimum of information about ASDs to give them an understanding of their neighbor and fellow citizen—which is one of the reasons why I wrote this book.

People who come across those who have an ASD in their line of work can read the chapters they think will help them most. In chapter 8, I have included a section that is helpful for the general public who may occasionally come across someone with autism: babysitters, recreation leaders, emergency responders, storekeepers, scout leaders, bus drivers . . . basically anyone who works with the public. With a diagnosis rate as high as 1 in 166, and in some places 1 in 150, everyone knows someone whose life is touched by autism, and your clients are some of them.

General education and special education teachers and administrators, job coaches, and other professionals who work in the field will find nuggets of information. This book is written simply, with practical tips, in order to point the reader in the right direction for more information if needed.

Adults who have been recently diagnosed will find information that is useful in different chapters. Hopefully, this book will provide some insight and support.

Parents, this book was written with the goal of saving you countless hours of precious time and heartache. You have enough to do! Having spent tens of thousands of hours learning about ASDs, how to navigate through the different systems in different places, and how to create what my son needs, it seems a waste to hoard all I have learned for the benefit of just a few people. Hopefully this book will also inspire you, and remind you that you are not alone. Knowledge is power, so use this guide to empower yourself.

I could have used a book such as this twenty-five years ago, when I tried to learn whatever I could to help my clients, and then again after having my son. I have written this book in the hope that it will inform and help many people.

NOTES ABOUT
THE BOOK

I have used the term "autism spectrum disorders" (ASDs) throughout this book to mean autism, pervasive developmental disorder (PDD), and Asperger's. If used, the word "autism" means autism spectrum disorders. When speaking specifically about people with Asperger's syndrome I have used "Asperger's." As three out of four people with an ASD are male, I have most often used the pronoun "he." I would ask the reader not to be put off by the third person construction, as in "the individual" or "the person." Most resources are listed in the main text; others are in the Resources section in the back.

This book has been compiled to serve an informational purpose. None of the information is meant to be legal, medical, or educational advice. Any treatments, therapies, or interventions should be discussed with a competent professional. Please consult your physician before changing, stopping, or starting any medical treatment. Laws and regulations change, and so the reader should get professional advice concerning matters of legal rights in terms of educational provision, health benefits, and any other benefits. The author and publishers disclaim, as far as the law allows, any liability arising directly or indirectly from the use, or misuse, of the information contained in this book.

The publishers have made every reasonable effort to contact the copyright owners of the extracts reproduced in this book. In the few cases where they have been unsuccessful, they invite copyright holders to contact them directly and corrections can be made in reprints.

For more information about the author, visit her website:
www.chantalsicile-kira.com

1

The Myths and History of Autism Spectrum Disorders

Beyond the world of what and why
Beyond the reasons and the concrete,
The "abstract" lies with a richer glory
Somewhere in imaginations deep!

—TITO RAJARSHI MUKHOPADHYAY, *The Mind Tree*

TWELVE years ago, we were in the local doctor's office in a small village in England, where we had just moved. I was trying to explain to the receptionist why my three-year-old was obsessively walking around and around the waiting room, touching each chair he passed, whether it was empty or not, and obviously disturbing the other patients sitting in those chairs. We'd been waiting almost an hour to see the doctor. "My son is autistic, he can't wait any longer," I said. The receptionist replied, "Well, if he is artistic, have him draw. Here are some crayons to keep him busy." As she walked away, she mumbled under her breath about how badly behaved some children were, and how impatient the parents.

The Myths about Autism Spectrum Disorders

Sad but true, this type of misunderstanding still occurs. However, as the number of people diagnosed escalates to epidemic proportions, most people today have come across autism spectrum disorders (ASDs). Still, as ASDs are mysterious and have attributes that can be strange, awe-inspiring, and unexplainable, there are many myths that abound. Here are a few of them.

Myth #1: *The* Rain Man *Myth—*
Everyone with an ASD Has a Special, Extraordinary Talent

In the movie *Rain Man,* Dustin Hoffman plays Raymond, a young man who has autism. He goes on a road trip with his brother, played by Tom Cruise. Raymond has an incredible gift with numbers. His brother discovers this, and takes him off to Las Vegas so he can gamble and win some money.

There are certainly individuals with ASDs who have extraordinary talent or, more usually, an inconsistent profile where they excel or do well in one area and have low performance in others. For example, years ago I worked with a young man who had a gift for memorizing and was infatuated with sports. On my first day of work at Fairview State Hospital, he came up to me and said, "I used to be a sports newscaster. Ask me any question about sports and I'll fill you in." He had memorized the pertinent statistics for all the World Series from the previous two decades. We talked sports and I did find him a bit odd. For a few minutes I entertained the thought that he was another employee, thinking what a dedicated person he must be to quit working for the media and join the staff at this hospital. Then I looked on my roster and realized he was one of my students for functional living skills. He definitely had a talent for sports statistics, but hadn't yet learned how to dress himself independently or tie his own shoes.

However, there are many more individuals with ASDs who have no particular special talent, any more than the rest of us do.

Myth #2: *Everyone Who Has an ASD Is a Genius,*
a Thomas Jefferson in Waiting

It is true that some people with ASDs are geniuses, but not everyone is. Thomas Jefferson, it appears, had characteristics of Asperger's, within the range of modern diagnostic criteria. Others such as Beethoven, Isaac Newton, and Einstein have all been mentioned as famous people who could have been diagnosed as on the spectrum. However, for every person with an ASD who is a genius, there are many more who are mere mortals like ourselves.

Myth #3: *Everyone Who Has an ASD Is Mentally Retarded*

First of all, because of the nature of ASDs, it is difficult to ascertain the cognitive level of people with these disorders. Many people with autism have communicated that they are sensory overloaded. Some or all of their senses are 100 times more sensitive than others, and therefore they process the environment differently from neurotypicals (i.e., individuals considered to be "normal"). People who are unable to speak, but have learned to type or write independently, express the difficulty they have in controlling their motor planning, i.e., sending signals to their muscles, much like people who have had strokes. In his book *The Mind Tree,* Tito Rajarshi Mukhopadhyay explains, "Of course from my knowledge of biology I knew that I had voluntary muscles and involuntary muscles. I also knew that my hands and legs were made of voluntary muscles. But I experimented with myself that when I ordered my hand to pick up a pencil, that I could not do it. I remember long back when I had ordered my lips to move I could not do it."

Secondly, if you start with the perception that someone is mentally retarded, the expectations for that individual aren't going to be very high, and he will never be given the opportunity to reach as far as he can go. Better to hope he's a genius and be disappointed than never to have given a person the benefit of the doubt. The reality is that the population of people with ASDs is much like the general population: some of us have special talents, some of us are geniuses, and some of us are retarded. But most of us are just average earthlings.

Myth #4: *Everyone Who Has a Symptom of an ASD Has an ASD*

If a person has one or two characteristics of an ASD, it does not necessarily mean he has an ASD. As explained in chapter 2, it is the number and severity of behavioral characteristics in the areas of social interaction, communication, and repetitive stereotypical behaviors that causes concern. That is why it is important to consult with a medical professional who is familiar with ASDs.

Myth #5: *There Is No Cure for (or Recovery from) ASDs*

Tremendous advances have been made in the field of ASDs over the last decade. Granted, there is still no magic pill that cures everyone. However, there are cases of children who were diagnosed as clearly having ASDs, and who are now considered to be neurotypical or symptom-free by professionals thanks to interventions they have received. Some of these cases have been documented in books (*Let Me Hear Your Voice* by Catherine Maurice; *The Sound of a Miracle* by Annabel Stehli). There are also accounts written by people who have recovered significantly from ASDs (*Nobody Nowhere* and *Somebody Somewhere* by Donna Williams; *Emergence: Labeled Autistic* by Temple Grandin and Mar-

Even People with Autism Can Change

"Over the years, I have read enough to know that there are still many parents, and professionals, too, who believe that 'once autistic, always autistic.' This dictum has meant sad and sorry lives for many children diagnosed, as I was early in life, as autistic. To these people it is incomprehensible that the characteristics of autism can be modified and controlled. However, I feel strongly that I am living proof that they can."

—Temple Grandin and Margaret M. Scariano, *Emergence: Labeled Autistic*

garet M. Scariano; *Thinking in Pictures* by Temple Grandin). Recovery means that they have to have overcome some of the symptoms they had that made it difficult for them to live full and successful lives in a world created by neurotypicals.

Myth #6: *People with ASDs Have No Emotions and Do Not Get Attached to Other People*

It is true that many people with an ASD show emotions in a different way from neurotypicals. However, just because a person does not show emotions in the way we are used to seeing them exhibited does not mean that they don't have feelings. One only has to read accounts by people with autism to realize that some individuals express emotions differently (*Nobody Nowhere* by Donna Williams) or are unable to show emotion at all because they are not in control of their muscles or motor planning (*The Mind Tree* by Tito Rajarshi Mukhopadhyay).

It is very clear from reading books by people with autism (*Your Life Is Not a Label* by Jerry Newport; *Pretending to Be Normal* by Liane

Does Autism Need to Be Cured?

Perhaps ethical consideration should be given to the concept of "curing" autism. Saying that autism needs to be cured gives credence to the idea that everyone has to be "normal," that there is something wrong with being different. Granted, many people would find life a lot easier if they did not have an ASD. But perhaps those who have extraordinary talents would not have those gifts, either. Would Beethoven have created his Ninth Symphony? Would Einstein have come up with his theory of relativity? Temple Grandin (who has designed one-third of all the livestock-handling facilities in the United States) believes that her talent for solving concept problems is due to her "ability to visualize and see the world in pictures," which can be attributed to having an ASD.

Jerry Newport is a fifty-two-year-old author with Asperger's syndrome, and was a speaker at the 2001 National Conference on Autism hosted by the Autism Society of America. His speech was entitled "Every Child with Autism Must Become a Success," and was inspired by his concern about the "unrealistic and divisive notion in our community that becoming normal is the only and optimal goal for our consumers." He said, "I will never be normal. I have become a success. I have acquired enough self-esteem to do my best in every endeavor. That is what former UCLA basketball coach John Wooden calls success. I will focus on how we can teach all of our children to have self-esteem, make the most of who they are, and lead full lives, normal or not."

Holliday Willey) that they are capable of forming attachments with other people, and do so. Some people with autism date, get married, and have children, just as we do. Perhaps they are less expressive than others about their feelings, but that does not mean they are not attached to others.

The History and Future of Autism Spectrum Disorders

The labels "autism" and "autistic" come from the Greek word *autos,* meaning self, and were coined in 1911 by a psychiatrist, Eugen Bleuler. He used the terms to describe an aspect of schizophrenia, where an individual withdraws totally from the outside world into himself.

The Early Days—Kanner and Asperger

In the early 1940s both Leo Kanner and Hans Asperger, pioneers in the field of autism, used these terms in their publications (independently of each other), describing children with the characteristics we recognize today as being autistic; hence, the label "autism" was born. Kanner, an Austrian psychiatrist based at Johns Hopkins University in America, was the first to identify autism as a distinct neurological condition in 1943, although he could not specify a cause. In 1944, Asperger, an Austrian pediatrician in Vienna, published a doctoral thesis using the term autistic in his study of four boys. Both professionals described children who developed special interests, but also had deficits in the areas of communication and social interaction. Kanner's description was of children with severe autism, with the conclusion that it was a disastrous condition to have. Asperger's description was of more able children, and he felt that there might be some positive features to autism which could lead to great achievements as an adult. For thirty years, Kanner's description became the most widely recognized.

The term "Asperger's syndrome" was first used by Lorna Wing in a paper published in 1981, in which she described children much like the more able boys Asperger had described many years earlier. Unfortunately, Asperger died in 1980, and never knew that a few years later a condition named after him would become well known worldwide.

The "Refrigerator Mother" Days—Bettelheim

Meanwhile, Bruno Bettelheim, a Hungarian psychotherapist, reared his head in the mid- to late 1940s, claiming that the source of autism was "refrigerator mothers": cold, unfeeling parents who pushed their children into mental isolation. Bettelheim had spent 1943 and 1944 in concentration camps, and he likened the mental isolation of these children to that of the prisoners of war released from such camps after World War II.

Bettelheim eventually moved to the United States and became director of the Sonia Shankman Orthogenic School in Chicago, where he was lauded for many years internationally. Sadly, his theories were widely accepted for two decades, though eventually his school fell into disrepute. Thanks to him, for many years autism was considered a mental illness (as opposed to a developmental disability), leading to limited treatment options for these children. Even as late as the early 1990s a few civilized nations (namely France and Switzerland) still considered autism a mental illness, offering psychoanalysis and psychiatric hospitals as the primary treatment.

In 1997, *The Creation of Dr. B: A Biography of Bruno Bettelheim* by Richard Pollack was published. Pollack, whose younger brother attended the Orthogenic School where Bettelheim was director, conducted extensive research for his book. He discovered that before emigrating to the United States, Bettelheim had worked in the family lumber business and earned a degree in art history, and in fact did not have any qualifications to run a school or theorize about the causes of autism. Pollack also revealed that as director of the Orthogenic School, Bettelheim was known for his volatile, sadistic nature. He terrorized and beat the children, and treated the parents with disdain, blaming them for their children's problems and only allowing them infrequent visits.

FOOD FOR THOUGHT

Shades of Bettelheim

My son was born in Paris, France. Having worked with individuals with ASDs in the United States, I recognized early on that he had autistic tendencies. We sought help and guidance, and although the professionals denied he had autism, they sent us to a psychoanalyst. The psychoanalyst had plenty of Bettelheim books on her shelves, yet was quick to explain that she did not subscribe to Bettelheim's "refrigerator mother" theory. However, after a few sessions of psychoanalysis, it was decided that my son had suffered separation issues from breast-feeding. This the analyst gleaned from watching him spin round objects (which reminded him of his mother's breasts) and chase after one that he had "lost" when it fell and rolled under a piece of furniture.

A Huge Step Forward—Rimland

We owe the dramatic change in psychiatry's perception of autism to Bernard Rimland, Ph.D., a psychologist and father of a son with an ASD. In 1964 Rimland wrote *Infantile Autism: The Syndrome and Its Implications for a Neural Theory of Behavior*, insisting that autism was a biological disorder, not an emotional illness. This book influenced the choices that were made in treatment methods for autism. Rimland is the founder of the Autism Society of America (ASA) (www.autism-society .org), the first parent-driven organization to provide information and support to parents and professionals. He also founded the Autism Research Institute (ARI) (www.autismresearchinstitute.com) in 1967, creating a worldwide network of parents and professionals concerned with autism. ARI sponsors think tanks where scientists and physicians can exchange ideas, and it also sponsors research projects that are geared toward helping children now. ARI also collects data on individuals who were diagnosed with an ASD and are now considered cured or recovered. (Note of interest: Rimland was technical adviser for the movie *Rain Man*.)

The Present—It's a Spectrum Disorder, and It's on the Rise

In the not too distant past, professionals used many terms, including autism, Asperger's, pervasive developmental disorder (PDD), PDD not otherwise specified (PDD-NOS), high-functioning, low-functioning, and others, when discussing ASDs. Most recently, these syndromes, and others that share some of the same symptoms, have been placed under the umbrella term "autism spectrum disorders." Some professionals still do not include Asperger's syndrome under the term "ASDs." However, because they share some of the same symptoms and therefore the same treatments, in this book the term ASDs is considered to include Asperger's syndrome.

Though the different ASDs may vary in the number and intensity of the behavioral symptoms they share, it is still the same three broad areas that are impaired: social relationships, social communication, and imaginative thought. These characteristics can be present in a wide variety of combinations. Two people, both diagnosed with the same label, can have varying skills, deficits, and aptitudes. One of them could be severely incapacitated, the other might appear only to be a bit odd and lacking in social graces. What it all boils down to is that there is no standard type or typical person with an ASD, just as there is no standard type of nonautistic or neurotypical individual. Thus, people with ASDs present a wide spectrum of abilities.

Another important development is the increase in the number of books written and websites created by those who have ASDs. Some books are about what it was like growing up with an ASD (*Pretending to Be Normal* by Liane Holliday Willey; *Nobody Nowhere* by Donna Williams; *Beyond the Wall* by Stephen Shore; *Emergence: Labeled Autistic* by Temple Grandin and Margaret M. Scariano). Others give advice based on experience and knowledge about what is helpful for someone with an ASD (*Freaks, Geeks and Asperger Syndrome* by Luke Jackson; *Autism: An Inside-Out Approach* by Donna Williams; *Thinking in Pictures* by Temple Grandin; *Your Life Is Not a Label* by Jerry Newport). The insights the authors share about what sensations they are feeling, why they act the way they do, and what has helped them in their struggles give us a glimpse of what it can be like to have an ASD. Such accounts and suggestions are invaluable in helping those trying to understand the behaviors of individuals who are unable to communicate about themselves, though it must be borne in mind that these experiences are personal and may not be true for everyone with an ASD.

Another change in recent years is the dramatic rise in the number of individuals diagnosed with ASDs, now said to be reaching epidemic proportions in the United States and in other countries as well. A U.S. Department of Education study from 1992 to 1997 reported a 173 percent increase in the number of children with autism in public schools, compared with a growth of all nonautism disabilities in the same population of just under 17 percent. In California, between 1987 and 2002, there was an increase of 634 percent in the number of people with autism in California's Developmental Services System (California Department of Developmental Services, April 2003). A study conducted in Atlanta showed that 1 in 300 children in metro Atlanta had autism in 1996, a rate almost ten times higher than the rates from studies conducted in the U.S. during the 1980s and early 1990s, but consistent with those of more recent studies (*Journal of the American Medical Association*, January 2003).

Studies in the UK, Iceland, and Japan have all recorded incidence rates of autism much higher than previously assumed. Studies done since 1985 in Europe and Asia have found that as many as 60 out of every 10,000 children have an ASD (the Centers for Disease Control and Prevention, December 2003). In the UK, in 1979, it was estimated that 35 children in 10,000 would be diagnosed with autism; by 1993 the figure had risen to 91 in 10,000 children (the National Autistic Society). (For more on the prevalence of ASDs, see pages 29–32.)

Another recent development is a dramatic shift in the age of onset of autism. According to data compiled by the Autism Research Institute, regressive, or late-onset, autism cases (in which a baby develops normally and begins to regress during its second year) currently outnumber early-onset cases by about five to one. This is in contrast to the 1950s, '60s, and '70s, when late-onset cases were almost unheard of.

Though some of the unprecedented rise in numbers can be attributed to changing definitions and better diagnosing, ASDs are clearly becoming the fastest-growing disability of this decade.

The Future

We are at the dawn of a new era. The last decade was encouraging in the wealth of knowledge that has been acquired, and in this next decade we are sure to discover the causes of ASDs. Since the mid-1990s there have been tremendous advances in the field of medical science. The growth of parent- and professional-driven ASD organizations, coupled with the ease of access to the Internet, has ensured a strong lobbying force aimed at encouraging scientists and politicians alike to devote resources to research into the causes of ASDs and how to help those with these conditions. There are many notable scientists and professionals worldwide who have done much to advance our knowledge of ASDs and continue to do so.

Since its inception, the Autism Society of America (ASA) has grown into the foremost organization in the United States for people with autism and those who care for them. Thanks to the ASA, the National Autistic Society (NAS) UK, Cure Autism Now (CAN), the Autism Research Institute (ARI), Defeat Autism Now! (DAN!), National Alliance for Autism Research (NAAR), UC Davis's MIND Institute, Families for Early Autism Treatment (FEAT), the Schafer Autism Report, the Organization for Autism Research (OAR), and many other organizations and selfless advocates too numerous to mention, research is being funded, findings shared, and information disseminated.

2

What Autism Spectrum Disorders Are and How to Know If a Person Has One

All people like to put things into categories. I do so with my buttons, ribbons, and bits of colored glass. As for people, I had only ever truly felt there were two categories: "us" and "them." Most people see things in these terms, too, but with different and more value-laden definitions.

—DONNA WILLIAMS, *Nobody Nowhere*

THE day my son's diagnosis was confirmed is indelibly etched on my mind. I was in the TV studio where I worked producing a soap opera when the operator announced that I had a call waiting from the hospital. Although I felt sure that my son was not developing properly, the medical professionals had up until now refused to listen to my concerns.

Somehow I held it together while the dramatic love scene was being taped, gave my nod of approval to the director, and headed for my office to take the call. When I was given the news about my son, I felt stunned, shocked, and unable to breathe. Although I had felt there was something amiss, I had wanted to be proven wrong. Now it was acknowledged and I had to deal with that reality.

I went back down to the studio floor to finish taping the day's show. Somehow I got through it. Over the next few days, it was a relief to go to work and throw myself into the make-believe drama, which now seemed quite ordinary compared to the real-life emotional drama I was living. After many weeks and many tears of frustration and sadness I thought that perhaps now, with a diagnosis, we could move forward.

Why Seek a Diagnosis?

If you have any concerns about your child, it is important that you consult with a medical professional who is experienced in ASDs. Hopefully, you will have worried needlessly. But if not, it is important that you have a diagnosis as early as possible, in order to access services. Research shows that early and intensive treatment works best in helping these children make sense of their world. The earlier a child is started on a course of treatment, the better the prognosis. However, research also shows that our brains have neuroplasticity, which means that they continue to reorganize themselves by forming new neural connections throughout life. So, no matter the age, learning can still take place, and parents of older children should not be discouraged from trying different approaches to help their child.

If you are an adult and think you may have an ASD, just knowing there are others like you can bring an extra dimension to your life. Perhaps exchanging information on skills you have developed to handle situations that are hard for you can be helpful.

People in the past were hesitant about applying a label because they felt that the label of autism was permanent and signified that there was no hope for that person. This should no longer be the case. In fact, since

1994, ASDs are now classified as pervasive developmental disorders, reflecting the medical profession's belief that intervention can lead to improvement and sometimes recovery.

Your Label to Use or Not

Having an ASD diagnosed can open doors for you that would otherwise be closed. Your child may be eligible for early intervention services and therapies from local agencies and treatment under medical insurance. It will also allow the parent and professional to search out more knowledge on what to do, using the label as a starting point to gather information. However, you must remember that you, as the parent or the person with an ASD, own the label. It is up to you to use it or disclose it when it is helpful, or not to use it if you are uncomfortable doing so, or if you feel it is not helpful or necessary. It is your information and your choice.

Be aware also that over time, the diagnostic criteria change, and the opinion of the experts as to what those criteria should be differs as well. So although a diagnosis is helpful and necessary to access services, as a parent you would do better to focus on the behavioral characteristics that tell you more about the child and how to help him than to get hung up on the diagnosis and what it means.

Sometimes it may take a long while for an official diagnosis to be reached. You will need the diagnosis to access services from government agencies; however, as a parent there are things you can be doing to help your child while you are waiting. Read chapter 6, on family life, for suggestions in this area. This is also a good time to be doing your own research; see chapters 3, 4, and 5.

Keep in mind that each person is unique, whether he or she has an ASD or not, as Jerry Newport (an adult with Asperger's) reminds us with the title of his book: *Your Life Is Not a Label.*

Characteristics of Autism Spectrum Disorders

Autism spectrum disorders are considered to be the result of a neurological disorder that affects the functioning of the brain. They are four times more prevalent in males than females and typically appear during the first three years of life. ASDs are some of the most common developmental disabilities.

If the last decade has been encouraging in terms of treatments and research findings, in the next decade we are sure to find the causes of these disorders and invent medical tests to diagnose them. Meanwhile, the definition and diagnostic processes of ASDs are in a state of flux and constantly being improved as discoveries are made. What you have here is a road map of what is currently known and used.

At this point in time, there is no medical test to diagnose for ASDs. Any diagnosis is based on observable characteristics, that is, the behavior that a person is exhibiting.

Because of the nature of the symptoms, ASDs are difficult to diagnose at a very early age. If the child is their first, the parents have no experiences with which to compare. Seeing other toddlers and children develop differently, they may start to worry. When voicing these concerns to relatives, friends, or neighbors, the parent will often hear things like, "She'll grow out of it." Sometimes parents will talk to their doctor about their concerns regarding the child's lack of verbal communication and eye contact, his failure to respond to his name, and his obsessive attachment to certain objects.

In many cases, a baby will develop normally and then start to regress at around eighteen months. These children are usually easier to diagnose because of the obvious difference in past and present behaviors which parents and professionals can attest from looking at photos, watching videos, and comparing observations.

Often the parents may be concerned because their child is a walking encyclopedia on a particular topic (such as trains), plays obsessively in

FOOD FOR THOUGHT

Getting Diagnosed

"All the insecurities and frustrations I had carried for so many years were beginning to slip away. I had not imagined a thing. I was different. So was my little girl. Different, challenged even, but not bad or unable or incorrect. I understood my husband's tears and his fear for our daughter's future, but I did not relate to them. I knew my innate understanding of what the world of AS [Asperger's syndrome] is like would help my daughter make her way through life. Together, we would find every answer either of us ever needed.

"I had finally reached the end of my race to be normal. And that was exactly what I needed. A finish—an end to the pretending that had kept me running in circles for most of my life."

—Liane Holliday Willey,
Pretending to Be Normal

the same way with the same toy, or will eat only certain foods. Perhaps it is the kindergarten teacher who notices that he does not appear to engage in conversation with his classmates and has a difficult time with any change in routine. Or a child may be considered "naughty" at school because of certain behaviors, and perhaps the parents haven't noticed anything amiss because he is an only child, or they think that boys mature less quickly than girls. This may be true, but it is better to be sure and investigate your concerns.

The doctor may be hesitant to jump to any conclusions, because not all reported observations are necessarily objective and they can be interpreted in different ways. Everyone knows someone who was a late talker. On the other hand, a parent may not listen to concerns voiced by a child-care worker, a teacher, or a neighbor. This is unfortunate be-

FOOD FOR THOUGHT

How I Got the Doctor's Attention

When my son was a baby, I worried because he would sit rather floppily, content to play with the same toy in the same spot for hours, enabling me to get a lot of my pre-production work done. When I shared my fears with family and friends, they inevitably replied, "So he takes after his dad! Not everyone has to be as energetic as you. He's a calm baby. Just be happy you can get your work done." The pediatrician was not very supportive of my concerns, so I invited him to my son's first birthday party. Seeing the contrast between my son and a room full of healthy babies, he was forced to face the fact that some tests might be in order.

cause the earlier the diagnosis, the sooner the intervention, the better the prognosis.

Some people with an ASD may reach adulthood without ever having been diagnosed. They may have always felt as if they were not on the same wavelength as others socially, emotionally, or sensorially. Perhaps they exhibit some of the characteristics listed on pages 21–23. In such a case, having a diagnosis would be useful in putting them in touch with information and organizations that may be able to help them.

Three Areas That Characterize Autism Spectrum Disorders

There are basically three areas of observable symptoms that characterize ASDs: impairment of social relationships, of social communication, and of imaginative thought. Some of the symptoms may be mild, others more obvious. It is the number and severity of these symptoms that leads to concerns on the part of the parent or the professional. Examples of behaviors that portray these characteristics are listed on pages 21–23.

Does This Person Have Autism?

Advice to parents: Follow your instincts. You are the expert on your child. If you have any concerns, voice them to your family doctor. Take notes on whatever behaviors (see pages 21–23) are of concern by keeping a notebook, listing the behaviors and their frequency. Find out which medical professional in your area is knowledgeable about autism and consult with them. It is better to have your child checked out than to lose precious time waiting for him to "grow out of it."

If you have any concerns whatsoever, ask your physician for a routine developmental screening. On the First Signs website (www.firstsigns.org), you can read about the developmental milestones your child should be reaching. First Signs is a national nonprofit organization whose mission is to educate parents and physicians about the early warning signs of autism and other developmental disabilities. For more information about knowledgeable physicians in your area, consult your local chapter of the Autism Society of America, which you can find listed at the group's website (www.autism-society.org). Another good resource is the diagnostic checklist provided by the Autism Research Institute (ARI). To obtain this checklist, go to ARI's website (www .autismresearchinstitute.com) and fill out the request form.

Advice to medical professionals, educators, and other professionals: Take care how you voice your concerns, but voice them! Better to be proven wrong than to say nothing. If you are unsure about the best way to screen for ASDs, go to Autism ALARM (www.medicalhomeinfo.org/screening/autism) or the First Signs website (www.firstsigns.org). These guidelines and tools were developed from key policy statements of the American Association of Pediatrics and the American Academy of Neurology, with the help of an autism expert panel. The goal of these tools is to simplify the screening process, to make sure that all children receive routine and appropriate screenings (necessary for timely intervention), and to establish standard practices among physicians.

You can also consult the Checklist for Autism in Toddlers (CHAT) on the website for the National Autistic Society (www.nas.org.uk). In Britain, this screening tool, which takes under five minutes to administer, has been shown to be highly effective in predicting which children tested will develop autism, PDD, Asperger's, or other developmental syndromes. You may also wish to obtain the diagnostic checklist provided by the Autism Research Institute (ARI) by going to www.autismresearchinstitute.com and filling out the request form.

Advice to adults who might have an ASD: The National Autistic Society has a section that is helpful to adults who think they might have an ASD and wish to have more information. The organization's website address is www.nas.org.uk.

Lorna Wing, M.D., FRCPsych, a founding member of the National Autistic Society, consultant psychiatrist at the NAS's Centre for Social and Communication Disorders, and author of *The Autistic Spectrum,* describes these areas of impairment:

- *Impairment of social relationships:* An individual may not use or understand nonverbal behavior or develop peer relationships that are appropriate to his developmental level, or may appear aloof and indifferent to other people.

- *Impairment of social communication:* There may be a total lack of or delay in the development of speech (with no attempts to communicate by gestures). The individual does not sustain or initiate conversation, or uses language in a stereotyped and repetitive manner.

- *Impairment of imaginative thought:* An individual may have an all-encompassing, intense preoccupation with one interest or topic; or have inflexible, nonfunctional rituals or routines. Repetitive motor mannerisms such as hand flapping or spinning of objects may be observed. Often there is a lack of make-believe or social imitative play.

Difficulties in one or more of the areas listed above are required for a diagnosis of an ASD, but several additional observable behaviors do not necessarily fit into any of the three. Although on their own they do not call for a diagnosis of an ASD, these other characteristics are often associated with ASDs, and they are important when evaluating and assessing for the purpose of putting together a treatment plan.

Behavioral Characteristics of Autism Spectrum Disorders

A word of caution: this list is not meant to be a diagnostic checklist, but is intended to give you some ideas of the types of behaviors someone with an ASD may exhibit. Remember, it is the number and severity of these behaviors that may lead to talks with a professional about performing a diagnostic assessment (see "Diagnostic Criteria" on pages 24–27).

Some of these behaviors are seen on one end of the spectrum (e.g., classic autism); others on the opposite end (e.g., high-functioning autism, Asperger's syndrome).

IMPAIRMENT OF SOCIAL RELATIONSHIPS

As a baby, does not reach out to be held by mother or seek cuddling

Does not imitate others

Uses adult as a means to get wanted object, without interacting with adult as a person

Does not develop age-appropriate peer relationships

Lack of spontaneous sharing of interests with others

Difficulty in mixing with others

Prefers to be alone

Has an aloof manner

Little or no eye contact

Detached from feelings of others

IMPAIRMENT OF SOCIAL COMMUNICATION

Does not develop speech, or develop an alternative method of communication such as pointing and gesturing

Has speech, then loses it

Repeats words or phrases instead of using normal language (echolalia)

Speaks on very narrowly focused topics

Difficulty in talking about abstract concepts

Lack or impairment of conversational skills

IMPAIRMENT OF IMAGINATIVE THOUGHT

Inappropriate attachment to objects

Obsessive odd play with toys or objects (lines up or spins continually)

Does not like change in routine or environment (going to a different place, furniture moved in house)

Will eat only certain foods

Will use only the same object (same plate or cup, same clothes)

Repetitive motor movements (rocking, hand flapping)

OTHER CHARACTERISTICS

Peculiar voice characteristics (flat monotone or high pitch)

Does not reach developmental milestones in neurotypical time frame or sequence

Low muscle tone

Uneven fine and gross motor skills

Covers ears

Does not respond to noise or name, acts deaf

Does not react to pain

Becomes stiff when held, does not like to be touched

Becomes hyperactive or totally nonresponsive in noisy or very bright environments

Eats or chews on unusual things

Puts objects to nose to smell them

Removes clothes often

Hits or bites self (hits head or slaps thighs or chest)

Whirls himself like a top

Has temper tantrums for no apparent reason and is difficult to calm down

Hits or bites others

Lacks common sense

Does not appear to understand simple requests

Frequent diarrhea, upset stomach, or constipation

Many of these behaviors are the person's responses to how he or she is processing the immediate environment. The typical meaning behind certain behaviors is discussed in chapter 3 (pages 45–51).

Diagnostic Criteria

Unfortunately, at this point in time there is no objective or medical test that can be given to an individual to diagnose an ASD. Rather, it is a process of elimination based on checking on any areas of concern (e.g., perhaps the child is deaf or hard of hearing and that is why he does not respond to his name) and observations based on the individual's development, as well as social and communication skills.

Medical Tests

The following are suggested medical tests for the purpose of eliminating other possible reasons for the person's behavior, or to see if other specific disorders and developmental disabilities exist. The doctor you consult may suggest other tests as well. Keep in mind that after a diagnosis, other evaluations and assessments will be necessary to give you the information you need to form a plan of treatment.

- *Hearing:* Tests such as audiograms and tympanograms can indicate if a child has a hearing impairment. Audiologists can test the hearing of individuals by measuring responses such as blinking or staring or turning the head when a sound is presented.

- *Genetic testing:* Blood tests can show abnormalities in the genes that could cause a developmental disability.

- *Electroencephalogram (EEG):* An EEG can detect tumors or other brain abnormalities. It also measures brain waves that can show seizure disorders.

- *Metabolic screening:* Blood and urine lab tests measure how a child metabolizes food and its impact on growth and development.

- *Magnetic resonance imaging (MRI):* Magnetic sensing equipment creates, in extremely fine detail, an image of the brain.

- *Computer-assisted axial tomography (CAT scan):* CAT scans are useful in diagnosing structural problems in the brain by taking thousands of exposures which are then reconstructed in great detail.

Behavioral Checklists

Because there is no medical test that can be given to diagnose autism, professionals depend on observing the behaviors of the person in question as well as the medical and developmental history. There are behavioral checklists available that are used to determine if the person has the specific number of characteristics as defined in the *Diagnostic and Statistical Manual of Mental Disorders* (DSM-IV), which is the standard reference for the definition of autism. A good diagnostic checklist is available through the Autism Research Institute (www.autism researchinstitute.com).

Diagnostic and Statistical Manual of Mental Disorders (*DSM-IV*)

This medical diagnostic handbook, currently in its fourth edition, is internationally used and recognized. When the *DSM* was revised in 1994, some changes were made. Previously, the category of pervasive developmental disorders (PDD), which includes autism, was coded or classified with other long-term stable disorders that have a poor prognosis. Now PDD has been classified with more transient, temporary, and episodic clinical disorders. This is a positive move that reflects what current research is now showing: that there is a possibility of improvement with intervention, and that symptoms can vary in intensity.

The diagnostic criteria for autism have changed slightly as well. In order for a person to be diagnosed with autism, he or she still needs to show deficits in the broad areas of social interaction, communication, and stereotyped patterns. However, the number of symptoms that fall under these categories has been reduced from sixteen to twelve, making this diagnostic category more homogeneous. A third change made was the addition of three new autism-related disorders: Rett's disorder, childhood disintegrative disorder, and Asperger's syndrome.

All individuals who fall under the PDD category in the *DSM-IV* have some communication and social deficits, but the levels of severity are different. Here are the differences between specific diagnoses that are used:

- *Autistic disorder (or classic autism):* A child with this disorder shows impairments in imaginative play, social interaction, and communication, with an onset before the age of three. The child exhibits stereotyped behaviors, activities, and interests.

- *Childhood disintegrative disorder:* The child develops normally and has age-appropriate verbal and nonverbal communication skills, social relationships, play, and adaptive behaviors for at least the first two years and then shows a significant loss of previously acquired skills.

- *Rett's disorder:* So far, only girls have had this progressive disorder. There is a period of normal development through the first five months and then a loss of previously acquired skills. The girl loses the purposeful use of her hands, which is replaced with hand wringing. There is severe psychomotor delay and a poorly coordinated gait. (It is now possible, thanks to the recent development of a new genetic blood test, to test for this disorder.)

- *Asperger's syndrome:* A child with Asperger's tests in the range of average to above average intelligence and has no clinically significant general delay in language. However, the child will show impairments in social interactions, including difficulty in using social cues such as body language, and has a restricted range of interests and activities.

- *Pervasive developmental disorder not otherwise specified (atypical autism):* A diagnosis of PDD-NOS may be made when a child

FOOD FOR THOUGHT

Is It High-Functioning Autism, PDD-NOS, or Asperger's Syndrome?

The terms "high-functioning autism" and "Asperger's syndrome" are sometimes used interchangeably by certain professionals and authors. Some people with Asperger's as well as various professionals and researchers consider that it is not part of the autism spectrum. Although Tony Attwood, a world-renowned clinical psychologist who specializes in the field of Asperger's syndrome, considers that technically Asperger's syndrome is part of the autistic spectrum, he feels it is important to recognize that the child with Asperger's does not simply have a mild form of autism, but a different expression of the condition. One of Attwood's concerns is the past negative connotations of the word "autism."

However, while in the old days the word put fear into everyone's heart, today we are on a different playing field. The word "autism," as in autism spectrum disorders, does not imply a bleak and meaningless life in isolation, separated from the rest of society. What is important is that people get the help they need, and that their treatment is based on the behaviors they are exhibiting, not on the label they have been given.

does not meet the criteria for a specific diagnosis, but there is a severe and pervasive impairment in specified behaviors.

You may wish to consult the diagnostic criteria from *DSM-IV* at www.psychologynet.org/autism.html or at www.pediatricneurology.com.

3

What Causes Autism Spectrum Disorders and Why Do People with ASDs Act the Way They Do?

Men and women are puzzled by everything I do. My parents and those who love me are embarrassed and worried. Doctors use different terminologies to describe me. I just wonder. The thoughts are bigger than my expressions to get a shape. Every move that I make interprets my helpless way to show how trapped I feel in the continuous flow of happenings. The happenings occur in a way that shows the continuity of cause and effect. The effect of a cause becomes the cause of another effect. And I wonder. . . .

—TITO RAJARSHI MUKHOPADHYAY, *The Mind Tree*

IT used to be that autism was pretty rare. Seven or eight years ago if I mentioned the word "autism," people would have heard of it, but nobody had ever encountered it except at the cinema by watching *Rain Man*. Now it seems everyone is related to or lives next door to someone with an ASD. Recently I had to take my son to the emergency room at the local hospital. While we were sitting in the waiting room one woman looked at us and turned to her companion, saying, "Seeing that boy over there reminds me, how is your friend's nephew doing, the one with autism?" Then we got called in for X rays and the technician looked at Jeremy and said, "So, what school district do you live in? Are you happy with his program? My son's ten and we finally got what he needed at school for him." When we got home, I called the airline to confirm reservations for a summer family vacation. When I told the reservation clerk I would be traveling with someone with autism and needed to make special seating arrangements, she said, "Don't say another word, dear, I know just what you need. My cousin's son has autism. . . ."

It's an Epidemic

There has been much discussion over the past few years about the reason for the rise in the numbers of those diagnosed with autism spectrum disorders in the US, the UK, and other parts of the world. Some would argue that ASDs are diagnosed better and earlier, resulting in higher figures than before. Others argue that there is a true increase in the number of children with autism. In order to have a better understanding of what is actually occurring, a close look at some official numbers and reports is in order.

Numbers in the United States

Figures from the California Department of Developmental Disabilities are often quoted because of the strict record-keeping necessitated by state laws. California is required under the Lanterman Developmental Disabilities Act to provide services to persons with developmental disabilities. These services are provided through regional centers that must keep accurate data on the number and type of clients they serve. The criteria for diagnosing cases are strictly adhered to, and have not changed over time.

The Department of Developmental Services is required (for budgetary reasons) to report to the legislature the incidence of autism and pervasive developmental disorders compared with other developmental disabilities. In March 1999, the department reported to the legislature that the numbers of persons entering the system and receiving services had jumped 210 percent between 1987 and 1998 ("Changes in the Population of Persons with Autism and Pervasive Developmental Disorders in California's Developmental Services System: 1987–1998"). The California legislature was surprised and concerned by these findings.

Debate immediately started among autism experts, government officials, and parent-driven organizations on why such high figures were being recorded in California, as well as in the UK and other parts of the world. Some discounted the increasing rates of ASDs, attributing the rise to better and earlier diagnosis, a change in definition that now encompassed the more able and those with Asperger's, and a migration to certain areas for better services.

The legislature therefore commissioned the University of California's Medical Investigation of Neurodevelopmental Disorders (MIND) Institute to investigate these findings. In October 2002, Dr. Robert S. Byrd and his colleagues reported back with results that made headlines all around the world.

Byrd and his colleagues found that the huge jump in autism rates from 2,778 in 1987 to 10,360 in 1998 could not be explained by changes in the criteria used to diagnose autism, or by an increased migration to California of children with autism. Nor could it be explained by statistical anomalies. The report also found that parents' reports of regression at an early age did not differ between the two different age groups studied; however, more parents of the younger group reported gastrointestinal symptoms in the child's first fifteen months of life.

Dr. Byrd's study clearly showed a tremendous increase in autism in California for some unknown reason. Meanwhile, in early January 2003, figures released by the California Department of Developmental Services showed an increase of 31 percent from the previous year of children diagnosed with level one autism, the most severe kind (these figures do not include persons with PDD-NOS, Asperger's, or any other ASD).

Other studies are showing increases as well. For example, a study by M. Yeargin-Allsopp et al., published by the *Journal of the American Medical Association* in January 2003, on rates of autism in the metropolitan area of Atlanta, Georgia, compared to the 1980s and 1990s confirmed that the apparent increase is real. It is certain that we are in the throes of a huge increase in autism. What no one knows is why.

The federal government is also concerned about the increase of autism diagnosis and what it really means. This concern is reflected in time, money, and energy now being spent on finding out all we can on ASDs. Some examples of what the government is doing:

- More and more money has been allocated to autism research by the government. The National Institutes of Health spent an estimated $81.3 million on autism research in fiscal year 2003, compared to $9.6 million ten years earlier in 1993.

- The Centers for Disease Control and Prevention included autism in the developmental disabilities surveillance program based in Atlanta in 1998, and then began to monitor the prevalence of ASDs in numerous states, and will continue to do so for many years.

- The Coalition for Autism Research and Education (CARE), the Congressional Autism Caucus, was started in 2001. It is the first Congressional Member Organization to focus on ASDs, and has members from most states. Its focus is to teach members of Congress about ASDs and to improve research, education, and support services for people who have an ASD.

- The Institute of Medicine (IOM), a branch of the National Academy of Sciences, established an independent expert committee to review immunization safety concerns about a possible vaccine-autism connection. The first report of this Immunization Safety Review Committee was published in April 2001, and a second one in Spring 2004.

- The U.S. Department of Health and Human Services and the U.S. Department of Education sponsored a two-day conference, "Autism Summit Conference: Developing a National Agenda," in November 2003. The conference addressed topics such as early screening and diagnosis, biomedical research, and improving access to services for people with autism.

Elsewhere in the World

In Canada, the rate of ASDs was 1 in 286 for the years 2000–2001, an average based on figures from the provincial departments of education. They also reported an average increase of 63 percent over a two-year period (Autism Society Canada).

The prevalence of ASDs in the UK in 1993 was estimated by the National Autistic Society at 91 in 10,000 children of all ages, compared with 35 per 10,000 in 1979. In 2001, the Medical Research Council, commissioned by the Department of Health to look at how many children had been recognized as having an ASD, estimated that 1 in 166 children under the age of eight was affected. However, teachers reported much higher numbers of children with ASDs than any of these estimates: an NAS survey of seven local education authorities found that 1 in 152 children had a formal ASD diagnosis, while 1 in 86 had an ASD-related special educational need.

What Causes Autism Spectrum Disorders?

In response to the question, "What causes ASDs?" the writer is sorely tempted to reply, "We don't know," and move on to the next chapter. However, no guide to ASDs would be complete without an attempt at explaining the causes of the most recent epidemic to hit our planet.

What Does Not Cause ASDs?

It is infinitely easier to talk about what we know does not cause ASDs. It is known for a fact that ASDs cannot be caught through osmosis, dirty doorknobs, or bad parenting. Other than that, nothing can be said for sure.

Where to Get Updates on the Latest Research

What follows is by no means an exhaustive look at the science behind the causes of autism. The interested reader can follow on a regular basis the latest discoveries and ongoing research. As mentioned in the box on page 34, it is best to read the actual study or report than to read summaries and news releases. In order to gain an understanding of this highly controversial topic, the reader is advised to consult a wide variety of websites and journals such as those listed below and form his own opinion:

- The National Library of Medicine Pubmed (www.ncbi.nih.gov/entrez/query.fcgi): Use the search engine to find abstracts of any research articles you are interested in reading concerning autism. There are tutorials on the site with instructions for more advanced search techniques. Some abstracts will link you to the full article on the website of the journal where it is published. Some journals will provide full text for free, while others require a subscription or fee.

FOOD FOR THOUGHT

Developing a Critical Mind

The reader needs to be aware that, unfortunately, just as in every field, there are politics and money at stake in autism and science. Each organization and government body has its own interpretation of research studies and what they mean. Scientists are quick to point out flaws in studies by other scientists that do not report findings they agree with. Sometimes they are right. This means that we all need to develop critical thinking skills and an analytical mindset.

Never rely on the media to tell you the full story on research findings. For example, in 2001, media reports and newspaper headlines and articles were saying that a report published by the Institute of Medicine (IOM) said that no link had been found between autism and vaccinations. Also stated in the report (but left unmentioned by the media) was that a possibility of a connection between the MMR (measles-mumps-rubella) vaccine and autism could not be disproved for a small number of children. However, when the media quoted that same IOM report in 2004, this possibility of a connection between vaccines and autism was mentioned as one of the reasons why the IOM was again examining this issue.

To form your own educated opinion on any topic, always go straight to the horse's mouth. With the Internet, access to original sources and studies is easy, cheap, and available to all. For those who are computerless, your library awaits you.

- The Medical Research Council (UK) (www.mrc.ac.uk): Information on current research funded by the MRC is listed on its website. The MRC published the "MRC Review of Autism Research: Epidemiology and Causes" in December 2001.

- The Schafer Autism Report is the largest daily (almost) newspaper on ASDs; edited by Lenny Schafer and available free through the Internet. To subscribe: http://www.sarnet.org. For archives: http://groups.yahoo.com/group/AuTeach/messages.

- The Autism Research Institute International Newsletter (www.autismresearchinstitute.com): Bernard Rimland, Ph.D., publishes a quarterly newsletter with summaries of current research. The ARI website has information on some research studies.

- The Autism Society of America (ASA) (www.autism-society.org) often has information about the most important ASD issues being discussed by the media.

What Is Known about the Causes of ASDs?

There is much discussion on this issue, and research studies are often published that are sometimes disputed or explained away by other research. However, there is strong evidence for a genetic component and a biological basis. Most researchers believe that ASDs have different causes that may be affecting the same brain systems or hindering development by disrupting the different abilities needed for communicative and social development. Here is what is known and accepted to be true by almost everyone:

- There is a genetic predisposition to autism. Regions of interest, sometimes called "hot spots," have been found on certain chromosomes, the most important so far on chromosome 7q, although others are involved. If one identical twin has autism there is a 60–95 percent chance of the other having it as well. However, identical twins with the same genetic makeup and the same physical environment may have different expressions of ASDs—one may be very able, the other very disabled.

• There have been a number of findings in regard to differences in brain activity, not all in agreement with each other. However, most scientists who study autism would agree that some brain circuits are different in a person with an ASD.

• Serotonin, a neurotransmitter important for normal brain functioning and behavior, has been found elevated in a subgroup of people with autism and in some first-degree relatives who are unaffected. This is the only key biochemical finding since the 1960s that has held up to be true over time.

• There is a large body of anecdotal findings reported by parents and medical professionals that some children with ASDs appear to have biochemical and immunological problems. Some possible causes being mentioned are: mercury toxicity, yeast problems, casein and gluten sensitivity, and viral infections.

• In some studies, different levels of environmental toxins such as lead, antimony (a flame-retardant chemical present in many household items), and aluminum have been found in hair and blood samples of children with autism than in those of nonautistic children. This leads to the hypothesis that some children with ASDs cannot detoxicate, and thus accumulate toxins in their bodies.

For a long time, the favored theory was that autism was all about the genes. It is true that genes come into play. However, the dramatic rise in recent years in ASDs cannot be attributed to a rise in genetic anomalies.

Perhaps we are seeing different disorders, each caused by a different problem but with symptoms resembling one another. Perhaps the differences are all being caused by a yet unknown single underlying cause.

It appears most likely that there is a genetic predisposition to autism spectrum disorders interacting with environmental factors that may play a key role in affecting the gastrointestinal tract, the immune system, the sensory nervous system, and the brain.

Vaccinations and Autism: Is There a Connection?

The possibility of a vaccination-autism connection has become highly controversial; there is intense debate going on among scientists. On one side, there is a growing tendency to blame the increased numbers of required or suggested vaccinations as well as the tendency to give multiple vaccines in one shot for all the cases of regressive autism in the past ten years (regressive autism is autism that appears in a child at around the age of eighteen months, after a normal development, causing the child to regress). However, vaccinations in themselves do not cause autism, or millions more children would be autistic. Neither does thiomerosal, an organic compound present in some vaccinations. But perhaps these are triggers for children who are genetically predisposed to have autism and who have immune systems that are not functioning properly.

On the other side are the government and the vaccine manufacturers stating that vaccines are safe, and that those refusing to vaccinate their children are putting the public's health at risk.

In reality, no one knows for sure. It is difficult for the average person to form an educated opinion just from reading the newspaper headlines. Many headlines in the UK and the United States over the past few years have stated that expert groups and panels have found no link between childhood vaccination and autism. In reality, a careful review of the different government and experts' reports actually show the following:

- The Centers for Disease Control and Prevention and the National Institute of Health in the U.S. asked the Institute of Medicine (IOM), a branch of the National Academy of Sciences, to establish an independent expert committee to review immunization safety concerns (the Immunization Safey Review Committee). The "Immunization Safety Review: Measles-Mumps-Rubella Vaccine and Autism," issued on 23 April 2001, stated that "Although the committee has concluded that the evidence favors rejection of the causal relationship on the population level between MMR vaccine

FOOD FOR THOUGHT

Autism: A Hit-and-Run Epidemic

Lenny Schafer is the publisher and editor of the world's largest daily publication about autism. More than twenty thousand people subscribe to the Schafer Autism Report, *which is free of charge. A Danish study published in the* New England Journal of Medicine *in November 2002 concluded that there was no basis for the belief that the MMR vaccine was responsible for the increase in autism. This created quite a stir in the autism community. Some applauded the study; others criticized it. Lenny had this comment to make (which still holds true):*

The autism epidemic is like an epidemic of out-of-control hit-and-run accidents. Something big and dangerous collides with your child and leaves him or her devastated from the assault. We don't know the offending vehicle nor the driver nor the time of the collision. But these cars don't wreak the same damage on everyone they hit. It seems some more than others, and most not at all. Our public health detectives arrive on the scene long after the perpetrators have fled and announce that they have no idea what caused all the damage, but decide that the main problem is that the bodies of those presenting the most damage are too weak to sustain the blows like the others because of their genes. "We do know that it's probably not a single gene behind hit-and-run-ism, but rather a few of them acting together," pronounces the chief detective.

Some noisy parents of the victims say that their kids got hit right after they saw a police car in the neighborhood. A lot of them are saying the same thing. "Go investigate police cars!" scream the parents. "My son was fine until a police car came around. You are supposed to protect, not hurt our children!"

"Hysterical mothers being driven by greedy lawyers and useless anecdotes," smirks one detective to another. "We're looking into this," assures the detective, "and we will spend some resources on research and find those bad genes. By the time your other children grow up and are ready to have children of their own," they continue, "we'll know which of them ought to consider adopting, by their genes. Problem solved."

In the meantime, the detectives assure them, "We've looked over some traffic reports and there really isn't any increase in hit-and-run accidents. It's just more pedestrian accidents being reclassified as hit-and-run because we're spotting them better."

Like with hit-and-run research, almost all the money that goes into autism research today, both public and privately raised funding, is used for finding the faulty genes and/or faulty body parts, not the perpetrators of the assault. Almost nothing comparatively goes into treatment research for our kids already afflicted. Even the familiar parent-run autism research fundraising groups like CAN, NAAR and the parent-influenced MIND Institute spend the bulk, if not all, of their funds on genetic-related, or like research.

(The exception here is the Autism Research Institute, which spends all of its research dollars on treatment-related issues. The ARI is somewhat of a maverick within the research community, willing to help parents experiment with anecdote-mostly-tested treatments at first, if necessary, and often with good results. This is risky stuff; few others are ready to help parents willing to go this course. But the ARI does not spend its resources researching the cause of autism, either.)

The problem here is that if vaccines do play a role in autism—and this Danish study doesn't eliminate a reasonable possibility for a genetic subset of the population—relying on the promoters of the same vaccines, such as government public health agencies, to find the "real" or even the "other" environmental factors causing this large upswing in autism and other immune disorders is akin to asking O.J. Simpson to find the "real" killers of his ex-wife and her friend.

Inherent to public health is politics. And the political reality of the autism epidemic is that the watchdogs, and the vaccine pharmaceutical companies and their agent researchers, have too many conflicts of interests for the issue to be settled by epidemiological research alone. This research only looks at the results of pathology upon a population, and does not easily prove or disprove cause. This allows too much wiggle room for self-serving spin (and counterspin). A growing number of citizen public health advocates find vaccines to be poorly tested, and sometimes dirty with toxins like mercury. Vaccine-strain measles virus is showing up in the cerebral spinal fluid of autistic children and nobody can tell us how it got there, if not via the MMR vaccine.

Genetic and epidemiological research are not the primary tools for finding the cause of autism. The final answers will come from biomedical and clinical research. Someone had better start examining these kids, and soon. Until we start seeing efforts and money spent to pay for the clinics to do this research (and also, along the way, to treat our children), all other research serves as little more than alibi research.

The murky vaccine-autism connection has been effective leverage by some autism research advocates for getting the public health watchdogs and the media to sit up and pay attention to autism. Soon this leveraging won't be necessary as the prevalence rates will reveal more and more autism-victimized sons and daughters and grandsons and granddaughters of congress-people, movie and sports celebrities, investors in pharmaceuticals, etc., people not so readily dismissed as anecdotal hysterics—and who in ever growing numbers will demand answers, not alibis. Not everyone is as willing as some autism research fundraisers to let vaccines off the hook just yet.

---

and ASD, the committee recommends that this issue receive continued attention. . . . Its conclusion does not exclude the possibility that MMR vaccine could contribute to ASD in a small number of children."

• The Medical Research Council in the UK published a "Review of Autism Research: Epidemiology and Causes" in December 2001. After noting that "It is important to recognize that epidemiological studies cannot prove that vaccines are safe but can only exclude specified adverse reactions with a certain degree of confidence," it goes on to state that "Currently there are no epidemiological studies that provide reliable evidence to support the hypothesis that there might be an association between MMR and ASD."

• In response to Petition PE 145, calling for an inquiry into issues surrounding the alleged relationship between the combined measles, mumps, and rubella vaccine (MMR) and autism, the Health and

Community Care Committee reported to the Scottish Parliament in 2001 that "What is clear to the committee is that while there is an absence of any scientific data of a causal link between the MMR vaccine and the onset of autism, it remains impossible to prove conclusively the absence of a link." The committee also called for further research.

• Another immunization safety review by an expert review committee is being conducted by the Institute of Medicine (IOM). This review had not been made public at the time of the writing of this book.

So all we know is that, so far, no connection has been proven for the vast majority, but nor has any connection been disproved for a subset of children who may be at risk. It is also difficult for the average person to know what the research studies we read about in the news really prove or disprove. As soon as the results of a study are published, another expert issues a statement questioning their validity or unveils a connection between the researcher and a drug company that produces vaccines.

For example, the largest study to date, a review of medical records of half a million Danish children born between 1991 and 1998 by scientists at the Danish Epidemiology Science Center, was published in the *New England Journal of Medicine* in November 2002. The report concluded that there was no basis for the belief that the MMR vaccine was responsible for the increase in autism cases. This led to newspaper headlines such as "Study finds no sign that child vaccine causes autism" (the *Boston Globe,* 9 November 2002). However, the Danish study raised several legitimate criticisms from other researchers and autism experts, including Dr. Andrew Wakefield (the autism researcher who found a potential link between the measles-mumps-rubella vaccine [MMR] and autism).

One of the criticisms involves a factor the author of the Danish study failed to mention: that they do not have the mercury-containing thimerosal in the pediatric vaccines used in Denmark, meaning that the study's findings are not applicable to the U.S. or the UK populations. Another is that the medical records reviewed were selected from psychiatric clinics and hospitals, and contained no data in regard to immune system dysfunction or inflammatory bowel disease.

What is real is the growing number of parents who have seen differences in their children before and after the MMR vaccine, and have photographs and videos that clearly document regression. This is a fact for those families that no government report will erase. Although it is true that this represents a small number of the total of children vaccinated, it should be of great concern to the medical community.

Everyone agrees on one point: that more valid, unbiased research is clearly needed. Some facts as well as areas of concern in regard to vaccinations are:

• One of the theories in the U.S. is that the rise in ASDs matches the increased exposure of young children to thimerosal, a preservative containing mercury, as the number of vaccinations required has increased over time from four in the 1950s to over twenty now. In the United States there is a much more aggressive vaccination schedule than in other parts of the world, including the UK. During most of the 1990s, many American six-month-olds were exposed to a total of 187.5 micrograms of ethyl mercury through vaccination. At that time, the Environmental Protection Agency's (EPA) daily "safe" dose for methyl mercury (a related compound) was 0.1 micrograms per kilogram of body weight.

• As mentioned earlier, regressive, or late-onset, autism cases currently outnumber early-onset cases by about five to one. In the 1950s, '60s and '70s, late-onset cases were almost unheard of (Autism Research Institute).

• In July 1999, the American Academy of Pediatrics (AAP), chaired by Neal Halsey, M.D., the Public Health Service (PHS) agencies, and vaccine manufacturers agreed to reduce or remove thimerosal from most vaccines. This decision was based on the assumption that the health risks from methyl and ethyl mercury were the same. It is now possible to get most (if not all) of the recommended schedule of vaccinations in the U.S. without thimerosal.

• There is concern in the U.S., that although thimerosal is no longer present in most vaccines, the actual number of vaccinations now required or recommended is in itself a health risk for a subset of children.

• In Canada, all vaccines for routine immunization of children have been available without thimerosal since March 2001.

• In the UK, thimerosal (known there as thiomersal) is currently used in some vaccines, such as the diphtheria and tetanus preschool boosters, although the MMR vaccine (triple or single) currently used in the UK does not have thimerosal as a preservative. In the autumn of 2002, the Department of Health in Britain backed the continued use of thimerosal-containing vaccines, stating that the alternative vaccines without the mercury preservative were less effective.

• It has been suggested by expert panels that when the MMR triple vaccine was first introduced, not enough testing was carried out to ensure its long-term safety in regard to the interaction between multiple vaccinations and potentially fragile immune systems.

• There is valid concern about the serious risk to public safety if children are not immunized. Until recently, mumps and measles were practically nonexistent, and these diseases pose serious threats to children. In the UK, the number of cases of measles has been climbing and the disease has been responsible for the deaths of some children.

• There is debate about what information medical professionals should divulge to families in their care about a possible vaccine-autism connection. Government and health officials say there is no connection between vaccinations and ASDs, so that is usually the message passed on to the health consumer. Should doctors tell parents that a connection between the two has not been proved, but has not been disproved either? What constitutes "informed consent"? If a physician suggests that a child should not be vaccinated, and that child then contracts measles or mumps, he would open himself up to the risk of litigation. In the U.S., some parents have been told by their pediatricians that if they won't vaccinate their children according to the recommended schedule, then they are no longer welcome as patients in that practice.

• In rare cases, the measles virus has been found in the fluid that bathes the brain and in cerebrospinal fluid. In some children, measles viruses have been found in the gut. It is theorized that these viruses cause inflammatory bowel disease, which in turn allows the peptides to cross the blood-brain barrier and affect neurotransmission, leading to some of the behaviors associated with ASDs. DNA analysis has shown that the strain of measles found in autistic children is from the vaccine, and not a wild virus.

To Learn More about Vaccines

Obviously, there is an urgent need for more research into vaccinations and a possible connection with ASDs, and any decisions regarding vaccination should be discussed with your family physician.

Meanwhile, parents need to educate themselves by going to the different sources and reading for themselves. As always, keep in mind each organization's or agency's mission when reading any articles or reports or analyzing research. Besides the scientific journals and government documents, here are some other sources of information:

• *What Your Doctor May Not Tell You about Children's Vaccinations,* by Stephanie Cave, discusses lucidly the pros and cons of the different vaccines and offers a risk-benefit analysis, as well as an alternative vaccination schedule that may minimize exposure to any possible risks.

• The National Vaccine Information Center (NVIC) (www.909 shot.com), a nonprofit educational organization founded in 1982, is the oldest and largest parent-led group in the U.S. advocating reformation of the mass vaccination system. NVIC is responsible for launching the vaccine safety movement in America in the early 1980s. Contact: National Vaccine Information Center, 421-E Church Street, Vienna, VA 22180; phone: 703-938-DPT3; fax: 703-938-5768.

• SafeMinds (www.safeminds.org) is a nonprofit organization that works aggressively with government agencies and legislators to facilitate the removal of mercury from all medical products, as well as to create awareness campaigns for families and physicians to educate them about the issue.

• The Institute for Vaccine Safety (www.vaccinesafety.edu) was established in 1997 at the Johns Hopkins University School of Public Health (now the Bloomberg School of Public Health). Its goal is to work toward preventing disease using the safest vaccines possible. Look on this website for information concerning vaccine schedules for infants and children, as well as the amounts of thimerosal (if any) in the different vaccines.

Why People with ASDs Act the Way They Do

As mentioned in the previous chapter, a diagnosis of an ASD is based on observable behavioral characteristics. We are beginning to have an understanding of why people have those observable characteristics, that is to say, why they behave the way they do.

From observation and written accounts by people with ASD, we can understand what some of the behaviors mean. This is helpful information for the general public so they can develop an understanding of why people with ASDs might act a certain way, and understanding is a near neighbor of tolerance! It is invaluable knowledge for parents, caregivers, teachers, and other professionals who are trying to decide what therapies, treatments, and interventions could help a person with an ASD.

Behaviors Are a Form of Communication

For the very young, and those who are nonverbal, behaviors can be the only way for them to communicate with us and the only way for us to understand what is going on with them. Some of these behaviors are avoidance behaviors. Other behaviors are indicative of the individuals trying to make sense of their surroundings. The brain structure of many people with ASDs is unlike ours, with some processing circuits wired differently, and it is important to realize that they cannot help what they are doing; they are not just "being difficult."

Parents, caregivers, and teachers can observe a person's behaviors and try to analyze the reason behind them. There is a certain amount of guesswork involved, but by systematically picking one behavior and writing down your observations, you will probably find a pattern.

For example, if a child keeps taking his clothes off, he is probably sensitive to the feel of fabrics on the skin. It would be helpful to observe and take notes on this particular behavior, such as whether he is doing it when he is wearing a certain type of fabric or a certain fit or cut of clothing. Identifying what he can wear will make it easier for him to be comfortable. Perhaps he can be desensitized by a sensory integration technique of "brushing" the skin with a soft plastic brush specifically made for that purpose.

Striking a Balance between Changing the Environment and Changing the Behavior

As parents and caregivers, we need to find the balance between trying to change the environment and changing the individual. Usually a bit of both will be in order. For example, if behaviors indicate possible food allergies, and tests indicate that that is so, a change in diet (the environment) is in order. However, the person may need to learn to tolerate (slowly, through desensitization) eating certain foods that perhaps he would not eat before if he is following a special diet to help his condition.

If a person has auditory and visual sensory processing difficulties, perhaps he can undergo auditory training or vision therapy and avoid spending too much time in noisy, bright environments. Classrooms should not be lit with fluorescent lighting, but the child also needs to learn an alternative appropriate behavior, such as requesting a break or permission to go for a walk, rather than having a temper tantrum.

Listed below are some behaviors and what they can mean. Keep in mind that these are generalizations and that everyone is different, so they may not be true for everyone. Nonetheless, this is a good place to start trying to analyze a person's behaviors. Then, when looking at treatments and therapies, you will already have an idea of areas in which you can help this person. Remember, too, that some behaviors can be indicative of different causes, so you need to look at the total person.

Some Observable Characteristics and What They Could Mean

Finicky eating
- Eating only from certain food groups can be indicative of food allergies. Sometimes the discomfort created by food allergies can cause other behavioral symptoms similar to sensory processing issues. Often, frequent diarrhea or constipation accompanies eating problems due to allergies.

• Eating only foods of the same texture, smelling the food before eating it, and not eating foods that produce a crunching sound can indicate sensory processing issues, as can chewing or eating unusual nonfood items.

• Eating only exactly the same foods, if accompanied by other examples of insistence on sameness, can show high sensory sensitivities or apprehension of the unknown.

Avoidance of auditory stimulation

• Covering the ears or appearing deaf (e.g., not responding when name is called) indicates auditory processing difficulties and a high sensitivity to sound. A person may cover their ears to try and block out the sound, or tune out completely.

• Leaving a room when people enter may be a way of avoiding too much auditory stimulation.

• Listening to and repeating TV commercials or songs could indicate that the person has gotten used to hearing those sounds, i.e., has desensitized himself to them. Listening to people talk is more difficult because people don't usually say the same thing twice, and no two people speak the same way.

• People with autism often have a monotone or peculiar intonations because they don't understand the concept of nuance, and that how you say something conveys an additional meaning to what you say.

No reaction, or else a strong reaction, to touch

• Some babies become stiff when you pick them up; some children will fall and cut themselves and not cry. Usually this indicates that their tactile sense is out of whack. Perhaps a child's tactile sensors are overly sensitive and he does not like to be touched, or they are very dull and he doesn't feel sensations the way most people do.

Removes clothes or shoes often

• A person may not like the feel of particular textures on their skin. Certain fabrics and shoes can make people with extremely sensitive tactile sensors uncomfortable.

Lack of eye contact

• People with visual processing problems find it hard to look at people straight on; usually they look from the side of their eyes.

Unusual body movements

• Rocking in a chair, or back and forth from one foot to the other, could be a stress release from too much stimulation, or not enough.

• Flicking of fingers could also be a release from stress, but if doing it in front of the eyes, it could be a visual processing stimulation.

• Awkward movements and running into furniture can be a symptom of poor body mapping, not knowing where one is in space, or poor fine and gross motor skills.

Does not play with or imitate others

• People with autism are often lacking in the social skills, interests, and understanding which the rest of us find so important. Also, a child with sensory processing issues will have difficulty being near other children who are, in his eyes, noisy and unpredictable, and who have textures and smells associated with them that the child with an ASD cannot tolerate.

Lines up objects

• This can show a need for sameness. Usually children who line up toys are also the ones who do not like change in their routine, may have repetitive speech, and do not like to see the furniture moved into a different pattern in their home.

• They may have a hard time making sense of their world, and so the sameness in certain areas provides a predictability and security missing from an existence which they are having a hard time comprehending.

Temper tantrums, hyperactivity, and aggression toward self or others

• Temper tantrums or meltdowns in children can be a reaction to sensory overload, or to a change in the sameness that provides security.

• Places with a lot of light and noise, such as supermarkets and waiting rooms with fluorescent lighting, are really hard on people with sensory processing issues.

• Aggression toward others could be for any number of reasons, such as sensory overload (e.g., a sudden loud noise near someone's ear could cause them to jump up and strike out at the person making the noise, as it can be very painful).

• Self-aggression could be due to seeking sensory stimulation, feeling pain, or frustration.

4

Newly Diagnosed Adults and Parents of Children with an ASD: After the Diagnosis

The book was finished and now I had a word for the problems I had fought to overcome and understand. The label would have been useless except that it helped me to forgive myself and my family for the way I was. . . . I wanted to meet the other autistic people I'd been told about and was surprised to find out that they were few and far between, scattered across the country and across the world. I was even in a smaller category. I had become "high functioning." Nevertheless, I needed to meet others.

—DONNA WILLIAMS, *Nobody Nowhere*

When you are a parent of a child who is developing more slowly than typical children, you may feel alone, but you are not. Knowing that you are not alone is a big part of the cure for the worry and pain. Parents whose children are not developing typically can greatly benefit from understanding the similarities between themselves and others. A lot of healing occurs when you exchange stories with others in similar circumstances.

—ROBERT A. NASEEF, *Special Children, Challenged Parents*

IT was hard for me to go to my first Berkshire Autistic Society meeting. I was taking another step toward acknowledging that my child had a disability and that it wasn't just going to go away. It felt as if I was becoming a member of a club that I didn't really want to join. The only thing I had in common with the roomful of people was the label our children shared, but even so our children were so different from each other. But we helped one another. We shared resources, information, anger, tears, and advice. We gave each other energy and the courage to do what was needed. We shared stories about our children that were too embarrassing to tell anyone else, and we laughed at the absurdity of our situation. And most importantly, the group developed resources that were nonexistent. We created change in the status quo.

You Are Not Alone

Because of the epidemic rise in the numbers of individuals diagnosed with autism spectrum disorders, you are not alone. Whether you are a parent or you are an adult with autism, having access to others like yourselves is necessary, not only for the sharing of information but also for your mental health.

There Is Power and Comfort in Numbers

In this chapter, suggestions and resources will be provided for the parents of children with ASDs and for the recently diagnosed individual. Professionals can also learn much by accessing the same sources. It is true that you are not alone: there are many organizations, associations, books, and websites ready to help you. Remember too that there is comfort to be had in meeting others experiencing the same situation as you. There is also power in numbers: the more people who get together, the more useful ideas float around.

Adults who have a diagnosis of an ASD may find support through local chapters of the Autism Society of America (ASA), www.autism-society.org. There are also many online resources and websites available to you that are run by people with Asperger's that can give you support and advice. They are listed in the Resources section at the end of this book.

Professionals who are new to the field of autism spectrum disorders would do well to read about the experiences of parents and to consult the resources available to parents in order to learn more about this disorder, as well as how it affects the family.

Parents and professionals alike would benefit and gain a greater understanding of autism and Asperger's by reading accounts by people with ASDs, either in books or on websites.

Empower Thyself—Seek Knowledge

The first step in gaining an understanding about ASDs is to gather knowledge. Here are some places to start:

Make contact with nonprofit organizations dedicated to ASDs. The first step should be to make contact with other people in the same situation, i.e., others who have an ASD, or other parents. The first place to start is the Autism Society of America. They have an excellent website (www.autism-society.org) with valuable information for parents, professionals, and adults with ASDs. The ASA also has local chapters, and you can get their contact numbers off the national ASA website.

Local chapters will be able to give you more localized information. Because each state has different ways of providing federally mandated early intervention and education, you will need to know how to access these services in your state. Also, local chapters often have guest speakers, and meeting other members can be a great way to get helpful information on local resources. You can find out about other autism associations that

FOOD FOR THOUGHT

Tips to Keep in Mind on Your Quest for Knowledge

• Make sure you are seeking information from reliable sources. Just because something is published on a website or in a magazine does not mean it is accurate.

• Take it one step at a time and seek only what you are ready to assimilate. Focus on the present. Learn what you can that will help you today or over the next six months. At this early stage, if you try to think too far ahead, you may feel overwhelmed. Do only what you feel capable of doing, and read only what you are ready to digest.

• Learn the jargon. If someone uses a word you don't understand, look it up or ask for an explanation.

• Ask questions if you don't understand. Ignorance is not bliss, and life will become a lot easier if you get used to asking questions. Before going to any meetings or appointments, write questions down. Ask and ye shall receive.

• What works for one child may not necessarily work for yours. Everyone is different; you need to find what is right for your child.

• Do not be intimidated by others. Some parents feel overawed by medical or educational professionals. There is no need to feel this way. They may be an expert in their field, yet you are the expert on your child. ASDs are very complex, and even educational and medical experts do not know everything. Together you can be a team.

---

may be helpful to you in your area, and many local chapters have a lending library of books you can borrow. This is a good way of filtering through the different books and only buying the ones you really will use over and over.

Another nonprofit organization that may have a chapter in your area is Families for Early Autism Treatment (FEAT), and you can find out by looking on their website (www.feat.org) which also offers excellent resources.

If you are looking for information more specific to those who have Asperger's syndrome, or those on the more able end of the spectrum, an excellent source of information is O.A.S.I.S. (Online Asperger Syndrome Information and Support) (www.udel.edu/bkirby/asperger), as well as the book *The Oasis Guide to Asperger Syndrome: Advice, Support, Insight and Inspiration* by Patricia Romanowski Bashe and Barbara L. Kirby.

Make contact with other families or adults diagnosed with an ASD. Through your local association or websites, make contact with others in your situation. If you are an adult who has just been diagnosed, you might find it helpful to contact another adult who has an ASD. This can be done on the telephone or online. Parents will find it helpful to talk to others who have been in the same situation or are going through it now.

Contact the Autism Research Institute (ARI). For over thirty-five years, Dr. Bernard Rimland's nonprofit organization (www.autism researchinstitute.com) has been a clearinghouse for all kinds information about the diagnosis and treatment of ASDs. Dr. Rimland's 1964 book *Infantile Autism: The Syndrome and Its Implications for a Neural Theory of Behavior* dramatically changed the accepted perception of autism. He is also the founder of the Autism Society of America, and initiated the Defeat Autism Now! project. Dr. Rimland analyzes research studies on ASDs conducted all over the world, and he compiles anecdotal information from parents and caregivers. He has amassed detailed case histories of over thirty thousand children with ASDs from more than sixty countries. This makes for an enormous body of information on ASDs, the only one of its kind.

Dr. Rimland also publishes the quarterly *Autism Research Review*

International, and his institute provides information packets, books, and videotapes, charging only the cost of the postage and materials.

Read Advice for Parents of Young Autistic Children (2004): Working Paper *by James B. Adams, Ph.D., Stephen M. Edelson, Ph.D., Temple Grandin, Ph.D., and Bernard Rimland, Ph.D.* This paper is geared toward parents of newly diagnosed children, and parents of young autistic children may find it useful. It is on the Center for the Study of Autism's website at http://www.autism.org/contents.html.

Read accounts written by adults with autism spectrum disorders. For everyone, reading books by people with ASDs gives an insight into what was helpful to them and explains some of their feelings and behaviors. For newly diagnosed adults, this may help you to understand that there are others out there with similar challenges, and perhaps their stories will hold tips to helping you live in a neurotypical world. See the Resources section for some recommendations.

Read books written by parents of children with an ASD. If you read only one book, make it *Facing Autism* by Lynn M. Hamilton. It is a particularly good book, full of valuable information about the latest methods shown to be effective with children with ASDs. Parents can take comfort from reading books by others who have been there, knowing that all have the same struggles and fears. The information that other parents have shared about their experiences can save new parents a lot of time and energy, and give you tips on all sorts of different aspects. See the Resources section for other recommendations.

Learn about any services or funding for which you or your child may be eligible. If you are not already, you and your child will soon be consumers of the various wonderful systems that are there to help you. This gives you certain rights as well as responsibilities (see "Where to Start Your Search for Services and Funding" on page 84). Your local chapter of the Autism Society of America (ASA) can provide you with the information you need to get started in your area. Educate yourself by talking to other parents who have been there before. Start the application process for anything you feel you are eligible for. Things take time.

Get on waiting lists. If your child is very young, you need to find out about early intervention in your area. For any age, it is important that you get your name on any lists for services you feel you may need to access at some point. Who knows what the future holds? You may need to get on lists for speech evaluations, respite care, an assessment of special education needs, or other services. If you are investigating applied behavior analysis (ABA), it's best to call a few providers and get on their lists. You may not want or need it in the end, but remember, it is easier to get off a list than to get a service when you haven't been on one in the first place.

Start keeping good records. Start keeping a record of all medical visits and professional appointments. Keep track of telephone conversations as well. Filing papers in a three-ring binder in chronological order is the best way to organize information. Do not separate papers by profession (e.g., speech assessment, psychological assessment), as a chronological order of all papers makes it easier to see a complete picture of the child at different ages.

Start keeping notes on your child. Make a journal about your child and start collecting data and making notes about developmental milestones, illnesses, bowel movement patterns, as well as health changes (if any) following vaccines, medications, and vitamins. Information recorded here about dietary habits; behaviors, including self-stimulatory ones; and the child's abilities and challenges can be useful in getting a full picture of your child and can help in identifying the best ways to help him.

Videotape your child. Our memories may fade, but videos don't lie. This is a good way of seeing how a child develops and progresses. Also, if ever you need to prove a point on how a particular method is working, a video can illustrate that and make a strong visual impression about the difference in your child.

Do whatever you can to interact with and teach your child. You may be waiting on lists for some time. Do what you can to connect with your child: read to him, sing to him, play with him. Don't wait for someone else to do it. Connecting with this child may not be the same as connecting with his siblings (if any), but you will connect.

Take care of yourself. Most importantly, stay healthy. Remember that you still have a life outside this child. Take time for yourself and for your partner as well as any other children. There is a whole world out there, and you need to recharge your batteries to keep things in perspective.

Seek out positive people. Stay away from negative people who sap your energy. Later in this chapter, we will discuss the grief cycle and how it affects people. Sometimes, in support groups you will meet individuals who are constantly depressed or you may have relatives who are handling the diagnosis worse than you are. Everyone is entitled to a bad day here and there where they feel as if they have hit rock bottom. However, the whole point of having a good cry is to get it out of your system, and then get on with your day. You need to save your energy to help your child, your own family, and yourself; don't let others drain it from you.

Who Said What? Buyer Beware

You will meet people at support groups, visit many websites, read books, get advice from professionals. All these sources of information are helpful, but you must be able to sift through the information and analyze what is valid for you:

• *Information from other parents:* Parents will say that a particular treatment worked or didn't work for their child. They may say a certain therapy is the best thing on the market since sliced bread. Remember, they are talking from their point of view, based on their child. Your child may share a common diagnosis or label, but that does not mean the children have the same treatment needs. You need to evaluate the information from the parent based on what you know about your child. Keep in mind that just as people have certain political or religious beliefs, they also have particular beliefs when it comes to autism and treatment.

• *Information from websites:* The great thing about the Internet is the accessibility to information and the ease of researching particular topics. The downside is that any Tom, Dick, or Harry can put up a website, and many of them have. The result is that while many websites are valid, informative, and based on fact, others simply put out information based on the particular bias of the individual or company that has set them up. You need to read everything with a grain of salt and learn to develop analytical skills if you don't have them already. I liken getting information from the Internet to talking to strangers in a bar. You never know who you are talking to until you investigate and ask a few questions. Would you take advice from a stranger in a bar? You would probably want to know more about him before you believed and acted on anything he said.

• *Information from books:* Books are generally good sources of information, though again you need to bear in mind who is writing the book and what perspective they are writing from. Also, look at when the book was published. If you are preparing for a meeting with your school district and have questions about your rights and responsibilities, you want to make sure you are consulting a recent publication that takes into account any recent changes in the law, and not something written five years ago.

• *Information from professionals:* Professionals are very knowledgeable people and can be experts in their field, but that does not mean that they are knowledgeable about the latest treatments and therapies for ASDs. Neither are they experts on your child; you are. Again, you need to know more about a professional's experience and training, and what biases they have. It does not mean that what they have to say is not valid, but like everyone, they are shaped by their experiences. Perhaps they have not yet worked hands-on with a child of your age or functioning level. If they have, did the children they worked with progress?

• *Information from autism organizations:* ASD organizations are wonderful sources of information. Just be aware that they have opinions, just as people do. Sometimes there can be the appearance of a conflict of interest. Unfortunately, autism is not free of politics. But remember that all organizations are doing their best to help people with ASDs; you just have to be able to gather information and make your own decisions about what is best for your child and your family.

For Parents: The Emotions

Life is a series of choices. Granted, as a parent you did not choose for your child to have an autism spectrum disorder. However, you can choose how to react to it and what you are going to do about it. The first place to start is to learn about the emotions you are feeling, and to understand that they are real and unavoidable, and that all parents will go through them at some time or another. These emotions need to be addressed. A good place to start is to acknowledge them and accept that it is normal to have them.

Loss of Expectation

"What it comes down to is that you expected something that was tremendously important to you, and you looked forward to it with great joy and excitement, and maybe for a while you thought you actually had it—and then, perhaps gradually, perhaps abruptly, you had to recognize that the thing you looked forward to hasn't happened. It isn't going to happen. No matter how many other, normal children you have, nothing will change the fact that this time, the child you waited and hoped and planned and dreamed for didn't arrive."

—Jim Sinclair,
"Don't Mourn for Us"

The Moment Your Life Changes Forever

There are certain events that change the course of world history; dramatic events that are indelibly etched in all our memories. And along with the memory of the actual event, there is the memory of where you were or what you were doing when you got the news. September the 11th and the terrorist attack on the Twin Towers; the day that John F. Kennedy was assassinated; Princess Diana dying in a car crash in Paris; *Challenger* exploding on takeoff are all events that we as members of the human race shared collectively.

After disastrous events, all of society grieves together; and though we are all different, we can mourn together and acknowledge the feelings the event has provoked. The day a parent learns that his or her child has a disability is like one of those dramatic event days. For some, it feels as if they have just been hit in the stomach and had the wind knocked out of them. Even if the parent suspected that there was something wrong with the child, they can't believe this is happening. For every parent of a child with a disability, this moment is forever etched on their mind.

The difference is that no one else is sharing your pain. When the parent leaves wherever it is that he got the news and walks into the street or parking lot, his whole world has changed, but there is no comfort to be had, no collective reaching out to one another. The other people in the street or in the other cars have the same life they had an hour earlier. Only the parent's has changed forever.

The Grief Cycle

In her book *On Death and Dying,* psychiatrist Elisabeth Kübler-Ross introduced her famous "stages of dying" or "stages of grief" model, in which she lists the five stages a dying person goes through when they are told about their terminal illness: denial and isolation; anger; depression; bargaining; and finally acceptance.

The emotions that a parent goes through when raising a child with a chronic health need or disability, including ASD, have been likened to Kübler-Ross's five stages of grief. The difference is that instead of going through each stage chronologically, parents are on a continual cycle, going through different stages at different times. They never graduate completely out of the grief cycle but do eventually learn to spend more time in the acceptance phase.

Why Do Parents Go Through the Grief Cycle?

First of all, parents are mourning the death of the child they never had, the death of the future they had envisioned sharing with their child. They have not actually lost their child, but they have lost their fantasy child, the one they had hoped for and dreamed about. As Jim Sinclair so rightly puts it in his article "Don't Mourn for Us," "Much of the grieving parents do is over the non-occurrence of the expected relationship with an expected normal child. This grief is very real, and it needs to be

You Never Get Over It, You Just Learn to Deal with It

It was one of those beautiful Parisian spring days that makes you feel that all is right with the world. I decided to stop at the café after a walk with my four-year-old son.

At the next table, a mother and her ten-year-old boy were laughing at a joke he had just told her. She asked him about his school day and he talked about the games he played at recess. When the waiter came to take their order, the boy grinned impishly at his mother and asked imploringly, "Maman, can I please have a pain au chocolat and a hot chocolate?" "It's going to ruin your appetite for dinner, but go ahead," she replied, ruffling his hair.

When the waiter came to take our order, I asked my son if he wanted a hot chocolate, as he stared at the speckles of dust in the air reflected by the light, his head cocked to one side, while spinning the spoon he had found on the table. He appeared not to hear me; it was as if I had not even spoken. I looked with envy at the other table, at that mother sharing an everyday ordinary moment with her child. And that now-all-too-familiar ache descended as I realized once again that I would never have a moment like that with my son; I would never sit and share a joke and have a conversation with him. I wondered if he would even ever look at me with the same interest he showed the spoon.

I reached for the spoon and started fidgeting with it. My son looked at the movement of the spoon. I picked it up and twirled it in front of my face. For an instant he looked into my eyes and smiled before fixating back on the spoon, melting my heart in the process. Perhaps, I thought, I will never be able to have a conversation with him about recess, but I know we will connect somehow; we will find a way, our way.

expected and worked through so people can get on with their lives—but it has nothing to do with autism. . . . It isn't about autism, it's about shattered expectations."

Second, parents go through this grief process because until recently autism was considered incurable, and parents were told to go home and accept that there was no hope for their child and to plan on institutionalizing their child in the future when life with autism got to be too much. The medical professionals had nothing to offer but condolences.

Third, parents who have children with regressive autism (a child who developed normally and then started regressing at around eighteen months) may feel the very real loss of the child they did have, of seeing their child slip away into autism.

However, a diagnosis of autism is no longer a diagnosis of despair and hopelessness. There is a chance of recovery and even cure for some individuals with the proper interventions. And for the rest, there is much that can be done to help them reach their potential. There are so many new treatments, therapies, and educational strategies out there. Dedicated parents and professionals have fought hard (and are still fighting) to get research funded, discoveries made, services provided, laws enacted, and information shared so that all individuals with ASDs can have a future. The grief cycle is still here, but the future looks brighter for all of us.

The Positive Aspects of the Grief Cycle

An important part of this grieving process is to realize that to grieve is normal and necessary. It is important for the well-being of the family that the parents recognize and acknowledge this grief as well as the emotions that will continually resurface. Each emotion on the grief cycle, if recognized, can be fuel for positive action. If you are at the anger stage, for example, you might use that anger to refuse to accept a third-rate educational program for your child and to request an appropriate placement. Parents need to learn to recognize where they are on the cycle, and how to use that emotion to gain knowledge and empower themselves. Then, on the days that they feel strong and capable, they will be ready for action.

Remember, when it comes to autism spectrum disorders, early intervention is the best intervention. The sooner you can use these emotions to help yourself, your child, and your family, the better off you all will be.

The Different Stages of the ASD Grief Cycle

Shock and disbelief. The first reaction a parent usually has when hearing the diagnosis, even if they suspected something was wrong, is disbelief. "There must be some mistake." "This can't be happening." At this point, the parent usually does not process exactly what has happened or the enormity of what has just been said. They often go into automatic-pilot mode and sit through the rest of the meeting without really taking in any more information. Some parents may even feel physical pain, as if someone has torn them open. They may feel as if they have been smothered in a dark heavy blanket and are unable to see or hear or breathe.

Tip for parents: Leave the meeting and allow yourself time to react to what you have heard. React however you want to react. Don't do anything or make any decisions until your body stops reacting. Make an appointment to come back another time, when you have had a few days to process the initial shock. Make a list of questions to ask. You may find it helpful to talk to close family and friends; you may wish to isolate yourself. Take time for yourself.

Denial. At this stage, parents think there is some mistake which will eventually be cleared up. Even though they may see the obvious and it has been confirmed by a professional, they still think, "There is nothing wrong with my child. They must have mixed up the test results." In denial, parents often seek second or third opinions, or some magical treatment that will "cure" their child.

Tip for parents: Use your denial positively: gather information and learn more about autism. Some parents start "shopping" for services, looking for that one treatment that will cure their child. You know there really is not a magic pill out there, but denial can fuel you to get informed and learn all you can.

Anger or rage. Once a parent has got through the denial stage after the initial diagnosis, they will often be angry. "Why me?" "How come there are people out there with perfectly healthy children and they don't appear to care about, and our poor child, who is the light of our life, has the disability?" Often, the professional who gave them the initial diagnosis bears the brunt of their rage. They may feel anger toward their spouse, toward God (if they believe in one), toward the child, or maybe even toward a sibling for being healthy and normal (which leads to feelings of guilt . . .). They will feel anger at the disability. At sensitive times, such as when seeking educational provision, this anger may flare up and be misdirected at representatives of the local educational authority.

Tip for parents: Feel angry! You have a right to be. But don't misdirect your anger at the people who are trying to help you. Anger carries a lot of energy with it that can be focused to enable you to be an advocate for your child. Learn to refocus your anger and do something positive with it: perhaps write those letters asking for services or more assessments— just wait a few days and reread them once you have calmed down, then tone down the inappropriate parts before sending them off.

Confusion and powerlessness. You are now entering a world you know nothing about, hearing new words that sound foreign. You are confused: "What does this really mean about my child?" "I don't understand what the doctor is talking about." And this confusion leaves you feeling powerless. Powerlessness results from feeling that now you have to rely on the advice and expertise of others, people you don't even know that well and have no reason to trust: "The specialist says this is the best method."

Tip for parents: Of course you are confused and feel powerless; you

FOOD FOR THOUGHT
Shame and Embarrassment

My son is fifteen now, and sometimes he finds it difficult to be in certain environments, and will start flapping one of his hands or will rock on the spot. I am so used to being stared at that I forget that people are looking at me because of my son's behavior and I start thinking, "Is there food on my face?" "Are my buttons undone?"

My son is usually good about keeping his hands to himself, but every once in a while he will get attracted to a pattern or a color or a shiny object and will touch someone's bag or sweater while we are waiting in line at the supermarket. Obviously we work hard at teaching him that this is inappropriate, but sometimes he sees something that is just too tempting. Of course I immediately stop him, remind him of what we said about doing that and apologize to the person in question. I often get them laughing by saying something like, "He knows quality when he sees it, he only goes for the top designers." Humor helps to put us all at ease.

---

have entered a territory you know nothing about. There is a solution: start learning the terminology and the subject, and little by little you will become knowledgeable. And knowledge is power. You will feel less and less confused and more in control once you have the knowledge to make informed decisions. It will take time, but you will get there.

Depression. Sometimes everything seems like a struggle. The struggles to try to cure or change the ASD lead to feelings of despair. The idea that this is not the life the parent had dreamed of, that this is not the family they had hoped for is more than can be borne. They realize that autism is 24/7, and that they are on a train they never wanted to board and there is no getting off. The lack of sleep does not help, either.

Tip for parents: This is when you need to take some time away from autism, even if it is only a few hours. Have a good cry and then pamper yourself. Call a friend and do something you really enjoy: meet for lunch, play some golf, go shopping. If talking to friends, family, or other parents is not helping you get out of your depression, contact a counseling service or ask your doctor to recommend a therapist, perhaps even a bereavement counselor.

Guilt. Parents feel guilt about having a child with an ASD. After the diagnosis, the guilt is typically expressed as, "What did I do to cause this to happen?" "Was it the glass of red wine I had at my birthday party when I was pregnant?" "I shouldn't have allowed the doctors to give him those vaccinations." "Am I being punished for something I have done?" Later on, when they revisit the guilt stage on the cycle, it revolves around, "I'm not doing enough for my child." "I should have taken a second mortgage on the house so he could have more therapy and alternative treatments."

Tip for parents: Don't beat yourself up. All parents do what they think is best at the time. It is not a good idea to use hindsight to try to analyze and critique the past. Nobody's perfect. Take the time to sit back and think about all the positive things you have done for your child, and how your child is growing and developing under your care. Pat yourself on the back for what you have done, and think about where you can go from here. The past is the past; focus on the present.

Shame or embarrassment. At some point parents will feel shame about not having a perfect child—"What will people think?" Later, as the child gets older, they are nervous about people's reactions to the child's behavior in public. They catch someone staring at their child. They think, "Gosh, I wish he wouldn't flap his hand while he is walking." "His lack of eating skills and his disruptive behavior is ruining everyone else's dinner at this restaurant." "People must think I'm a terrible parent when he acts this way." And then, of course, they feel guilty about feeling shame, which puts them on another part of the cycle.

Tip for parents: Get over it. Do not worry about what others are thinking. In the big picture, it doesn't matter. Think of it this way: your child is different and interesting and your life with him will not be boring. Develop a sense of humor. Stand straight and tall, look confident. Just think about making this a positive experience for your child, not about the others. When people see that you are at ease with your child in public, or see that you are trying to cope with a challenging behavior, they will respect you.

Fear and panic. Parents will inevitably feel fear and panic: "What will happen to my child?" Times of transition can bring about these panic attacks. "How will he adjust to the new school?" "Another new teacher! Is she going to understand his learning style?" "What will he do after high school?" and of course the biggest panic attack comes from the dreaded, "What will happen to him and who will look out for him when we are dead and buried?" or "I want him to live with us at home but we can't handle it anymore. Is there a good safe place for my child?"

Tip for parents: Take some time for yourself, take a few deep breaths, or practice your favorite relaxation technique and then acknowledge that what you are feeling is fear of the unknown. Use the fear and panic to propel you toward gathering knowledge about the choices you have in regard to whatever issue you are feeling fear about. Write down everything you think the new teacher should know about your child and give her the letter with a smile, telling her you hope it is helpful information. Find out about his options after high school. Visit group homes or residential schools to see what they are really like. Just having the knowledge about the options will make you feel better. If you are not happy with the options, perhaps you will find yourself at the anger stage and that will propel you to organize with other parents and advocate for better choices or, better yet, create them.

Bargaining. After a while parents start to bargain with whatever higher intelligence or God they believe in. "If the forty hours of behavioral therapy per week for two years cures my son, I will adopt a poor family to send money to every week for the rest of my life." "If it is only autism, I can accept it, but if it's mental retardation as well . . ." "If he can learn to communicate in some way . . ." The process of bargaining is a way for the parent to accept a part of the problem without taking on the whole problem.

Tip for parents: As time goes on, you will find that you are bargaining less and less as you start to have more acceptance of your situation and get to know your child, his personality and potential, as well as the options out there.

Hope. Parents have moments when they feel hopeful. "We may make it through this." "This diet/therapy/medication seems to be helping our child." "He is getting this concept." "He's keeping his behaviors under control." Just like any parents, there are times when we are encouraged by the accomplishments of our child or we meet professionals or treatments that are having a positive impact on him.

Tip for parents: Celebrate and cherish each and every one of these moments. Tuck them away and pull them out on the days when you feel bleak and could use some hope. These are the moments that make you feel that life is good. Treasure them, and share them with those who have shared your sorrows so they can also share in your joy.

Isolation. Sometimes parents feel isolated—"My child is the only one who is not acting appropriately." Or they seek isolation because they do not want to see the reminders that they have a different child or a different life from everyone else's, or because they feel that they must protect their child.

Tip for parents: Sometimes you feel an overwhelming need to isolate yourself from others because the pain of seeing other parents interacting normally with neurotypical kids is too great. It is not a good idea to stay isolated, however. To get through this, use local associations to find other families who have children with ASDs or other disabilities. You will feel more comfortable with them, as you will understand each other's concerns. Eventually, over time, you will come to feel more comfortable spending time with other families who are not in the same situation as you.

Acceptance. Parents will feel acceptance of their child's ASD only after having experienced and worked through some of the other emotions discussed above. Acceptance means that they are feeling some control over the situation and their feelings about it. The challenges may not be solved to the level that they wish, but they see that they are able to cope and live with the hand they have been dealt. Acceptance also means that they realize that there will be days filled with anger or grief, and days that they will have strength. On any given day they will be in one spot on the grief cycle or another, but it's OK. The parent is learning to cope and knows it's all right to have those emotions. Also, accomplishments that may seem ordinary and small to others will be moments they savor and cherish. Acceptance also means that they look at their child and see a person, not a disability.

For Adults with ASDs: Getting Diagnosed Later in Life

In the past, many individuals with ASDs on the very able end, or with Asperger's syndrome, who were able to function pretty well, did not get diagnosed at all or until later in life. However, many felt that they were in some way different and, once diagnosed, reported feeling relieved at knowing that there were others out there like them and that there was a reason why they never fitted in.

Knowing that there is a name or label for what you have gives you the option of looking up information and seeing what strategies are out there to help with some of the challenges you may face. Being diagnosed

Don't Mourn for Us

This is an excerpt from an article published in 1993 in the Autism Network International newsletter, Our Voice *(vol. 1, No. 3). It is an outline of the presentation Jim Sinclair gave at the 1993 International Conference on Autism in Toronto, and is addressed primarily to parents. Jim is autistic.*

Autism is not death. Granted, autism isn't what most parents expect or look forward to when they anticipate the arrival of a child. What they expect is a child who will be like them, who will share their world and relate to them without requiring intensive on-the-job training in alien contact. Even if their child has some disability other than autism, parents expect to be able to relate to that child on the terms that seem normal to them; and in most cases, even allowing for the limitations of various disabilities, it is possible to form the kind of bond the parents had been looking forward to.

But not when the child is autistic. Much of the grieving parents do is over the non-occurrence of the expected relationship with an expected normal child. This grief is very real, and it needs to be expected and worked through so people can get on with their lives—but it has nothing to do with autism. . . . It isn't about autism, it's about shattered expectations.

I suggest that the best place to address these issues is not in organizations devoted to autism, but in parental bereavement counseling and support groups. In those settings parents learn to come to terms with their loss—not to forget about it, but to let it be in the past, where the grief doesn't hit them in the face every waking moment of their lives. They learn to accept that their child is gone, forever, and won't be coming back. Most importantly, they learn not to take out their grief for the lost child on their surviving children. This is of critical importance when one of those surviving children arrived at the time the child being mourned for died. . . .

That isn't the fault of the autistic child who does exist, and it shouldn't be our burden. We need and deserve families who can see us and value us for ourselves, not families whose vision of us is obscured by the ghosts of children who never lived. Grieve if you must, for your own lost dreams. But don't mourn for us. We are alive. We are real. And we're here waiting for you. . . .

---

allows you access to support groups and information you did not know existed.

You may wish to read books by people with ASDs who give suggestions on how they cope with some of the challenges they face, or look up information on the Internet. Some of the books listed in the resource section in the back were written by people who were diagnosed with an ASD later in life, such as Liane Holliday Willey and Jerry Newport.

If you wish to look into support groups for you or your family, check out Tony Attwood's website (www.tonyattwood.com.au) and click on the "Support Groups" link, as well as the link "Websites for People with Asperger's." There are many good resources on Tony's website as well as on the O.A.S.I.S. website (www.udel.edu/bkirby/asperger) under the link "Adult Issues."

There are many more resources you may find useful in chapter 9. You may also find this next section helpful in your quest for more information.

Marshaling Your Resources to Get Support, Services, and Funding

Most parents or adults with ASDs will need at one time or another to ask for support or advice. In this section, developing the survival skills that will make you an effective advocate is discussed, followed by some basic information on where to start looking for the services and funding that can help you.

FOOD FOR THOUGHT

Liane Holliday Willey recognized that she had Asperger's syndrome at the time her daughter was diagnosed. In her book Pretending to Be Normal, *this is what she has to say about realizing she had Asperger's as well:*

Yet, no matter the hardships, I do not wish for a cure for Asperger's syndrome. What I wish for is a cure for the common ill that pervades too many lives; the ill that makes people compare themselves to a normal that is measured in terms of perfect and absolute standards, most of which are impossible for anyone to reach. I think it would be far more productive and so much more satisfying to live according to a new set of ideals that are anchored in far more subjective criteria, the fluid and the affective domains of life, the stuff of wonder . . . curiosity . . . creativity . . . invention . . . originality. Perhaps then, we will all find peace and joy in one another.

How to Develop the Survival Skills You Need

Working through the educational systems in three different countries has provided me with untold opportunities for observing and learning about how systems work and don't work, the politics involved, and how to ask the right questions. This has been helpful in developing strong survival skills and enabled me to become an effective advocate for my son.

Think of the work you do, and about what skills you used to get and keep your job. Think of the skills used by other people working in the same company. All these skills are the kind you will need either as a parent of a child with an ASD or as an adult with the condition. Applying the skills used every day in work situations will help you obtain the services you or your child needs and keep good relationships with all the people involved.

For example, the skills I developed while producing TV shows are the same skills I used to obtain my son's educational needs: gathering information, analyzing data, listening to consultants' and other team members' expertise, using good clear communication, learning to negotiate, preparing for meetings, deciding what was worth fighting for, working as part of a team, expecting professional behavior, monitoring progress, forgiving honest mistakes, and rewarding a job well done. Sometimes people had to be kicked off the team or there were major disagreements, but at the end of the day, there was a show in the can.

Communicating. Every job involves communicating, whether it is with the public, clients, or fellow workers and the boss. Even if you work the graveyard shift as a security officer, at some point you need to be ready to communicate in case of an emergency. Communication is the major building block of all relationships, and relationships are critical for you to develop in order to get the help you need or the educational program that is appropriate. Being effective at communicating means being able to listen as well as to talk. It means being polite and respectful, and clear about what you are talking about.

Planning. Every company has a business plan, and every worker has a plan of action for what they will do that day, whether it is putting hamburgers together or marketing software. Whether you are dealing with the school district, the medical profession, or social services, planning should now be a part of your life. Planning means looking at what your needs are today and will be in six months, next year, five years from now, and so on. What do you envision for your child or for yourself? How are you going to make that happen? How can the services on offer help you reach your goals? All the decisions you make are about reaching the dream or vision you have for the future.

Researching and analyzing. Before making major decisions at work, you have to research your options and then analyze the information. If you are a chef, you may research where to buy the supplies you need to prepare certain meals, and then analyze the information you have uncovered to come up with the place that best suits your needs and your customers' requirements. If your company needs a photocopy machine, you research the different suppliers and analyze the various options. As a parent, or an adult with an ASD, you need to research the different treatments and diets, education, and work opportunities available. You also need to research what funding options are open to you. Then, analyzing the information will help you decide what plan of action is best for you.

Marketing. If you have a new product to sell, you have to convince your clients that it is the best thing on the market since sliced bread. At work, when someone has a plan of action they want adopted, the whole team has to be convinced to jump on the bandwagon, or the plan will not fly. To sell the idea to colleagues, marketing needs to take place. The person with the idea goes around to his colleagues and persuades them of the benefits of his plan. The same needs to be done once you have developed a plan of action: you need to convince the other team members (e.g., the school district, your doctor) on the merits of your plan. In getting what you need, you will need to market your ideas (using those effective communication strategies) and present the information and analysis as to how you came up with this plan and why.

Negotiating. At work, you may have to negotiate time off with your boss. With clients, you may negotiate different prices or marketing plans. Either way, you have to be prepared to discuss your needs, and to know how far you are willing to go to get what you feel you need. When it comes to services, you may not have as much room for negotiation, but in some cases you may. With the school district, for example, you may be able to negotiate for an educational program they are hesitant to provide due to cost or lack of experienced personnel. Keep in mind that doing this is not easy, but it is possible.

Acknowledging and rewarding. Once you have obtained what you wanted at work, or at least been given the opportunity to present your point of view, you need to reward the people involved by acknowledging the time they spent considering your proposal. The same holds true if you have negotiated and signed a deal with a client, or even if you didn't come to any agreement. A simple "Thanks for taking the time to listen to me" or "I appreciate your support," whichever the case may be, is in order. The same applies to the people you, as a parent, or an adult with an ASD, have been "negotiating" with, even if you don't agree with the results.

Perhaps, as an adult, you didn't get the results from a social worker you had hoped for; but remember, you may be asking that person for help again down the line. If you are a parent, you will be in touch with your local school district for many years, so it is better even in disagreement to acknowledge their efforts. "It looks as if someone took a lot of time out of their schedule to do this assessment and I appreciate the effort" is a good way of acknowledging the effort made before announcing that, unfortunately, the assessment did not address the real issue.

Monitoring. Every business has to have some form of monitoring put in place. The person making french fries has to monitor the amount of fries needed, the temperature of the oil, and how long the fries have been in the fryer. A doctor has to monitor the health of his patients postoperation. Even after your child has an Individual Education Program (IEP) and everyone leaves feeling satisfied that he is going to receive the support service he needs, monitoring must take place. This is where good communication skills are really necessary, as sometimes a gentle nudge is needed to get a service started.

For example, perhaps as an adult with an ASD you have been assured a promised service or some funding to begin at a certain date. If it

FOOD FOR THOUGHT

"When my daughter was diagnosed with Asperger's syndrome, her doctors gave me one outstanding piece of counsel. They told me that my husband and I would now become the experts on AS. We, in effect, would stand as her greatest advocates. The truth of their prophecy has been shown virtually every day. The general public is largely uneducated in AS. I have grown to believe that this is the single most damaging element to the AS cause, that is, understanding and acceptance. Without knowledge of the symptoms, outcomes and even confounding attributes, it is nearly impossible for others to recognize and support AS individuals."

—Liane Willey, *Pretending to Be Normal*

does not, you may need to make a few phone calls to find out what the status is, and what can be done to get the support in place.

How to Get the Information You Need

In an earlier section, we talked about the need to find out about services and start the paperwork, as well as finding out about possible funding. Here are some other tips.

Find out what is available. All therapies cost money. Adults may need funds to supplement their wages. If you are not independently wealthy, someone in the family will need to become the designated expert on "how to get the treatment without it coming out of the family budget." This person will need to learn about their rights in terms of education, social services, and the health system. If you have private insurance, find out what it will cover. Find out all you can about any financial support you may be eligible for.

Learn to ask questions. Do not suppose that social services, early intervention services, the school district, private insurance, or whatever agencies you are turning to for help will automatically tell you what you have a right to. Dare to ask questions. They have budgetary concerns. Sometimes they will tell you only what they are offering on a regular basis—what they wish to provide—not what you are entitled to. Most people have not been taught to think "outside the box." You will need to learn to ask the right question to get the right answer. Think of it as playing detective. Often a case is cracked when the detective asks a question that brings out information that people did not volunteer, as they felt it was unimportant or did not concern the case. The same can be true when looking for funding, employment support, or an appropriate education. As a parent, or an adult with an ASD, you will need to be proactive, and learn to communicate in an assertive, nonaggressive manner. Always be polite. The people on the other end of the phone or the other side of the counter are only doing their job as they have been taught.

Talk to others in the same situation. Ask other parents or adults with ASDs in your area for some ideas about what they have been able to obtain. There are many options for help out there. Each agency has a brochure explaining clients' rights and lists advocates to turn to for help if necessary.

Learn to ask for and accept help. When you are used to being self-reliant, it is difficult to ask for help or to accept help that is offered. My advice to you is: get over it! Remember the times you have helped others and keep in mind that you will help others in the future. Now is not the time to have a stiff upper lip and be too proud to accept help.

Learn how to answer questions in a way that fully explains your situation. For example, at some point when answering questions on a form regarding your child's level of need, you may be asked, "Can your child

On Taking Charge and Making a Difference . . .

BY LINDA LANGE

Early in my journey into parenthood and autism, I received vital advice from a caring and experienced mother with a Down syndrome child. She was the neonatal nurse in charge when my two-week-old infant was having seizures. She handed me a book on seizures while emphasizing that I must get educated to be my child's advocate in order to make informed decisions. She explained that, although there were many dedicated professionals, no one would ever care about my child's outcome more than I.

Parents of autism face a maze of biomedical and educational treatment options. We bounce around from one professional specialist to the next in search of answers and solutions. The process is a necessary evil, but the end result can lead to an unhealthy mindset of overreliance upon doctors, therapists, teachers, etc., which can leave a parent feeling even more helpless and ill-equipped to steer their child's treatment direction.

A professional's role is to provide advice, assistance, and teaching, but parents should never become so dependent upon others that they lose sight of their child's best interests.

Because my daughter Madison's seizures began at birth, we had the "benefit" of knowing about a potentially bumpy road ahead. We plunged into biomedical information and options, especially when we learned about the Defeat Autism Now! (DAN!) movement, which has been a journey and a story in itself.

At the same time, Madison received early childhood intervention services in occupational therapy, physical therapy and speech therapy. In addition, I did the National Association for Child Development (NACD) home program (an offshoot of Doman's Institutes in Philadelphia), in which we did a checklist of daily sensory, cognitive, and physical exercises, including "patterning" for crawling and walking.

We decided to try a home-based ABA [applied behavior analysis] program when she was four, but Madison's admission to [O. Ivar] Lovaas's Wisconsin replication site was denied because her IQ test scores came in below

50. That same month, we learned of the opening of a private Applied Verbal Behavior school program for ASD kids opening in Austin, Texas, a two-hour drive from our home. We moved so she could attend.

Madison was four and a half when she started the Horizon Program at Capitol School of Austin. Joyce Gruger was the parent impetus behind Horizon's inception. She had encouraged therapists from her home-based ABA program to work with Capitol School (which serves kids with language and learning differences, aged two to eight) and the Grugers provided training funds and support to help start a special class for young ASD kids.

Madison, who remains nonverbal, had some immediate success at Horizon, acquiring functional skills and modified sign language that allowed her to communicate some basic desires. Her accomplishments only made me hungry for more, and after three years at CSA, I was anxiously searching for an educational route that would help get her to the next level, into academic skills like spelling, reading, and writing. I was also painfully aware of the ticking clock—Madison was close to aging out of that program, which only goes up to age eight. We knew she still needed individualized teaching and that she was not ready for inclusion in a mainstream public school, so my husband and I chartered a nonprofit called HALO (Helping Autism through Learning and Outreach) and began to stir up local interest in developing a program for older ASD students.

After *60 Minutes II* featured Soma Mukhopadhyay, I rushed out to see Soma work at Carousel School in Los Angeles. I was encouraged to see that Soma was having unprecedented success teaching kids whom many consider and write off as the "worst outcome" students. I invited Soma to come to Austin for a few days to train teachers for our would-be ASD school program, which we had hoped to start in August 2003 under the guidance of the special education department at the University of Texas. Shortly after, the UT initiative screeched to a halt when the lead professor announced his intended departure.

So I changed Soma's Austin visit. She worked one day with students in Madison's school; Soma's sessions with ten kids "wowed" observers. I edited my videotape footage down to a thirty-minute tape (different types of learners and topics), which we showed the day during Soma's half-day workshop, attended by more than 240 professionals and parents from all over Texas. The workshop could not have happened without the help of many generous parent volunteers, like Frank and Gwen Milano who secured the location and provided refreshments.

Later in fall 2003, Soma indicated that she needed help in meeting the demand of students all over the United States, so we decided to collaborate on goals under the mission of our nonprofit organization, HALO. HALO now provides organizational support for Soma to spread her trademark Rapid Prompting Method.

Our family has experienced success with Madison using RPM [Rapid Prompting Method] at home, and our vision is for HALO to help provide improvements in communication and academic success for many persons all over with ASDs.

The neonatal nurse's advice (and that of clinicians like Dr. Sidney Baker, and too many other family members and friends to list) stuck with me through the years. Just when I settle into a comfortable place, it's time to forge ahead into the next unknown territory. I try to remain flexible and to make constant adjustments to Madison's medical and educational goals. And though I frequently feel unsure of what should come next in my daughter's treatment plan, I remain resolved that I am in charge. It is a heavy burden, but I would rather feel empowered to make decisions than enslaved by someone else's agenda which may or may not be right for my child.

Linda Lange is president of Helping Autism through Learning and Outreach (HALO), a nonprofit organization dedicated to providing exemplary learning opportunities and innovative teaching techniques to individuals with autism and similar disorders.

walk?" Most people would reply "yes" if the child is not physically handicapped. However, some children with autism do not follow instructions and are not safety-conscious; some will run into the street, others may have a tantrum. The real question in your mind should be: "Is my child capable of getting somewhere independently without adult prompting of any sort?" If the answer is "no," the correct response to "Can your child walk?" is, "My child needs help to move from one place to another."

Where to Start Your Search for Services and Funding

Having an ASD or having a child with an ASD can be mind-boggling and expensive. Knowing what options are available medically, educationally, and financially is a great source of comfort. Knowledge is empowering, and gathering information is the first step toward making you feel that you are in the driver's seat and that you have choices about which direction you want to go.

Although there are federal mandates, you need to know about how these are applied in your state, so check your local state agencies. Because each state is different, some more complex than others, various sources are listed below and some may be redundant. However, it is better to have too many places to look for the information you need than not enough. Here are some places to start information gathering about services and funding:

Contact your local Autism Society of America chapter and/or Families for Early Autism Treatment (FEAT). Your local chapter should be able to give you advice on a local level. To find out what chapters are in your area, visit their websites (www.autism-society.org and www.feat.org).

Find out your rights and responsibilities. Contact the protection and advocacy agency in your state, and obtain a copy of whatever information they have in regard to your rights in the state where you live. To find your state's agency, go to the Autism Society of America (ASA) website at www.autism-society.org, which has all of them listed by state, or the NICHCY website listed below.

Look on the NICHCY website for your state agencies. The NICHCY website (www.nichcy.org) has a link to "State Resources," and you can find many useful agencies and contact information for your area. For example, under California resources contact information is listed for (among others): "Programs for Children with Disabilities: Ages 3 through 5"; "Programs for Infants and Toddlers with Disabilities: Ages

Birth through 2"; "State CHIP Program" (which is health care for low-income uninsured children); as well as services for teenagers and adults. Protection and advocacy agencies are listed here as well.

For services regarding babies and young children look up the FICC. The Federal Interagency Coordinating Council (FICC) (www.fed-icc.org) facilitates federal, state, and local activities related to serving infants, toddlers, and preschoolers, from birth through age five, who receive services under the Individuals with Disabilities Education Act (IDEA), as well as other federally funded programs such as health care, child care, and social services. This website has links to state resources.

Find out about possible medical and Medicaid benefits. It is best to contact your state agencies; however, if you wish other information you can contact the U.S. Department of Health and Human Services through its website (www.hhs.gov).

Find out if you or your child is eligible for other services by contacting your local State Council on Developmental Disabilities. Go to the Administration of Developmental Disabilities website (www.acf.dhhs.gov/programs/add) to find your state council.

Find out if you or your child is eligible for Supplemental Security Income (SSI). Adults are eligible if considered disabled. For low-income families there may be some possible funding for children. Contact the Social Security Administration (telephone: 800-772-1213, or website: www.ssa.gov) for more information, or your state agency.

Find out your rights in terms of private insurance coverage. If you have questions and concerns about insurance issues, there are state agencies that should be able to answer your questions. These agencies are listed on the Autism Society of America website (www.autism-society.org).

5

Treatments, Therapies, and Interventions

"Therapies," "techniques," and "treatments" used with people with "autism" present themselves like shops along the High Street; they have little relationship to one another and each shop will encourage you to shop at their store and tell you why their product is THE product.

But each of these shops sells something quite different from the next. Some deal with behaviors, some with brain development, some with biochemistry, some with cognition or with the mind and some with the soul—and some don't deal with anything but make a good job of appearing to.

The problem with services behaving like High Street shops is that people with "autism" don't just have problems with behavior or communication or perception or their senses or with brain development or with biochemistry, or with stress levels or with troubled souls. Because people with autism are whole beings, most of them have trouble with the whole lot, which all interconnect and feed into each other at some point.

To get any all-round service, people with autism don't need a High Street of competing shops, they need a department store where each department is aware of what the others offer and points people in the direction of other services which complement their own.

—DONNA WILLIAMS, *Autism: An Inside-Out Approach*

WHEN Jeremy first stood up and walked on his own, his first steps were not toward me. He got up and followed the patterns in the rug. We were living in Paris at the time, and psychoanalysis was the treatment on offer to cure Jeremy's autism. When my husband was offered the opportunity to work on Legoland in Berkshire, we jumped at the chance to move to England, where at least Jeremy could attend a special needs school. Soon after arriving in England, I read *Let Me Hear Your Voice* by Catherine Maurice, and I also met Cathy Tissot, whose autistic son attended the same school as mine. We discussed the book a few times, saying how we would like to try the Lovaas program (a home-based applied behavior analysis program described in the book; see page 94), but we felt it was a lot to take on. Frankly, we were both overwhelmed with our respective situations; not only were we mothers of children with severe autism, we were also foreigners, far from family and friends, with no close circle of support to rely upon.

Meanwhile, Jeremy did not progress at school. While helping out in his class, I witnessed what I considered to be physically abusive and unsafe treatment of a child. That, coupled with the headmaster's seeming indifference and refusal to look into the situation when confronted, did it for me. I knew I had to remove my son from school and try to teach him myself. At the time, practically no one was doing the Lovaas program in England, but Cathy and I decided we would give it a try. I remember going to her house one evening, trying to get the nerve up to call the Life Institute, the Lovaas center in California, to find out if there was a consultant who could come and put on a workshop to train us and students to work with our children.

Making that phone call changed my life. That was the moment when I stopped being a victim of the systems in place, took control, and realized I was not powerless to help my son. I was lacking in knowledge, but I would learn whatever I had to. I knew my son was severely autistic, but I also knew he could learn, and that he should be given the opportunity to reach his potential, whatever that would be. Now I was going to learn strategies to teach my son and help him make sense of the world.

How to Know What Will Help

In the past, there were practically no options for people with ASDs in terms of treatments, therapies, and interventions, and this was the source of much anguish and stress. Nowadays options abound, and the challenge is more about getting information about them and trying to decide what best fits the needs of the person with the ASD, before figuring out how you can access that treatment or therapy.

In chapter 4, where and how to get information was discussed. In this chapter, you'll learn more about how to know what can help a particular person with an ASD, and about many of the different treatment and therapy options that are available.

Knowing about the Person with an ASD

The first thing to do is to look at the person with an ASD, whether it's yourself, another adult you're helping, or your child. Here are some things to consider:

- *The age of the person.* A person who is diagnosed at age ten or sixteen or twenty-five or even forty-five will have different therapy and treatment needs from a child diagnosed at two or at five. For example, a toddler may need intensive early intervention to learn to speak or develop a system of communication. An older child may have language skills but no social skills. Adults may have sensory processing issues that could be helped through physiologically oriented therapies. Remember that although for a long time people have been talking about the early years as the "window of opportunity" for learning, recent research has shown that brains have neuroplasticity, which means that they continue to reorganize themselves by forming new neural connections throughout life. As more is discovered about the brain, we are finding out that you can teach an old dog new tricks.

• *What the person is like in terms of functioning level or ability.* ASDs cover a wide range of functioning in terms of behavioral characteristics, communication and social awareness, and sensory integration issues. If a formal diagnosis has been made, any assessments made at that time may give you more information about yourself or the person you're helping. There are many different assessments that are used, depending on the age and ability of the person: speech and language, occupational therapy, functional behavior analysis, neuropsychiatric tests, and developmental, intelligence, and academic tests. A parent of a child with an ASD has a good knowledge base of what their child is able or unable to do just from living with him and observing his capabilities and deficits.

• *The person's behaviors.* A diagnosis of autism is based on observable characteristics, and it is important to look at a child's behaviors and try to understand what they indicate. Is the child covering his ears frequently when there is a lot of activity in the room? Does he often have diarrhea? Does he have tantrums when you change his routine? Is he always trying to remove all his clothes? Does he appear clumsy and uncoordinated?

• *Whether the person is a visual or an auditory learner.* Many people assume that all people with ASDs are visual learners and therefore that visual strategies will work with everyone. This is not the case, as some people are auditory learners. It is helpful to establish which sense you or your child uses best.

• *What the person's strengths and weaknesses are.* Every person has strengths, and if you can identify them, you can build on them to fortify the weaknesses.

• *What goals this person has, or you have for your child.* Each person needs to think about what their overall goal is. Perhaps it is a general goal of "recovering" a child from autism; perhaps it is to

have the child reach his potential. Perhaps it is addressing one particular area of a person's life or skill area where he needs to learn
practical or coping skills.

• *What treatments the person has already had (if any).* Looking at
what has been helpful and what has not can be useful at times in analyzing whether or not a particular treatment is worth pursuing.

• *Whether or not it is time to reevaluate.* Is the person changing,
growing? Perhaps a treatment appropriate at one time is no longer
the case. Every once in a while it's a good idea to step back and decide whether the current treatments are still useful or appropriate. It
may be time to change or "tweak" a current treatment.

As Donna Williams suggests in the quote taken from her book
Autism: An Inside-Out Approach at the beginning of this chapter, all
these therapies, treatments, and interventions truly need to be looked at
with a department-store mentality, rather than a High Street approach.
ASDs are all-invasive, and rarely does one therapy alone provide all the
help a person needs. Therapies or treatments are not exclusive of others, and a visit to different departments or types of therapies is often
needed.

Knowing What to Ask about a Treatment Option

After looking at the needs of the person with an ASD, there are other
factors to consider before deciding on what treatments and therapies to
pursue at this particular time. Here are some things to consider when
looking at treatment options:

• *The potential risk to the individual.* Does the therapy have side
effects? Is it risky to mental or physical health? Do the possible
risks outweigh the possible gains? Does it use any form of punish-
ment?

FOOD FOR THOUGHT

If I were the parent of a very young child, and this were a perfect world, I would do the following:

• Start an applied behavior analysis program (page 94) with trained therapists and proper supervision for thirty to forty hours a week, with a parent doing at least six hours. Research has shown that this method of teaching is effective. It is not a "cure" for all children, but every child can learn and progress. A parent who is involved and keenly aware of the program will be able to help the child generalize skills, and get to know the child's strengths and weaknesses.

• Learn the Floor Time approach (pages 128–31) and use it.

• Start a sensory integration program (pages 112–13) tailored to the child's needs, overseen by a professional who is trained and experienced in sensory integration. Almost everyone with an ASD has sensory integration difficulties in one area or another. This can make it difficult for a child to focus and learn.

• Follow the DAN! (Defeat Autism Now) approach. If a child is having allergic reactions or intolerance to some foods, if he is not metabolizing enough of the nutrients his body needs, if he has toxins in his system—any or all of these could affect his health, his brain functioning, his sensory processing, and his ability to learn.

• Try supplements such as vitamin B_6, magnesium, and DMG (page 124). Data based on thousands of cases and twenty published studies show that these supplements have helped 50 percent of the children who have tried them.

• Engage the child in fun activities, such as music or singing or horse riding.

• Involve the child in physical therapy or exercise. If my young child were behind in his developmental levels for gross motor skills, I would find a physical therapist to show me what I could do to help strengthen his muscles. If that were not an issue I would make sure my child got plenty of exercise, doing something he enjoys.

The reality is, this is not a perfect world, and each family must decide what the needs of the child are, what the needs of the family are, and what they feel capable of taking on.

• *The family.* ASDs are a family thing, as they affect everyone in the household either directly or indirectly. But so does the treatment. The parents have to think about how the treatment or therapy fits into the family. What kind of involvement is expected from others? How will this treatment affect any siblings? Is the family going to be able to follow through with whatever the professional deems necessary (e.g., giving supplements on a regular basis, sticking to a diet, generalizing skills learned)? Can the family commit to the prescribed treatment or therapy for whatever time it takes or is recommended? Are all responsible adults in the household in agreement about the particular treatment and supportive of seeing it through? If the treatment fails, how will it affect the family?

• *The financial cost of the therapy.* Money does not grow on trees. Do you have to sell your home to provide this therapy or intervention? Is insurance going to cover it? Are you asking for the school district or private health insurance to fund the treatment? If yes, do you have the tenacity to advocate effectively to obtain the appropriate type of service?

• *Can the treatment be integrated into whatever existing program the child already has, and if so, how?* For example, in the case of a special diet, can it be carried over to all of the child's environments? Will the treatment's inclusion be at the expense of other equally important aspects of the child's program?

• *What evidence exists to validate this method of treatment?* Is the therapy being touted as a miracle cure for everyone? Is there scientific validation of this treatment? What does the anecdotal evidence have to say?

• *Is this treatment or therapy autism-specific and, if not, has it proved effective with individuals with ASDs?* Some treatments may not be specifically created with ASDs in mind, but can be very beneficial. However, it is important to verify how others with an ASD have done with this treatment. For example, early intervention is a great concept. However, some programs do not work well with all children with autism, because most children with ASDs do not imitate or tune in to social cues the way other developmentally delayed children do, and therefore need first to be taught how to imitate or understand those social cues.

• *How is the effectiveness of the therapy going to be measured?* With any treatment or therapy, there should be record-keeping in order to track effectiveness. Parents need to ask who is responsible for taking data, how data is taken, how often it is recorded, and how often it is reviewed.

• *What is the track record of the provider of the therapy or treatment?* How long have the practitioners been doing this therapy and with what age group? What level of ability has this person worked with? If it is dietary supplements, is it a reputable company that is making them?

• *Does the person prescribing the treatment or supervising the course of treatment have all pertinent information about the person being treated?* Make sure the person knows as much about the individual in question as possible. It's a good idea to write down anything you think the provider should know, especially if she is dealing with a young child or someone who is unable to communicate independently about himself. Information that is helpful includes other treatments that may have been tried, the person's likes or dislikes, and particular behaviors the practitioner should know about. Any allergies to food or medication, phobias, chances of seizures, special diets, and so on are all valuable information.

Treatments, Therapies, and Interventions

This is not meant to be an in-depth overview of all the treatment options, but rather a brief explanation about the most well known or currently popular ones. Resources are included for those who want more information. Therapies and interventions are listed here for informational purposes only, and this does not mean that they are endorsed by the author or that they are prescribed for any particular person. The reader should investigate further the treatments that interest them and make an informed decision with professionals and others who may be concerned.

Skill-Based Treatments

Listed here are programs that look at what the person is able to do, and work on specific skills to improve their level of functioning. Relationships and emotions are considered important, but the basic premise is to start working on specific skills the person needs to acquire in order to be able to learn and live in society.

Applied Behavior Analysis (ABA)

This has proven to be the most effective way to teach young children with ASDs. Specific skills are taught by breaking them into small steps, teaching each step one at a time, building on the previous one. Different methods are used to help the child learn, such as prompting (helping the

She Had Experience, Just Not the Right Kind

My son is very challenged by sensory integration issues and has many fine and gross motor problems. One year he came home from school with rug burns on his chest and back, the result of an inexperienced occupational therapist's attempts to perform sensory integration on him. After a few phone calls (and I must say no apology from the therapist or the school district in question), two Individual Educational Program (IEP) team meetings, a sensory integration (SI) and occupational therapy (OT) assessment, another occupational therapist was brought into the picture. At this point, concerned not only about the quality of my son's educational experience but also for his safety and comfort level, I asked specific questions of the therapist they were proposing about her experience. The therapist said she had a few years of experience with sensory integration, as well as working with adolescents with autism. All seemed well with the world.

After a few months, I received reports from school that the therapist was concerned about the occupational therapy goals for my son. She felt the goals were unrealistic, and that he was not progressing on any of them. The goals the IEP team had identified were fastening buttons and snaps on his pants and learning to cut with a knife. I met the therapist to ask how I could help. After chatting with her, I realized that though she had worked with adolescents with ASDs, they had been able students who could follow instructions and did not have the same level of motor difficulties as my son. The therapist had not needed to teach these skills before and was unable, in spite of her professional training, to figure out a way to teach my son these basic tasks. I had not thought before to ask about the ability level of the children she had worked with, thinking that as a professional she could figure things out for varying levels of ability.

The therapist was at a loss about how to teach my son, even though he had a well-trained school aide who was more than willing to help. Needless to say, my son learned to fasten the snaps on his pants after the aide analyzed the different steps, identifying which ones were creating difficulty for him, and then wrote up a task analysis and worked on teaching him this skill in a systematic manner.

So, the moral of the story is, ask the right questions. No matter how long my son has been in the system, I am always learning a few more questions that I should have asked.

---

child by guiding him through the desired response), shaping, and rewarding (for correct responses). ABA has been used for many years to successfully teach individuals of varying abilities, and can be used to teach in all skill areas, including academic, self-help skills, speech and language, and socially appropriate behavior.

B. F. Skinner is the grandfather of ABA, thanks to his study of "operant conditioning" and his book *The Behavior of Organisms* published in 1938. ABA is based on the theory that all learned behaviors have an antecedent (what happened before the behavior was exhibited) and a consequence (what happened after the behavior was exhibited) and that all such behavior is shaped by the consequences of our actions, meaning that we are motivated by the consequence to repeat that behavior. For example, most adults work because they are rewarded by a wage or salary. If they stopped receiving that wage, they would stop working.

Some of the terms used in ABA include:

• *Task analysis.* This consists of analyzing a skill or task that needs to be taught, by identifying each step of the skill, and which steps the person needs to learn. For example, if teaching someone at home how to set the table, you would analyze the whole sequence: walking to the cupboard, opening the cupboard with the right hand, picking up a plate with the left hand, closing the cupboard with the right hand, walking to the table, and so on.

• *Discrete trial teaching (DTT).* This is a method of teaching that is very systematic and consists of the teacher's presentation or request, the child's response, and the consequence to that response (i.e., a reward if correct); a short pause, and then the next trial. Each trial is "discrete"—that is to say, separate—so it is clear what is being requested of the child, and what is being rewarded.

• *The Lovaas method.* This is an intensive ABA program, aimed at preschool children, developed by Dr. O. Ivar Lovaas at the UCLA Young Autism Project. In 1987 Lovaas published a study that showed dramatic results on nineteen children with autism who had received intensive ABA therapy: the average gain in IQ was twenty points, and 47 percent of the children (nine of them) completed first grade in a mainstream class. In 1993, eight of the nine were still enrolled in mainstream classes and had lost none of their skills.

• *Verbal behavior therapy.* This is ABA therapy as it pertains to language behavior and is based on Skinner's behavioral analysis of language.

• *Errorless learning (no-mistake learning).* When a new behavior is taught it is important for the student to be successful from the beginning. Thus, teachers *prompt* a successful behavior, phyically motoring the student through if necessary. The prompts are gradually removed so that the behavior will eventually occur simply in response to a request or some other cue.

Care should be taken when choosing ABA providers. For more information on board-certified providers, go to the Behavior Analyst Certification Board's website (www.bacb.com).

Listed are a few well-known ABA providers who provide services nationally and internationally. Contact them for more information about whether or not they provide services in your area.

Applied Behavior Consultants (ABC)
Joseph Morrow, Ph.D., BCBA
4540 Harlin Drive
Sacramento, CA 95826
Phone: 916-364-7800; fax: 916-364-7888
Website: www.abcreal.com

Center for Autism and Related Disorders (CARD)
Doreen Granpeesheh, Ph.D.
19019 Ventura Boulevard
Tarzana, CA 91356
Phone: 818-345-2345; fax: 818-758-8015
Website: www.centerforautism.com

Autism Partnership
Ron Leaf, Ph.D., and John McEachin, Ph.D.
200 Marina Drive #C
Seal Beach, CA 90740
Phone: 562-431-9293; fax: 562-431-8386
E-mail: info@autismpartnership.com
Website: www.autismpartnership.com

Life Institute
Dr. O. Ivar Lovaas
Website: www.lovaas.com

The ME-List (a Lovaas therapy discussion list on the Internet)
Website: http://php.iupui.edu/~rallen/me_list.html

BOOKS ABOUT ABA

Teaching Developmentally Disabled Children: The ME Book by O.
   Ivar Lovaas

*Facing Autism: Giving Parents Reasons for Hope and Guidance for
   Help* by Lynn M. Hamilton

Let Me Hear Your Voice: A Family's Triumph over Autism by Catherine Maurice

Behavioral Intervention for Young Children with Autism edited by Catherine Maurice, coedited by Gina Green and Stephen C. Luce

A Work in Progress: Behavior Management Strategies and a Curriculum for Intensive Behavioral Treatment of Autism by Ron Leaf and John McEachin

Rapid Prompting Method (RPM)

RPM is a method used for teaching academics by eliciting responses through intensive verbal, auditory, visual, and/or tactile prompts. RPM aims to increase students' interest, confidence, and self-esteem. Prompting is intended to keep students focused while allowing students to be successful. This is a very low-tech method requiring only paper and pencil. A lesson might begin with a teacher's simple statement, followed by a question about what was just said. Next, the teacher writes possible answers and spells the choices aloud. Students learn to select answers by picking up choices and eventually pointing to letters on an alphabet chart or keyboard to spell answers. RPM was developed by Soma Mukhopadhyay (see box, pages 117–18). Originally Soma taught her son and then tried her method, improving and adapting it to different learning styles (e.g., auditory or visual; left brain/right brain), in a classroom of severely autistic children in Los Angeles for two years. Soma has since used RPM with more than two hundred individuals with an ASD. More empirical study is needed but anecdotal evidence from parents and professionals indicates that RPM is a viable means for improving communication and academic success for persons with autism. This method appears to be most helpful for those who are nonverbal or lacking in conversational skills. Soma is currently writing a manual about

On Generalization

BY JOSEPH MORROW

Often children with autism will learn a task in a particular situation but will be unable to perform that same task in a different situation. For example, in a discrete trials situation at a table, children may learn to hand over a spoon when it is requested, but as one moves to the kitchen and requests that they hand you a spoon, they do not. In an incidental learning situation the children may learn, at home, to point to an item when one asks, "What do you want?" Asking the same question in the grocery store may not result in pointing.

At Applied Behavior Consultants School, we have found that generalization of a learned task does not necessarily occur without special instruction. Once a student learns a task, we begin a systematic generalization procedure to try to ensure that the task will be performed in all situations. For example, suppose we are trying to teach the concept "wiggle." We may start with a prompt such as "wiggle your fingers" and provide an example. When the right response is given, we will reinforce it with a desired item. After several successes, we begin to vary the prompt. We may say, "Do this with your fingers" and show an example. Later we may prompt the student to "wiggle your toes." Soon we move away from the original situation to a different location and continue to teach the response.

We may continue to teach the response while adding distracters such as a loud TV or other children playing. At a still later stage we continue to teach "wiggle" with fewer tangible reinforcers and more social ones.

The final stages of the generalization process involves integrating "wiggle" into some natural day-to-day situations. For example, the children's song "If you're happy and you know it . . ." (which is followed by some request such as "clap your hands") can be used to strengthen generalization by singing "If you're happy and you know it . . . wiggle your . . ." Lastly, we try to involve peers in the process. When our student responds appropriately to a peer request involving "wiggle," the generalization training is complete.

This process can be used with all the concepts we teach. Teaching children to discriminate the color "green" becomes meaningful when they can respond appropriately to "Where is your green crayon?" or "Do you like your green sweater?" or "What color is the grass?"

Children with autism require structured teaching, and providing the education that makes generalization across situations possible can be made a part of that structure.

Joseph E. Morrow, Ph.D., is a professor of psychology at California State University in Sacramento, as well as the cofounder of Applied Behavior Consultants (ABC). ABC is an eighteen-year-old ABA firm specializing in autism treatment, with three schools and numerous in-home programs. ABC provides behavioral services to school districts, community care facilities, and regional centers, and conducts workshops on autism treatment both nationally and internationally.

RPM with Portia Iversen, cofounder of the Cure Autism Now Foundation. For more information, contact:

Helping Autism through Learning and Outreach (HALO)
P.O. Box 303399
Austin, TX 78703
Phone: 512-327-4250; fax: 512-327-4495
E-mail: information@halo-soma.org
Website: www.halo-soma.org

Picture Exchange Communication System (PECS)

This is a practical communication system that allows a person to express his needs and desires without being prompted by another person, by using pictures or a series of pictures to form a sentence. The child first learns to communicate by handing someone a picture of the object he wants, then sentence strips, and so on. Not only does this facilitate communication, it motivates the child to interact with others. PECS is easy to incorporate into any existing program, and does not require expensive materials. Behaviorally based instructional techniques are used to implement the program (such as prompting, shaping, fading, and so on). Basic concepts such as numbers, colors, and reading can be taught using PECS, and the picture icons can be used for visual schedules to help the child. Codeveloped by Andy Bondy and Lori Frost, this method helps relieve the frustration of those unable to speak and does not inhibit a child's ability to acquire and use speech. Many children who began with PECS have gone on to develop verbal language.

Pyramid Educational Consultants
226 West Park Place, Suite 1
Newark, DE 19711
Phone: 888-PECS-INC (888-732-7462); fax: 302-368-2516
E-mail: pyramid@pecs.com
Website: www.pecs.com

BOOK ABOUT PECS

A Picture's Worth: PECS and Other Visual Communication Strategies in Autism by Andy Bondy and Lori Frost

Facilitated Communication (FC)

This is a type of communication that was originally developed for use with individuals who had problems controlling or using their muscles (such as cerebral palsy sufferers) and therefore were unable to communicate independently. A facilitator holds the communicator's hand or arm in a certain manner, thus allowing the communicator to point to letters on a letter board or keyboard. In Australia, Rosemary Crossley tried using this method with people with autism. By the early 1990s the use of facilitated communication became widespread in other places in the world. Many nonverbal people with autism were soon able to communicate with a facilitator.

However, this method became controversial because of the lack of research proving that it was the individuals who were communicating and not the facilitators. There have been about fifty studies carried out on FC, but none of them has been able to prove scientifically that it works.

Recriminations continue. Critics of FC say there is no research backing up the claims of its supporters and the supporters criticize the research methods used to explain the failure of the studies to prove the authenticity of the communicators' responses.

The goal of facilitated communication was for the individual to eventually be able to communicate independently, without the use of a facilitator. However, there are few reported cases of individuals who have become independent. Whether this is due to the facilitator not working toward independence by withdrawing support over time, or the inability of the person to communicate on his own, is unclear.

Facilitated Communication Institute
370 Huntington Hall
Syracuse University
Syracuse, NY 13244-2340
Phone: 315-443-9657; fax: 315-443-2274
E-mail: fcstaff@sued.syr.edu
Website: www.soeweb.syr.edu/thefci/fcfacts

Social Skills Training

Social skills are a difficult area and need to be taught for those with an ASD. Research has shown that many people with autism have mind-blindness. That is to say, they do not understand that people think differently than they do, that they have their own plans and points of

Facilitated Communication: Its Rise and Fall

BY BERNARD RIMLAND

Can some autistic children who cannot speak communicate meaningfully in writing?

I was probably the first person to discuss this question publicly, in my lectures and writings, starting in the early 1970s. I reported that a very small percentage of autistic individuals are able to express their own thoughts in writing but not speech. I referred to these individuals as "autistic-crypto-savants": crypto meaning the ability was hidden, waiting to be discovered. I discussed and described several such rare individuals whom I had encountered during a period of several decades and urged that efforts be made to identify and encourage them.

In the mid-1980s I began to hear from colleagues in Australia about Rosemary Crossley, the director of the DEAL Center in Melbourne, who was using a technique she called "facilitated communication" to elicit writing—usually very sophisticated and highly literate—from severely handicapped, non-speaking autistic and mentally retarded clients. Facilitated communication (FC) was based on the assumption that these autistic or mentally retarded individuals had very little control of their hand and finger movements, and therefore needed the help of trained "facilitators" to support their hands, while they used their fingers to spell words on a keyboard or a letterboard.

Crossley's work also attracted the attention of Douglas Biklen, a professor at Syracuse University in New York, who spent a month at the DEAL Center in 1989, and returned to the U.S. with bombshell news: virtually all autistic and mentally retarded persons were very capable of expressing themselves fluently, usually immediately, if they were provided with a skilled facilitator. The media were ecstatic. The major magazines and all the television networks featured Douglas Biklen and the miraculous breakthrough he had brought with him from Australia. Many parents were also ecstatic—their beloved nonspeaking children were able not only to communicate, but to communicate eloquently. Academia joined the celebration. Conferences held at major universities and elsewhere were attended by standing-room-only crowds.

But things were not very rosy in Australia. The government-sponsored Intellectual Disability Review Panel investigated Crossley's methods and claims and was not impressed, noting that intellectually disabled individuals are "extremely susceptible to influence by people who may be unaware of the extent to which they may be influencing decisions."

I began receiving clippings of newspaper articles from Australia saying a number of parents had been charged, by their own children using facilitated communication, with physical and sexual abuse. In one such widely publicized case, a twenty-nine-year-old mentally handicapped woman, Carla, had been forcibly removed from her home by the police after she had allegedly accused her parents of sexually abusing her. After more than a year of the parents fighting these charges, the court awarded them full guardianship of Carla, concluding that the allegations made through FC were untrue. During the trial the facilitator demonstrated to the court how skillfully Carla could answer various questions. She was able to give an anatomically correct description of sexual intercourse, for example. However, when the defense asked Carla "What is the name of your dog?" there was no answer.

There were a number of such alleged abuse cases in Australia, then very quickly the same phenomenon began in the U.S., where parents, teachers, and others were being accused via FC of sexual and physical abuse.

The courts were confronted with a number of questions: Is FC a valid technique? How can we be sure that the communication is coming from the handicapped individual, rather than from the facilitator?

The controversy over FC raged on for a number of years. Numerous experimental studies were undertaken to determine its validity; many of them by the facilitators themselves, who wanted to prove, under carefully controlled circumstances, that the messages they believed they were eliciting from their clients were in fact coming from their clients, and not from themselves.

To date, approximately seventy such studies have been published, involving some five hundred mentally handicapped individuals. The major outcome of all this research is very clear: it shows overwhelmingly that if the facilitator does not know the answer to a question, the client cannot respond correctly. Further, the more carefully the study was done, the more likely FC was to be found invalid. The few studies which the authors claimed to support the value of FC tend to be poorly designed and poorly executed. Even the results that are said by FC proponents to show that FC is valid are very weak. (For example, the client might be able to point to the letters C-A-T when shown a picture of a cat. This is a far cry from the ability to "express his own thoughts in his own words," as originally claimed by Crossley and Biklen.)

The consistently negative findings from the research studies, as well as the consistently anti-FC decisions of the courts, have led most major organizations that advocate for the developmentally disabled to condemn FC as being an invalid method of communicating. These include the American Academy of Child and Adolescent Psychiatry, the American Academy of Pediatrics, the American Psychological Association, the American Speech and Hearing Association, and the American Association on Mental Retardation.

But a few nonspeaking autistic persons can write. I am aware of at least three books that were written by autistic individuals who could write but not speak. The autistic author of one of these books learned to write via facilitated communication. The other two authors emphatically deny that their writing is the result of their having been exposed to facilitated communication.

Howard Shane has been directing a clinic for nonspeaking children at the Boston Children's Hospital (Harvard University Medical School) for twenty-five years. He is considered to be an expert on the use of augmentive means of communication for nonspeaking children, including autistic children, having worked with hundreds of autistic children during this time. I asked him how many nonspeaking children were able to write meaningfully. He replied that perhaps three or four of the hundreds of children he had seen, or approximately 1 percent, could do that. But if the question were very simple, such as "What is this?" ("D-O-G") or "What color is this?" ("R-E-D"), the number might be 5–10 percent. However, he said, FC was quite unnecessary in teaching such children, since if they are interested in words or letters, they tend to learn on their own, or with encouragement from their parents or teachers.

Let us now consider the specific question: How can you tell if it is your child or the facilitator who is communicating by FC? Use the same method that many of the courts have used: Send the facilitator to another room so he cannot hear what is being said. Select several objects that you can show and describe to the child, for example, a comb, a five-dollar bill, and perhaps a picture of a horse. Hide the objects, invite the facilitator back into the room to help the child answer, and ask the child, "What did we discuss while [the facilitator] was gone?"

An even simpler method: the facilitator helps the child name objects on flash cards visible to both him and the child. Then move the cards to where only the child can see them and see how accurate the responses are.

In one case in Massachusetts, a man who had been in jail for eight months because of allegations made via FC that he had sexually molested his girlfriend's child was immediately released when the facilitator was totally unable to assist the child in spelling the names of any of the several objects that had been discussed during the facilitator's absence from the room.

The bottom line: be careful!

Bernard Rimland, Ph.D., is the director of the Autism Research Institute.

---

reference. This may be why they are unable to anticipate what others may say or do, which creates problems in social behavior and communication. There are different methods of teaching social skills. Here are some of them:

Social stories. This method promotes desired social behavior by describing (through the written word) social situations and appropriate social responses. Developed by Carol Gray, social stories may be applied to a wide variety of social situations and are created with the learner, who takes an active role in developing the story.

Social stories usually have descriptive sentences about the setting, characters, and their feelings and thoughts, and give direction in regard to the appropriate responses and behaviors. Comic strip conversations are illustrations of conversations that show what people say and do, as well as emphasize what people may be thinking. Social stories and comic strip conversations can be adapted to many functioning levels and situations, and anyone can learn to create them. They are particularly useful for learning how to deal with unstructured time such as recess and lunchtime.

BOOKS ABOUT SOCIAL STORIES

Comic Strip Conversations: Colorful Illustrated Interactions with Students with Autism and Related Disorders by Carol Gray

The New Social Story Book by Carol Gray

The Original Social Story Book by Carol Gray

Social skills groups. These teach specific social skills by breaking them down and providing practice in a "safe" environment. Depending on the age or grade level, different social skills are emphasized, including making conversation; taking turns; joining a group; dealing with bullying; friendship; and understanding facial expressions. Social skills training usually takes place in groups of four to six children and is usually beneficial for the more able person with an ASD. Social skill development is one of the biggest challenges children with ASDs face, and a well-structured social skills group can be beneficial. For more information, see www.udel.edu/bkirby/asperger/social.html.

Circle of friends. The object of a "circle of friends" is to make sure each child is included in activities and feels a part of the group. A social "map" of the child, listing his social contacts, is prepared with his help. Then classmates are identified who would like to help the child and be placed on the "map." A facilitator helps with the circle of friends, and the classmate volunteers act as mentors to the child in teaching appropriate social skills in social situations, such as greeting the child, walking to class with him, and being helpful and friendly in other ways. In 1997, the Leicestershire Autism Outreach Team in the

UK established seven such circles. The results were very promising. Not only did the child with an ASD show benefits, but so did the six to eight children who volunteered to form each circle. The benefits also extended beyond the immediate circle. For more information read the article on the O.A.S.I.S website (www.udel.edu/bkirby/asperger/social.html).

BOOKS ABOUT CIRCLES OF FRIENDS

Common Sense Tools: Maps and Circles for Inclusive Education by Marsha Forest and Jack Pearpoint

Relationship Development Intervention (RDI). Developed by Dr. Stephen Gutstein, the primary goal of the RDI program is to systematically teach the motivation for and skills of experience-sharing interaction. It is a parent-based clinical treatment and begins at each child's level and teaches skills to the next level.

Connections Center
4120 Bellaire Boulevard
Houston, TX 77025
Phone: 713-838-1362; fax: 713-838-1447
E-mail: administrator@connectionscenter.com
Website: www.connectionscenter.com

BOOKS ABOUT RDI

Relationship Development Intervention with Young Children: Social and Emotional Development Activities for Asperger Syndrome, Autism, PDD, and NLD by Steven E. Gutstein and Rachelle K. Sheely

Relationship Development Intervention with Children, Adolescents and Adults: Social and Emotional Development Activities for

Asperger Syndrome, Autism, PDD, and NLD by Steven E. Gutstein and Rachelle K. Sheely

OTHER BOOKS ABOUT SOCIAL SKILLS TRAINING

Teaching Children with Autism to Mindread: A Practical Guide for Teachers and Parents by Patricia Howlin and Simon Baron-Cohen

Autism: A Social Skills Approach for Children and Adolescents by Maureen Aarons and Tessa Gittens

Incorporating Social Goals in the Classroom: A Guide for Teachers and Parents of Children with High-Functioning Autism and Asperger Syndrome by Rebecca A. Moyes and Susan J. Moreno

The Autism Social Skills Picture Book by Jed E. Baker

Social Skills Training for Children and Adolescents with Asperger Syndrome and Social-Communications Problems by Jed E. Baker

Do-Watch-Listen-Say: Social and Communication Intervention for Children with Autism by Kathleen Ann Quill

Thinking about You, Thinking about Me by Michelle Garcia Winner

Inside Out by Michelle Garcia Winner

O.A.S.I.S. (Online Asperger Syndrome Information and Support) has a section on "Social Implications and Strategies" which has useful websites and books. Visit the website at www.udel.edu.bkirby/asperger/social.

Physiologically Oriented Interventions

Effective teaching methods are extremely important, but so is the child's physical and neurological health. If an individual's body and/or brain is not working properly, learning will be that much more difficult, and for some, close to impossible. Scientists are hard at work discovering all the secrets the brain has to offer, and much is still unknown. However, as there is a definite connection between the body and the brain, a healthy body is a priority.

This category of treatments, including therapies that address sensory issues as well as dietary and biomedical interventions, holds many possibilities. Bear in mind that this list is not exhaustive. Some of these treatments have no side effects and some do. Some are expensive, some are cheap. Some have empirical research to back them up, some of them have only anecdotal reports.

Before starting any of these interventions, data should be taken over at least a two-week period on all of the person's negative (tantrums, hyperactivity, bedwetting) and positive (communication, staying on task, eye contact) behaviors. This will give a baseline of the behaviors before treatment. During and after treatment, the same types of notes should be taken. This will enable you to judge whether or not the treatment is having an effect.

Physiologically Oriented Interventions: Therapies That Address Sensory Issues

Jean Ayres, an occupational therapist, first described sensory integration dysfunction as a result of inefficient neurological dysfunction. The auditory, visual, tactile, taste, and smell senses are what give us information about the world around us. Individuals with sensory disorders have senses that are inaccurate and send false messages. Children and adults with hypersensitivity overreact to stimuli, while others have hyposensitivity, which prevents them from picking up information through their senses. Sensory malfunction can also be an inability to understand and organize sensory information when it is received. Sensory integration dysfunction symptoms are many and varied, depending on which sense or senses are perturbed. When he has auditory sensitivities a child may cover his ears, overreact or underreact to noise, or try to escape from groups. Tactile sensitivities can be indicated by a seemingly high tolerance for pain, refusal to keep socks and shoes and sometimes clothes on, difficulty in brushing teeth and hair, or dislike of having hair washed. Visual issues may be apparent if a child is sensitive to light, likes to watch things spin or move (tops, hands on a clock), spins himself or other things, or turns lights on and off. These are a few examples of behaviors that display sensitivities in certain areas; however, you may wish to consult Lynn M. Hamilton's book *Facing Autism* for a more complete list.

Sensory issues are not autism-specific, and therefore the methods below were not specifically developed for people with autism. Many children and adults who have sensory disorders do not have an ASD. However, all the books that I have read that were written by adults with an ASD describe sensory impairment of one kind or another, and all the children with autism whom I know appear to have some sort of sensory issue. It is important that you choose therapy providers who have experience with ASDs and the age group of the person seeking treatment.

Sensory Integration (SI)

This is practiced by occupational therapists, who contend that many behaviors exhibited by children and adults with autism are an attempt to avoid certain types of sensations or seek preferred stimuli in order to balance out their nervous system. There are different strategies that are used. Occupational therapists who are well trained in sensory integration have designed individual programs that have led to improvements in behavior and skills by assisting individuals with ASDs to process and use sensory information. Data from patient records show these improvements. SI can be a valuable intervention, integrated into a child's program, depending on the person's sensory issues.

Sensory Integration International
P.O. Box 5339
Torrance, CA 90510-5339
Phone: 310-787-8805; fax: 310-787-8130
E-mail: info@sensoryint.com
Website: www.home.earthlink.net/~sensoryint/

BOOKS ABOUT SI

The Out-of-Sync Child by Carol Stock Kranowitz (website: www.out-of-sync-child.com)

The Out-of-Sync Child Has Fun by Carol Stock Kranowitz

Facing Autism by Lynn M. Hamilton

Auditory Integration Training (AIT)

These methods, developed by Dr. Guy Berard and Dr. Alfred Tomatis, are based on the theory that some people have hypersensitivity toward certain sound frequencies, making some common sounds painful to hear. In AIT, individuals wear headphones and listen to modulated sounds and music, with certain frequencies filtered out. This is done over a period of time. It is not known exactly how it works, physiologically speaking; however, individuals have reported benefits from these listening methods. Other listening programs have been developed that can be used at home without any special equipment.

The Society for Auditory Intervention Techniques is a great resource for information on various types of auditory therapies. A review of twenty-eight reports of studies on AIT, as developed by Dr. Berard, was undertaken between January 1993 and May 2001. The authors of the review, Dr. Stephen M. Edelson and Dr. Bernard Rimland, concluded that "The balance of the evidence clearly favors AIT as a useful intervention, especially in autism." However, the Tomatis method does not appear to be supported by any published research studies.

Society for Auditory Intervention Techniques
P.O. Box 4538
Salem, OR 97302
E-mail: info@sait.org
Website: www.sait.org

BOOK ABOUT AIT

The Sound of a Miracle by Annabel Stehli (about her daughter's recovery from autism through AIT)

Listed below are some of the programs that have been developed for home and school use. For more information, read more about the different types of programs and ask professionals and parents who have used them about the benefits and drawbacks of each of the different methods.

Samonas Auditory Intervention
Phone: 800-699-6618
E-mail: poaUS@samonas.com
Website: www.samos.com

The Listening Program
Phone: 888-228-1798; fax: 801-627-4505
E-mail: info@advancedbrain.com
Website: www.advancedbrain.com/autism

Vision Audio Inc.
Phone: 888-213-7858
E-mail: visionaud@earthlink.net
Website: www.vision-audio.com

BOOK ABOUT THE SAMONAS METHOD

Samonas Sound Therapy: The Way to Health through Sound by Techay Verlag

Irlen Lenses

These were developed by Helen Irlen for individuals with a sensory perceptual problem known as Irlen syndrome. Irlen's theory is that people with reading problems and perceptual difficulties are very sensitive to white-light spectrum wavelengths, which overstimulate certain cells in the retina, resulting in incorrect signals being sent to the brain. She found that by placing different-colored overlays on printed pages, light sensitivity and perceptual distortions were reduced. These colors were then applied as a tint on glasses. There is no strong empirical research to support the use of Irlen lenses as an autism-specific therapy; however, colored overlays on printed matter and tinted glasses have been shown to be helpful for a number of schoolchildren. There is anecdotal evidence that some people with ASDs have light sensitivity, and have reported a major difference in their sensory processing when wearing tinted glasses. It would be interesting to study if tinted lenses available for use as sunglasses have the same effect as Irlen lenses.

Website: www.irlen.com

BOOK ABOUT IRLEN LENSES

Reading by the Colors by Helen Irlen

Physiologically Oriented Interventions:
Dietary and Biomedical Approaches

What follows is a basic overview of some of the dietary and biomedical interventions that are being used to treat ASDs. Some of these interventions have empirical research to back them up. Some have much anecdotal testimony. Some of these interventions are noninvasive and worth trying; others should only be done under the care of a knowledgeable health professional.

These types of interventions are effective in helping people whose metabolic systems may not be functioning properly. It may be that their systems are not processing essential nutrients properly, possibly because of a food allergy or intolerance, a "leaky gut" (where the wall of the intestine does not do its job of keeping its contents separate from the bloodstream), or high levels of mercury or other toxic metals. It is possible to check for food allergies by adding or removing the suspected culprit from the person's diet and taking data before and after on their behavior. Essential nutrients can be tested in the same way. However, there are specific tests and analyses that can be done which are more indicative of what is going on in the metabolic system.

More and more health practitioners are learning about these interventions and how to treat patients with ASDs from a dietary and biomedical perspective. In the last few years an increasing amount of credence has been given to the positive effects of these interventions on many individuals with ASDs. And although more research is needed, it is important to note that the discovery of many of these interventions has been due to a strong collaboration between parents and medical professionals. At times it was parents who convinced health practitioners or researchers to think "outside the box" in searching for answers to their child's behaviors. At other times it was medical professionals who dared to look beyond the confines of traditional medicine. Together they have formed a strong partnership, widening the prism through which

Tito and Soma: Never Underestimate the Power of a Parent

Tito Rajarshi Mukhopadhyay is a teenager from India who is severely autistic and writes eloquently. His mother, Soma, raised him and educated him with little help from anyone else. When he was two and a half he was diagnosed as autistic and she was told to keep him busy. Soma did just that. She read to him from textbooks on subjects ranging from science to literature when she wasn't engaged in teaching him other skills. Any physical activity, such as riding a bicycle, she had to teach him by physically motoring his body through the motions. She taught him to write by attaching a pencil to his fingers with a rubber band as he was unable to hold it on his own. She taught him to point to numbers and letters, also by physically prompting him through the tasks. By age six he was able to write independently.

In December 1999, Soma took Tito to England, to Elliot House (the Centre for Social and Communication Disorders run by the National Autistic Society), where he was observed and assessed by Drs. Lorna Wing, Beate Hermelin, and Judith Gould, among others. Tito at the time was eleven, yet reached the level of a nineteen-year-old on the British Picture Vocabulary Scale administered by Dr. Gould. His story, from India to the UK and back home again, is the subject of a BBC program, *Inside Story: Tito's Story*. The National Autistic Society subsequently published a book written by Tito entitled *Beyond the Silence: My Life, the World and Autism*. The revised U.S. edition of Tito's book, *The Mind Tree*, penned at the ages of eight and eleven, provides valuable insight into the life and mind of persons with little to no expressive language.

In autumn 2001, the Cure Autism Now Foundation (CAN) invited Soma and Tito to move to Los Angeles so that Soma could try her teaching techniques on U.S. students with autism. In addition, Tito graciously consented to undergo extensive testing by experts such as Dr. Michael Merzenich, a neuroscientist at the University of California at San Francisco Medical School. Merzenich's tests helped validate and clarify Tito's written experiences, while shedding light on the brain function of people with severe autism. For example, in perception testing where lights are flashed on a computer screen at the same time as the sound of beeps is issued, most people can sense the beep and the light at the same time. However, Tito cannot see the light on a computer screen unless it appears a full three seconds after the beeps. He explains that he can only use one sense at a time, and has chosen to use his ears. This is in marked contrast to the experience of Temple Grandin, a professor at Colorado State University who holds a doctorate in animal science and has autism. Dr. Grandin explains that she thinks totally in pictures, that thinking in language and words is incomprehensible to her, and that she has difficulty with her ultrasensitive hearing because she cannot tune out unwanted noise the way most of us can.

Soma worked for two years with a class of severely autistic children using the method she developed with Tito, which she calls Rapid Prompting Method. Soma teaches academics by simultaneously stimulating auditory, visual, and kinesthetic channels. She elicits responses from children at a rapid pace, which keeps students focused on the lesson at hand.

Soma has since worked with more than two hundred individuals with autism in the United States and adapted her method to different learning styles. Now Soma is educational director of the nonprofit organization Helping Autism through Learning and Outreach (HALO), which provides individual instruction for students and training for parents and professionals interested in RPM.

Neuroscientists such as Dr. Merzenich are hopeful that this teaching method will help many.

---

autism is viewed and treated from the medical perspective. To them we owe a resounding thank you.

Dietary and biomedical interventions can be confusing for anyone who is not medically inclined. Please keep in mind that what follows is not a complete analysis of all the possible interventions, and that interventions are constantly being improved upon, so the reader will need to get the most up-to-date information available. Before attempting any of them, I would strongly suggest that the reader obtain a more complete understanding of this area of intervention by reading or consulting the following:

• *Facing Autism* by Lynn M. Hamilton. As mentioned earlier, her explanations about dietary and biomedical interventions are easy to read.

• *Biomedical Assessment Options for Children with Autism and Related Problems—A Consensus Report of the Defeat Autism Now! (DAN!) Scientific Effort Autism Research Institute.* This is the most complete and detailed of the resources. Some of it is easy to read and some is a bit mind-boggling for the nonmedically inclined. The Autism Research Institute has a website (www.autismresearch institute.com) and more contact information is in the Resources section of this book.

• *Parents' Ratings of Behavioral Effects of Drugs and Nutrients.* Also from the Autism Research Institute, which since 1967 has been collecting information on the usefulness of the interventions parents have tried on their children.

• For those wishing to read studies regarding dietary and biological interventions for ASDs, Karyn Seroussi of the Autism Network for Dietary Intervention (ANDI) has compiled most of them on the group's website (www.autismndi.com/studies.htm). Research results are also available from the Autism Research Institute.

Gluten Free/Casein Free (GFCF) Diet

This has been developed for individuals who have allergies or a toxic response to gluten (found in wheat, oats, rye, and barley, among others) and casein (found in dairy products). Some indications of allergy or a toxic response to gluten and casein are diarrhea, constipation, hyperactivity, red face or ears, breaking wind frequently, and pale skin. (However, it is important to note that these symptoms can be an indication of other problems.) Basically, peptides that are derived from an incomplete breakdown of certain types of food are affecting neurotransmission within the central nervous system. Research studies as well as hundreds of anecdotal reports have shown dietary intervention as a useful treatment for alleviating some of the symptoms of autism in children. It is less clear what the effect is on adults.

This type of treatment, though constraining in terms of diet, is not harmful and it may be worth removing your child from gluten and casein to see if it has an effect on his behavior. There are urine and blood tests which can show the level of peptides your child has, which are helpful indicators of before and after trials to see if the diet is helping.

There are many interesting books on gluten- and casein-free diets, as well as recipe books. The websites and books listed below them are good resources.

Website: www.gfcfdiet.com (about a GFCF diet)

Website: www.celiac.com (celiac disease and gluten-free diet online resource center)

Website: www.autismndi.com (Autism Network for Dietary Intervention [ANDI])

BOOKS ABOUT THE GFCF DIET

A User Guide to the GF/CF Diet for Autism, Asperger Syndrome and AD/HD by Luke Jackson and Marilyn Le Breton (This book is by a teenager with an ASD who is on this diet.)

Unraveling the Mystery of Pervasive Developmental Disability by Karen Seroussi

Special Diets for Special Kids by Lisa Lewis

FOOD FOR THOUGHT

The Power of Sharing Knowledge

"Thirty years later, Dr. Rimland and I had lunch down the street from my home and office in Connecticut. I expressed how inadequate I felt in understanding the digestive and immune system problems of the autistic children I was seeing in increasing numbers. I asked Dr. Rimland if he could gather some smart people to brainstorm the problems. I knew one smart person, Jon Pangborn. Bernie knew dozens around the world. Within a few months he had organized and named the first DAN! (Defeat Autism Now!) meeting, an extraordinary gathering of 30 practitioners, researchers, and parents who found common ground in a new map of the landscape that emerged from the mirage that once simply cast blame on mothers."

—Sidney MacDonald Baker, M.D.
from the *Defeat Autism Now!*
2002 Conference Presentations Book

Anti-Yeast (or Antifungal) Diet

This is helpful for those individuals who have an overgrowth of yeast (*Candida albicans*) in their system. Children who have autism and have had frequent ear infections treated by antibiotics may be likely to have an overabundance of yeast in their gut. While the antibiotics may reduce the bacterial flora naturally present in the gut, the candida increases, as it is not affected by the antibiotics. Physical symptoms of yeast overgrowth may include gastrointestinal distress, headaches, and skin rashes; behavioral symptoms may include irritability, confusion, and hyperactivity. As these may be characteristics of other difficulties, testing for yeast overgrowth is advisable.

Anecdotal reports show that this diet has been effective in over 50 percent of cases. There are some antifungals that may be useful for more persistent yeast overgrowth.

BOOKS ABOUT THE ANTI-YEAST DIET

Feast without Yeast by Bruce Semon and Lori Kornblum

The Yeast Connection by William Crook

Biological Treatments for Autism and PDD by William Shaw

The Feingold Diet

This diet was developed by Dr. Ben Feingold to treat hyperactivity in children. In his book *Why Your Child Is Hyperactive,* he recommends removing artificial colorings and flavorings, salicylates, and some preservatives from children's diets. Salicylates are a group of chemicals related to aspirin and found in certain fruits and vegetables. His hypothesis was that more and more children were being seen and treated for hyperactivity at the time the book was published, due to the increase in artificial ingredients being added to our food and the increase in the consumption of processed foods.

Website: www.feingold.org (the Feingold Association of the United States)

BOOK ABOUT THE FEINGOLD DIET

Why Can't My Child Behave? Why Can't She Cope? Why Can't He Learn? by Jane Hersey

The Ketogenic Diet

This diet has been developed for people who have seizures. It is high in fat, low in protein and carbohydrates. When the body burns fat instead of carbohydrates for energy, it creates ketone bodies, which in turn suppress seizure activity. This is not a healthy, balanced diet; it is difficult to undertake, and it has to be tailored specifically for each person. It is usually considered to be a last-ditch effort when medications are no longer effective, and should not be attempted without the supervision of a neurologist and with the help of a knowledgeable dietician.

Website: www.standford.edu/group/ketodiet (Pediatric Neurology Division at Stanford University School of Medicine)

BOOK ABOUT THE KETOGENIC DIET

The Epilepsy Diet Treatment: An Introduction to the Ketogenic Diet by John M. Freeman, Millicent T. Kelly, and Jennifer B. Freeman

Mercury Detoxification Treatment (Chelation)

There has been growing concern over the last few years about a possible connection between mercury and ASDs. Mercury is present in dental amalgam, certain types of seafood, and in thimerosal, a preservative found in some vaccines. It is highly toxic and some individuals are extremely sensitive to it. If the mercury exposure has been fairly recent, urine, hair, and blood analysis may show some trace. However, provoked excretion of mercury and heavy metals is necessary to estimate the amount in the body. Defeat Autism Now! and the Autism Research Institute brought together the expertise of twenty-four experienced physicians and researchers to come up with a mercury detoxification protocol, published in June 2001. It is suggested that before starting the mercury detoxification treatment, patients correct as much as possible any nutritional disturbances or "leaky gut" problems. This is because many of the drugs and supplements used for mercury detoxification can increase the growth of bacteria and fungi.

Web page: www.autismresearchinstitute.com/ari/mercury/consensus .html (This is the "Mercury Detoxification Consensus Group Position Paper.")

Vitamin B$_6$ and Magnesium

This is one of the treatments you can try without worrying about possible negative effects. Since 1965, twenty studies on these supplements have been published. These studies have shown benefits to taking vitamin B$_6$ (often combined with magnesium), and none have shown harm. Some of the benefits reported have been: improved eye contact, improved language, reduced self-stimulatory behavior, reduced aggression, and reduced self-injurious behavior.

Website: www.autismresearchinstitute.com (Autism Research Institute)

Dimethylglycine (DMG)

This is a naturally occurring substance in the body and is implicated in a number of important biochemical reactions. Much anecdotal evidence exists that DMG has been helpful for some people with autism, although there have been no scientifically valid trials to show efficacy. Reported benefits are: positive changes in behavior, improved language, and even, in some cases, reduction of seizures. Some parents have reported increased hyperactivity, and in those cases it is suggested that small amounts of folic acid be added to alleviate the problem. As DMG is not harmful, it is one of those therapies worth trying. For information, contact the Autism Research Institute (www.autismresearchinstitute.com).

Fatty Acids

It has been recognized that fats have a very important role to play in the metabolism and development of the body. However, due to the way our foods are now processed and the widening use of antibiotics that alter the intestinal flora, plus the fact that we do not swallow a daily spoonful of cod-liver oil the way our grandparents did, it has become apparent that most of us are not getting the fatty acids our bodies need.

Omega fats, cod-liver oil, and evening primrose oil may be of benefit to all individuals, not just those with autism. Cod-liver oil has the added benefit of containing vitamin A.

Sulphate Ions

Dr. Rosemary Waring of the University of Birmingham is the first researcher to produce scientific evidence of abnormally low sulphate levels in children with autism. (It was the UK parent group Allergy Induced Autism that first brought concerns of a possible link between sulphation and autism to the attention of Dr. Waring.) Some children with ASDs show a deficiency of sulphates in their plasma. Sulphate is a substance the body produces that helps break down and get rid of compounds it no longer needs, such as the residues that are left once medication has done its job. This deficiency may contribute to "leaky gut." Sulphates appear to be important for hormone effectiveness as well as good intestinal function. As sulphate ions are not easily obtained from food but may be absorbed through the skin, magnesium sulphate (Epsom salts) is added to bathwater as a way of facilitating absorption.

Enzymes

The stomach enzymes of some people with autism may not be working properly. It could be that in some there are insufficient levels of peptidase enzymes, or insufficient acid in the stomach for the enzymes to break down proteins. Some parents of children with hyperactivity have for many years been using enzymes taken orally to help with some of the problems associated with hyperactivity. Enzyme therapy is usually administered in conjunction with other dietary interventions.

Secretin

This is a hormone involved in gastric function. It stimulates the pancreas to produce substances that aid in the process of digestion, among other functions. It was originally made from the intestines of pigs. Secretin as a therapy for autism was discovered by accident in 1996 as a result of an endoscopy performed on Parker Beck, a nonverbal child with autism who suffered constant chronic diarrhea. Parker's parents noticed dramatic changes in their child after this procedure, in which secretin had been used, and they pushed for medical professionals to look into the possibility that it might be beneficial to other children. Some doctors and parents have seen dramatic changes in some children with autism after treatment. No one really knows how or why it works. Neither studies of secretin nor clinical trials of Repligen (synthetic secretin) have been encouraging. However, secretin has been of help to a small subset of children.

> Website: www.autismresearchinstitute.com
> Website: www.repligen.com (about the synthetic secretin Repligen)

Intravenous Immunoglobulin (IVIG) Therapy

IVIG is a blood product that is tested and processed and given to the person over a period of months. No one is quite sure how it works, but it appears to have an effect on the immune system.

More Resources for Biomedical Interventions

The Autism Research Institute (ARI) also sponsors think tanks where scientists and physicians exchange ideas, and there are Defeat Autism Now! (DAN!) conferences held several times a year where much can be learned about possible new interventions. New interventions are constantly being explored, so the only way to keep current is to attend DAN! conferences or obtain the conference papers from them.

For those interested in consulting medical professionals who implement the Defeat Autism Now! suggested biomedical interventions, the Autism Research Institute has posted a physician referral list on its website (www.autismresearchinstitute.com).

GENERAL READING ON BIOMEDICAL INTERVENTIONS

Biological Treatments for Autism and PDD by William Shaw

Children with Starving Brains: A Medical Treatment Guide for Autism Spectrum Disorder by Jaquelyn McCandless

Treating Autism: Parent Stories of Hope and Success edited by Stephen M. Edelson and Bernard Rimland

Psychopharmacologic Treatments (Traditional Medications)

Medications can be used to treat some of the behaviors associated with autism. Certain drugs are used to control seizures. For some people, drugs can be helpful for reducing anxiety, obsessive-compulsive behaviors, hyperactivity, self-injurious behaviors, attention deficits, and depression. Medications used include anticonvulsant drugs, stimulant medications, tranquilizers, antidepressants, and opiate antagonists. No medication should be tried without the advice of a knowledgeable physician familiar with ASDs and the person being treated. Most of these medications should be tried in very tiny doses, less than the manufacturers' recommendation. Care should be given especially when treating young children, as many of these medications have been researched for use in adults only.

For more information on particular drugs, read the book *Essential Psychopharmacology* by S. M. Stahl or the sections on medication in the book *Autistic Spectrum Disorders: Understanding the Diagnosis and Getting Help* by Mitzi Waltz.

Also, the Autism Research Institute has developed a chart outlining how parents rate the effectiveness of many drugs and nutrients they have tried (see the Resources section for the complete contact information).

Treatments Based on Forming Interpersonal Relationships

These treatments are mainly concerned with facilitating attachment and bonding as well as a sense of relatedness, which are seen as the cornerstone on which the normal development of the child is built. These approaches vary in how they can be used in conjunction with other therapies and how they are accepted and utilized by the majority of families and professionals.

The Floor Time Approach

This was developed by Dr. Stanley I. Greenspan as part of his developmental approach to therapy. Parents and Floor Time therapists help children master the emotional milestones needed to develop a foundation for learning. The approach is based on his belief that emotions give meaning to our experiences, as well as a direction to our actions. Floor Time seeks to have the child develop a sense of pleasure in interacting and relating to others, and is done through play, based on the child's interests, and through creating an increasingly larger circle of interaction between the child and an adult. Parents and therapists work on four goals: encouraging attention and intimacy; two-way communication;

Tips from Temple Grandin

Temple Grandin is a woman with autism who has a successful international career designing livestock equipment. Temple has a Ph.D. in animal science from the University of Illinois and is now an associate professor of animal science at Colorado State University. She credits early intervention, starting at age two and a half, for her recovery from autism.

Temple has written two books, Thinking in Pictures *and* Emergence: Labeled Autistic *(with Margaret Scariano), as well as many informative articles, which can be found on the website of the Center for the Study of Autism (CSA) at www.autism.org.*

Over two phone conversations, Temple shared with me the following important information about what can help people with autism spectrum disorders to learn.

Therapies, treatments, and interventions: As every person has different areas of strengths and challenges, what works for one person may not work for the next. For each person, finding the right balance of strategies is important. Donna Williams, who has many sensory challenges, uses a combination of strategies to offset the difficulties she encounters. She wears Irlen lenses, is on a gluten- and casein-free diet, and is now taking a tiny daily dose of Risperdol (a quarter of a milligram a day), an antipsychotic. Temple takes Norpramin, an antidepressant, and still uses the "squeeze machine" she invented years ago. Temple designed and built this machine as a teenager after observing the calming effect a squeeze chute had on animals at a relative's farm. This was in response to her need for deep pressure, under her control, that she craved and that helped her cope with anxiety.

Educational strategies: Temple has accumulated much information and experience over the years about what is effective in helping others to learn (see box on pages 228–29). The most important point she makes is that intensive and early intervention with the right kind of teacher is crucial, more important than the type of program.

Medication: Temple reports that medications have helped her tremendously over the years. In her book *Thinking in Pictures,* she includes a chapter on the different kinds of medications and how they can be helpful. She has recently reviewed this chapter and found the information still to be valid, although more recent developments, such as the newer atypical antipsychotic medications, are not listed. When treating with medications it is important to look at the benefits of the medication versus the risks—especially with children, whose bodies are still not fully developed—and to start with tiny doses. Temple says that a good rule of thumb in deciding whether or not to continue using the medication is to look at the "wow" factor. If a child is put on a medication and there is an obvious dramatic, positive change in him (e.g., a nonverbal child can now speak), then the benefit may outweigh the risks.

For example, Temple told me that she recently attended a conference with Donna Williams and was amazed at how Donna was able to tolerate sitting and having dinner with her and other people in a noisy environment. If Donna lapses from her gluten- and casein-free diet now, the effects are not so severe. This way she can travel and eat in restaurants. She attibutes her improvement to the tiny amount of Risperdol she takes daily.

However, it is important to find a doctor who is knowledgeable about autism and medications, and to try medications only under the guidance of such a person. Ask your local autism chapter for names of doctors who are familiar with medications, doses, and the effects on people with ASDs, as again, this treatment needs to be individualized for each person.

encouraging the expression and use of ideas and feelings; and logical thought. This method is often used as the play component for children who are in ABA programs. An analysis of the charts of two hundred children has provided some data to validate its effectiveness. Floor Time looks promising for helping children with autism relate to others. As this is a relatively new technique, more empirical research is needed.

Stanley I. Greenspan, M.D.
4938 Hampden Lane, Ste. 229
Bethesda, MD 20814
Phone (Dr. Greenspan's office): 301-657-2348
Phone (Conference-Training Course): 301-320-6360
Website: www.stanleygreenspan.com

BOOKS ABOUT THE FLOOR TIME APPROACH

The Child with Special Needs: Encouraging Intellectual and Emotional Growth by Stanley I. Greenspan and Serna Wieder

The Boy Who Loved Windows: Opening the Heart and Mind of a Child Threatened with Autism by Patricia Stacey

Son-Rise Program

This therapy is not autism-specific but was developed by the parents of a child diagnosed with autism. They spent every waking hour with their son with the goal of developing a bond. Since the least stimulating room in the house was the bathroom, that was where they spent most of their time, and they started out by imitating his ritualistic behaviors. After three years, he no longer showed any signs of autism and is now an Ivy League university graduate. The key to this treatment is to join in the child's repetitive behaviors, showing unconditional love, thereby enticing the child to emerge from his world, and eventually utilizing his motivation to advance learning. The Option Institute offers training programs in this method for parents, and they are expensive. There are some case studies and testimonials claiming that other children with autism have improved dramatically. However, research has yet to be done on the effectiveness of the method, which appears to be more about making parents feel good about themselves than actually teaching the child.

Autism Treatment Center of America (The Option Institute)
2080 S. Undermountain Road
Sheffield, MA 01257
Phone: 413-229-2100; fax: 413-229-3202
E-mail: correspondence@option.org
Website: www.son-rise.org

BOOKS ABOUT THE SON-RISE PROGRAM

Son-Rise and *Son-Rise: The Miracle Continues* by Barry Neil
Kaufman

Holding Therapy

This is based on the belief that body contact and physical contact must
be reestablished with the child who is refusing to make eye contact with
the parent (usually the mother). Advocates of this therapy believe that
autism results from a broken symbiotic bond between mother and child,
and that when the child begins to cuddle and make eye contact with the
parent, his development will proceed normally. This therapy is touted as
a "cure" although few studies have been done. Again, this appears to be
one of those "let's make the parents feel better" methods. (Holding therapy is not to be confused with deep-pressure, or "squeeze" therapy,
which Temple Grandin advocates and which has a physiological basis.)

Psychoanalysis

Until recently this was the main treatment on offer in some countries,
namely France and Switzerland. Up until the mid-1990s France still
considered autism to be a mental illness rather than a developmental disability; children with autism were denied an education, and psychoanalysis was the recommended treatment. As late as 1993, some parents

in the UK were led to believe by certain professionals that their child's autism was due to bad parenting. Not only did psychoanalysis cause the parents to feel guilty, it offered no practical strategies to help them with their children. Although counseling and psychoanalysis may be used as a treatment for depression in people with ASDs, it is not to be considered as an effective treatment for autism in itself.

Combined Treatments

In this category are placed the better-known programs that use a combination of different approaches. These programs work on improving skills, include physiologically based approaches to help with behaviors, and have a relationship component to them.

TEACCH

The "Treatment and Education of Autistic and related Communication handicapped CHildren" was developed by Eric Schopler at the University of North Carolina at Chapel Hill in the early 1970s. TEACCH started out as a parent and child psychoanalysis group and quickly became a skill-based approach dependent on a strong parent-professional collaboration. It focuses on teaching functional skills while modifying the environment to facilitate the needs of the individual. Structured teaching and the use of visual materials and schedules are used to enhance the acquisition of skills, by providing a stress-free environment. Vocational preparation is a strong component of this program.

The effectiveness of individual components of TEACCH has been validated in a number of studies. However, there appears to be a lack of research in terms of individual gains. Adapting the environment for the person does make it easier for them, but in doing so it may remove some of the natural "stresses" that create opportunities for learning. TEACCH strategies are very useful for the visual learner, but may not be as suitable for those who are auditory learners. Sometimes classrooms based solely on TEACCH principles appear to be about making the class easier for the teacher to handle, and appear to lack social interaction and social skills development, which many individuals with autism need.

> Division TEACCH Administration and Research
> CB# 7180, 310 Medical School Wing E
> The University of North Carolina at Chapel Hill
> Chapel Hill, NC 27599-7180
> Phone: 919-966-5156; fax: 919-966-4003
> Website: www.teacch.com/

Daily Life Therapy

This treatment originated in Tokyo with Dr. Kiyo Kitahara over thirty years ago. It was introduced in the United States when the Higashi School in Boston was opened in 1987, and a number of schools in the UK have also incorporated some of the approach into their curriculum. Daily life therapy incorporates physiologically based interventions and skill-based treatments using systematic instruction. An important focus is physical education, which is viewed as a bridge to social development. Vigorous exercise helps the children to gain control of their bodies and sleep better, and leads to a decrease in self-stimulatory behavior as well as hyperactivity. Children learn self-help skills and the ability to follow directions, as well as language, math, art, and music, depending on the interests of the child. This therapy is lacking in objective scientific validation; however, its effectiveness is supported by numerous testimonials from parents. More information can be found at www.boston higashi.org.

Other Therapies

Listed here are some adjunct therapies, usually used to target a particular skill area or as part of a wider program, and potentially extremely useful depending on the individual's needs. Again, it is important that the therapist be knowledgeable and experienced with ASDs.

Speech Therapy

Language delay is often one of the primary concerns that parents of a young child raise that may lead to assessments and diagnosis of an ASD. Speech therapists play an important role by evaluating the child's level of functioning, using a developmental approach. Once in school, speech and language therapy should be a part of the child's educational provision.

> The American Speech-Language-Hearing Association (ASHA)
> 10801 Rockville Pike, Rockville, MD 20852
> Phone (professionals/students): 800-498-2071 (voice or TTY)
> Phone (public): 800-638-8255 (voice or TTY)
> E-mail: actioncenter@asha.org
> Website: www.asha.org

Occupational Therapy

Depending on the age, ability, and need of the individual, occupational therapists provide different services. Their aim is to help the person meet goals in areas of everyday life that are important to them, such as self-care, work, and leisure. Assessments are carried out initially to discover the needs of the individual and provide support to learn skills in those areas. Some therapists are specifically trained in sensory integration.

American Occupational Therapy Association
4720 Montgomery Lane
P.O. Box 31220
Bethesda, MD 20824-1220
Phone: 301-652-2682 (voice), 800-377-8555 (TDD); fax: 301-
    652-7711
Website: www.aota.org

Music Therapy

Most people respond favorably to music, including people with ASDs.
Music is motivating and enjoyable. In music therapy, goals are tailored
to the needs of each individual and may include: increasing nonverbal
interaction, such as turn-taking and eye contact; exploring and expressing feelings; and being creative and spontaneous. Some parents have reported that their children began to learn to speak as a result of being
taught nursery rhymes and other songs. Research shows that there are
some favorable benefits to music therapy.

American Music Therapy Association
8455 Colesville Road, Suite 1000
Silver Spring, MD 20910
Phone: 301-589-3300; fax: 301-589-5175
E-mail: info@musictherapy.org
Website: www.musictherapy.org

Assistive Technology and Computer Programs

Broadly, assitive technology means any item, piece of equipment, or
product system that is used to increase, maintain, or improve the
functional capabilities of a person. It can be a high-technology item
such as a Lightwriter to help someone type what they cannot say ver-

bally. Or it can be low technology such as picture icons used to communicate something a person wants, or larger letters on keyboard keys. Check with knowledgeable speech therapists and your school's assistive technology expert to see what items they have found useful, as well as with the latest research and computer specialists to see what is new.

Some children with autism can easily use computer programs and learn by using them. Others struggle with the sensory issues of too much to look at and too much to listen to. Some programs have been designed for students with autism in mind. This area is in constant evolution as advances in technology continue. Although not ASD-specific, here are good places to get information:

The Alliance for Technology Access (ATA) is a network of community-based centers, vendors, and professionals.

Alliance for Technology Access (ATA)
1304 Southpoint Boulevard, Suite 240
Petaluma, CA 94954
Phone: 707-778-3011 (voice), 707-778-3015 (TTY);
fax: 707-765-2080
Website: www.ataccess.org

Techable provides individuals with disabilities, their families, and support professionals information and access to assistive technology devices.

Techable
1114 Brett Drive, Suite 100
Conyers, GA 30094
Phone: 770-922-6768; fax: 770-922-6769
E-mail: techweb@techable.org
Website: www.techable.org

Inclusive Technology, the Special Needs People—this website has a comprehensive list of different types of programs for people with special needs and is updated regularly.

Website: www.inclusive.co.uk/catalog/softlist.shtml

BOOK ABOUT ASSISTIVE TECHNOLOGY

Autism and ICT: A Guide for Teachers and Parents [ICT stands for Information and Communications Technology] by Colin Hardy, Jan Ogden, Julie Newman, and Sally Cooper

There are some service providers who offer a variety or combination of treatments and therapies for individuals with autism spectrum disorders. An example of one based in Southern California is ACES Inc. (Comprehensive Educational Services), founded by Kristen Farmer, M.Ed.

ACES Inc.
3731 Sixth Avenue, Suite 100
San Diego, CA 92103
Phone: 619-278-0884; fax: 619-3278-0885
E-mail: info@acesangels.com
Website: www.acesangels.com

6

Family Life

Family life can be a test of love and resilience, so taking good notes and understanding each other's needs and wants are vital to the success and survival of any marriage. After children arrive, there is a balancing act between caring for their needs and putting time and effort into the maintenance and growth of the marriage. This rite of passage in the development of family life is challenged still further by disability or chronic illness.

—ROBERT A. NASEEF, *Special Children, Challenged Parents*

I was raised in a French Catholic family, one of six children. As my parents had emigrated to the United States from France, we had no extended family, but we were very close. We did everything together: ate dinner as a family every night, rode our bikes, played tennis, watched TV (the few hours a week we were allowed), went to church, and socialized with other families. We had very little time on our own and were not encouraged to join clubs that would take us away from our family activities.

So I had always expected that when I had a family, though it would be much smaller, it would be the same kind of close-knit family life with shared activities. This was important to me. However, having two children who are basically living on separate planets (one is severely autistic, with poor motor skills; the other is very social and athletically gifted) makes it tough to have the kind of family life I grew up with. I had to learn to let go of my expectations, change my perception of what family life meant, and figure out what we could still do together as a family and what we would have to do separately. We have had to create our own version of family life. But we are still a family; we just do things differently.

Autism Spectrum Disorders and the Family

Having a child with an ASD has a major impact on the family. Besides the stress associated with bringing up a child who needs more attention and care, children with autism are not as social as other children and do not reach out to parents in the same way that other children do. This lack of spontaneous signs of affection from one's own child is very difficult for a parent.

Often families tend to isolate themselves either because of concern over their child's socially inappropriate behaviors or from fear of being embarrassed by some of the child's behaviors or because of the extreme fatigue most parents of children with an ASD suffer from. Families stop doing what they did before the ASD was very apparent. Single-parent families find themselves alone with their hands full and no free time to keep up any kind of social life, increasing their isolation. Being a single parent, adoptive parent, stepparent, foster parent, or grandparent raising a child with an ASD adds even more difficulties to an already precarious situation.

A marriage or relationship with a significant other can deteriorate due to added stress, fatigue, and differences of opinion on how to handle certain situations. Often one or both parents are having difficulties coming to terms with having this child and are on different parts of the grief cycle. Add to that the searching for support and trying to get an appropriate education for the child, and it is easy to see how many couples come to call it quits.

Siblings can suffer from being raised in a family with a child who has an ASD. Not only do they have a sibling who is hard to understand, has limited interests, and is not social; they also have to deal with some pretty wild behaviors. And they also feel the stress their parents are under, as well as the fact that inevitably more of the parents' attention is taken up by the sibling with an ASD.

Extended family members such as grandparents also have a difficult time in dealing with ASD. Some refuse to face the facts, others don't know what to say or what to do. Again, as the parents, it is up to you to decide when and what information you want to share. Much depends on the type of relationship you have with your relatives and how close you are to them.

It is difficult bringing up a child with an ASD. But first and foremost you are raising a child, not a disability. No matter how bad the behavior or situation, there is always a solution. And mainly it is the parents' attitude that will make the biggest difference. In this section, practical suggestions on family life are offered.

Family Life with Children with ASDs

The sooner you realize that your family life will not resemble the Waltons', the better off you will be. Take heart from knowing that your family life would probably never have resembled that perfect ideal, and if it had, you would have been bored out of your skull. Think of the Addams's family and how much more fun they seemed to be having regardless of the daily household disasters.

Life for your family will never be boring from this point on. It may

Beam Me Up!

It's a Wednesday morning and I am volunteering at the jog-a-thon at my daughter's school. As we await the start of this event, other mothers are standing around talking. I approach a few I know and hear a bit of their conversation: "I hear Pasqual got voted off." "Oh, no, he was my favorite!" "Mine, too." I move in and ask, "What are you talking about?" They look at me as if I have just landed from another galaxy, and say, *"Survivor!"* I say, "Oh, you have time to watch that?" and as they look at me, one replies, "We make time, the whole family!"

They continue to talk about *Survivor* and I drift away. I am left with the usual feeling of being an alien on another planet. Is it because I have a son who is severely handicapped by his autism, leaving me with a lack of time for trivial time-fillers, that I don't fit in?

It's hard to feel as if you fit in when you don't have the same points of reference. The parents huddled around, waiting to pick their children up after school, talk about their daughter's latest piano recital, her high scores on her SATs, or how their son is representing the school at the county science fair. Somehow, the highlights of my fifteen-year-old son's week (he sat in his mainstream class and participated appropriately for a one-hour stretch, and hasn't wet the bed once) don't seem like the kind of information that I can just slip into the conversation and share as an accomplishment.

What are my time-fillers? Filling out paperwork to explain why I still need respite and other services; preparing for my son's annual review at school and documenting why he needs occupational therapy and applied behavior analysis; explaining to the medical insurance company why my son needs a certain treatment; attempting to keep him from "redecorating" the family room; making picture icons; trying to reach the neurologist about seizure medication; reading up on the latest research; making my son clean up the mess he made when he did redecorate; sending letters to politicians; attending voluntary board meetings; taking my son for a swim or a run because he is too hyper; cleaning spots off the rug, the couch, and the walls you really don't want to know about; and oh yeah—trying to earn a living.

I don't share the same cultural points of reference as most of the other inhabitants of this suburb. My reference points are those of autism: talk to me about ABA, OT, MMR, IEP, NAS, GFCF, DTT, ASD; I'm sorry, I don't know how to talk reality TV.

---

get monotonous, but it will not be boring. Start buying rubber gloves, cleaning liquids, disinfectants, and carpet stain removers in wholesale quantity, as you will be using them often. I wonder if the sales figures for cleaning materials rise at the same rate as ASDs diagnoses. But I digress.

It is not easy striking a balance between family life and all that is inherent to having a child with an ASD. It is true that you probably will not have the family life you envisioned. But many people who do not have a child with an ASD do not either. People get divorced, lose a partner or a child. They grieve, but then they move on and rebuild another kind of family life. And families with a child with an ASD need to do that as well. Grieve about the loss of your expectation for the family life you envisioned, and then start building the one you will have. You owe it to the rest of the family. It will be hard work, but you can do it.

You may find some of the books listed in the Resources section helpful to you. To start with, here are some basic guidelines to keep in mind:

Do not isolate yourself and your child. Primarily, parents must take care that the family does not become isolated. This is vitally important for all members of your family. Now, more than ever, you need to be surrounded by relatives and friends, and so does everyone in your family. Isolation occurs because you are too tired to go out, you cannot handle your child in public, or you are embarrassed by your child's behaviors. People soon stop inviting you over, either because you have previously turned down invitations from them or because of your child's behavior or because you are obsessed about ASDs and that is all you can talk about. You stop inviting people over because you are too exhausted to play hostess and you are embarrassed by your child's behaviors. Do not be one of those people who says, "I remember when I used to have a social life. Look, I even have pictures to prove it."

Get over caring what other people think. Do not be intimidated by looks and remarks when you go out in public, and do not feel you have to justify your actions to family members and friends. If you are too embarrassed to take your child out in public, then you need to analyze why you feel that way. If it is because of your child's behaviors, and they are very disruptive or unsafe, then you need to work on those behaviors. If it is because you feel uncomfortable that your child appears "odd," then I suggest you get over it. Your child is here to stay, and he needs your support. And the general public needs to be reminded that none of us is perfect.

Get your child's worst behaviors under control. This is never easy and can sometimes be extremely difficult. However, this child is your responsibility now. You need to help him. First you need to try to understand what is causing the behavior. If you can eliminate the cause, that's great. If not, you need to try to get disruptive behaviors under control. It is not fair to the rest of the family, nor will it make you friends out in the community. There are positive behavior techniques that can be used to decrease and eventually eliminate the worst behaviors, and with practice a parent can learn how to use them. Your pediatrician or local ASA chapter should be able to provide you with a professional who can help you. If not, there are various books you can consult that will explain in simple terms what to do. They are listed in the Resources section at the end of this book.

Keep your sense of humor and take time to laugh. Surround yourself with uplifting media. No matter how bad things are, you can and will make it through today. Play good upbeat music, not the tunes that make you feel even more depressed. If you have ten minutes to read or watch TV, make sure it is something amusing. Don't waste it on reading or watching the news. Usually the news is depressing, and you can't do anything about it. Keep entertaining videos around the house, as well as light reading. Humor helps, even if it is gallows humor. You may not be able to control the situation you are in or solve your problems, but keeping your mood uplifted will help you have a more positive frame of mind.

Do what you can to stay healthy. Take care of your physical health. Try to eat properly, catch up on sleep when you can, and exercise regularly. Even just a twenty-minute walk three times a week will keep your body healthier and will make you feel better. Your physical health affects your mental health, which in turns affects the whole family.

Remember that you are only human. You may try to act like a superhuman and do the impossible. That is OK, if you are feeling up to it. However, watch out for burnout. Revert to acting human and do not feel guilty for only doing what you can. Think of all you have accomplished, not what you wish you had done.

How to Continue Doing the Family Activities You Enjoy

Most parents think that family activities should be done as a unit. Parents of a child with an ASD may try to include the child in all family outings, hesitating to leave him at home while everyone else is out enjoying themselves. Others may rarely take their child out in public. What is needed is a balance. Pick activities to share as a family unit that will be enjoyable to all, and schedule other activities or family outings that can be done separately with individual members of the family.

Parents need to look at the activities they enjoyed doing before and what they would like to continue doing now. See how you can adapt them for the home life you have now. Analyze whether it is easier to change the activity or to change your child's behaviors or to drop the activity. You will probably have to do a bit of all.

Managing Your Energy

BY MARSHA MARKLE

As parents of special needs children, we require plenty of energy to meet the series of unique challenges we may face. Self-care becomes an essential part of our healthy functioning. Without appropriate self-care we risk becoming physically exhausted, emotionally isolated, mentally scattered, and spiritually depleted.

In order to manage our lives and have a reserve of resourcefulness to use in service of our mission, we must learn to give ourselves intermittent renewal. Research reveals that when you expend a lot of energy you must institute habits that replenish that energy. You need to put yourself on the front burner for at least fifteen minutes a day and increase that time or frequency as you develop these new habits. Don't wait for that once-a-year vacation. If you feel overwhelmed at the thought of fitting self-care into your day, then that is a sure sign that you need to do just that.

If you want to live your life by design, not default, plan ahead to give yourself renewal in all the energy resource domains: physical, mental, emotional, and spiritual. Start by identifying your core values. Check your daily activities to see how much time and energy you are spending within those values and how much is squandered on nonessentials. Imagine what you can say "no" to so that you can begin to make the time and energy for self-care. What is zapping your energy that you might be able to eliminate?

What gives you healthy energy that you can add to your lifestyle? Get the help of your partner, family, and friends to get these needs met. If necessary, find a personal coach to assist you in this endeavor.

You'll have more energy, power, patience, and sustainability when you can take care of your needs as well as those of your loved ones. Without self-care and managed energy you will be at risk for burnout, irritability, and feeling the effect of things outside your control. Exercise your self-care muscles to create a healthy balance for yourself.

Marsha Markle, M.A. Communications, M.A. Psychology, Ed. S. School Psychology, is a personal coach specializing in self-care for parents of special needs children and is on the Adjunct Faculty at National University in the special education and school psychology departments. Marsha was a school psychologist for twenty-two years and is the parent of an adult son on the spectrum.

The following basic suggestions will be helpful to some of you, especially parents of younger children and children severely impaired by an ASD. These strategies are included here for those who have no supervised behavior program and need to teach their child some basic skills. If your child has a behavior program, he is probably already learning these skills.

Teaching Your Child Basic Communication

The first skill your child should learn is how to communicate. Some children with ASDs are verbal and are able to communicate effectively; others may have enough speech to at least get their basic needs met. Many have no speech whatsoever, or had speech and then lost it.

Not being able to communicate is very frustrating and can lead to major tantrums and disruptive behaviors. Teaching some basic communication skills can alleviate a lot of this frustration. PECS is a wonderful system for helping children to communicate (see pages 101–2). At the basic level it teaches the child that by giving you a picture of an item that he wants, he will get that item. Without professional help, you can teach your child to give you or point to pictures that represent what he wants or needs. This will not inhibit him from learning to speak and is a good practical starting point to help you at home.

For example, start by cutting out the labels of food or drink items your child enjoys. When you first introduce this concept, have another person help you. The first step is to pick a moment when you know he wants a particular item. Make sure you have a picture of that item. Hold up the item, and have the other person physically help the child to hand you the picture. In exchange you can immediately give him the desired item. This will only work if he really wants that item, and if he can't reach it without your help. You can add more pictures, perhaps laminate them, and put them somewhere easy for the child to find— perhaps stuck to the refrigerator or on the kitchen table. You can keep adding pictures so that he can request to go outside, have a ride in the car, watch TV, listen to music.

If you wish to learn more, look on the PECS website (www.pecs .com) to find out when a workshop is planned for your area.

Teaching Your Child to Wait

Another skill your child will need to master to make home life easier is waiting. At home, he needs to wait for someone to help him, he needs to wait for dinner, he needs to wait to go out. In the community he needs to learn to wait at the doctor's, wait at the supermarket checkout, line up to get on a bus or a plane. Learning the concept of waiting (you will get what you want eventually) will help to lessen the number of tantrums.

Make or find a picture that will represent "waiting" to your child. We have used a simple line drawing of a person sitting in a chair, with the face of a clock next to it. Write "waiting" clearly on the card. Laminate the picture and place a piece of Velcro somewhere on it. Next, make sure you have pictures of whatever items your child usually requests or wants immediately (favorite food, toy, ride in the car), backed with Velcro, and a seconds timer. The next time he requests an item put the relevant picture on the Velcro on the waiting card, then turn the timer on for a few seconds. Say, "We are waiting" or "Waiting" and point to the card. When the timer goes off, immediately fulfill his request.

Some children need to start with a wait of only three seconds, and work on up from there. Some can start at ten seconds or more. Once your child has learned to wait for those few seconds, add more. You know your child, so you will have to gauge where to start. Eventually, he will understand that he will get what he wants, it is only a matter of time.

Creating Schedules

Another helpful tried and trusted method is schedules. Posting pictures or words about the day's activities in the kitchen or by the front door can be helpful for a child having difficulty making sense of the world around him. Knowing what will happen and in what order is comforting. You must be sure to explain verbally what the words and pictures mean, otherwise children who are auditory learners may not make sense of the schedule.

Scheduling also helps those who have sensory problems in some areas to get ready for a not so pleasant onslaught of sensory input. For example, I have noticed that if my son is forewarned that he will be visiting the dentist or the hairdresser, he appears to have an easier time of it, as if he has prepared himself mentally. If I have forgotten to put it on the schedule earlier in the day, and then show him the picture just before leaving the house, he appears to be anxious and unhappy, often refusing to get in the car, which he usually loves.

If your child is very young and home all day, you may find it helpful to establish a routine of activities that will fill part of his day and use a schedule to show what that routine is (eating, getting dressed, free play inside, napping, TV).

Being Consistent

For any behavior changes that you are trying to make with your child, it is important that you follow through and be consistent, and that the other family members do so as well. If you introduce a way to commu-

FOOD FOR THOUGHT

Learning to Share

"Having to SHARE my parents with two older brothers was the main thing. I see too many families where the needs of the autistic person run the day. There has to be a balance, between that very needy person and needs of parents and siblings. I don't care how needy he is, he has to learn that he is not the sun with the rest of the world as planets revolving around his every tantrum. I was very lucky to have two older brothers and two parents whose egos weren't totally tied up in what I thought of them or how I succeeded."

—Jerry and Mary Newport,
Autism-Asperger's and Sexuality

nicate and then do not respond to his attempts to approach you, you will be doing your child a disservice. If you teach him to wait, but do not give him the item he is waiting for, he will not learn the concept, and will be even more confused.

Handling Family and Social Gatherings

Over the years when we get together with other parents of children with autism, we joke that we used to have a social life and we have pictures to prove it! In reality, although it is true that it is harder to participate in family and social gatherings, it can be done. Gatherings can be overwhelming, and attending with your child requires a certain amount of preparation on both ends, depending on the type and size of the gathering. This is a balancing act between making your child comfortable, making the other guests and the host comfortable, and ensuring you will be invited back. Here are some guidelines:

• Prepare your relatives and friends about how your child might act and what it means. For example, if your child runs immediately out of the room when there are more than a few people, explain that it is not personal, but that your child cannot tolerate noise because his hearing is oversensitive.

• Make sure they understand that your child is not "misbehaving" but that you will be keeping an eye on him and you are teaching him to control his behaviors, but it takes time.

• If there are breakable items sitting around, you may want to ask if you can move them out of reach.

• Ask which rooms or areas are "off-limits" and make sure you enforce that.

• Just like a designated driver, you need a designated child watcher. If you are going with another adult, decide who will be keeping an eye on your child, and when.

• If your child is on a particular diet, you will need to bring plenty of food that she is fond of. Depending on how well you know the others and how they may react, you might ask about not leaving certain foods out to munch on, and bring something to share that all can enjoy.

• Look at the traveling tips below, and follow some of the ideas to familiarize your child with what is going to happen and who he is going to see, such as showing pictures and talking about who is going to be there and the schedule of activities for the day. If you anticipate noise, make sure you tell your child a few times in the days ahead. If you know certain holiday music will be played, you can put some on at home every day for a short while so the child can get accustomed to it.

• Bring some familiar toys and favorite items to make the child feel comfortable and more at home.

Traveling and Going on Vacation as a Family

Traveling can be trying even at the best of times when you have small children. Traveling with a child with an ASD can be even more of a challenge. Airports and train stations are areas that involve lots of waiting. Leaving the security of home for a new place can be off-putting for a child with autism. How you prepare your child depends on his age and how the ASD affects him. Some suggestions are given here that you can adapt for your own child's needs and level of ability. Remember that the first time you use this he may not understand, but over time, he will.

- Teach your child the "waiting" skill if he does not have it.

- Put up a monthly calendar and check off each day until it is time to go. Bring the calendar with you and mark off the number of days in the new place, always having the departure date indicated.

- Put together a "travel book" of pictures (and/or words) of the means of transport you are going to be using to travel (airplane, boat, train), who you are going to see (relatives, friends), where you will sleep (hotel, Grandma's house), and what you will do or see at your destination (swimming, playing outside, visiting monuments). Go over this with him as often as you like in preparation for the trip. A three-ring binder is best, because you can add extra pages or insert the calendar mentioned above for use on the trip.

- Put together a picture or word schedule of the actual journey to take with you on your trip. Add extra pages to the travel book. Use Velcro to attach pictures or words in sequence. Add an empty envelope to put the "done" pictures in when you have finished that step of the journey. For example, if you are flying to Paris, start with a picture of the taxi or car that will take you to the airport. When you are at the airport, have him remove the taxi picture and put it in the envelope. Then have a picture of the airport, followed by the "waiting" picture, and then the airplane, and so on.

• Think of your child's daily routine and the items he likes or needs for it, and bring them along to make him feel more at home. Bring whatever foods and drinks will keep him happy on the trip.

• Buy some small inexpensive toys that he can play with. If he only plays with one favorite item, try to find a duplicate and see if you can "break it in" before the trip. Do not wash any toys before you go, as your child may find comfort in the "home" smell of his cherished item.

• When staying in a hotel, it is a good idea to call ahead and ask for a quiet room. You may wish to explain about your child's behavior if there is a good likelihood of him exhibiting it in the public part of the hotel. The same with a friend or relative's home. It can be a bit disconcerting for everyone concerned if your older child takes his clothes off and races through a friend's house stark naked.

• Make sure your child has an ID tag attached to him somewhere, with current phone number and "autism" written on it. You can order medical bracelets, necklaces, and tags to attach to shoelaces. If you can persuade your child to keep it in his pocket, also make an ID card with current photo and date, plus home and mobile phone numbers and the number of where you are staying. Indicate that your child has autism. Be sure to add any other important details: allergies, medications, and any specific information—for instance, whether the child is nonverbal.

TIPS FOR TRAVELING BY PLANE

• Call the airlines as far in advance as you can, and tell them you will be traveling with someone who has special needs. Some airlines have "special assistance coordinators." You may wish to explain about your child's disability and some of the behaviors that may inconvenience other travelers (for example, rocking in the seat).

• If you will need help because you have other children and some carry-on luggage, and your child is a handful, request that assistance be provided after you check in to get to the gate, and ask that assistance meet you at the airplane upon arrival. Remember that the person may not understand about your needs. They may ask you questions and say that assistance is only for the physically handicapped, so you may need to explain in concrete terms why you need help (e.g., your child cannot move from one place to another without physical assistance). Always be polite but insistent.

• On the day of departure, talk to the airline agent at the check-in counter as well as the security agents about avoiding the long lines. If they are unable to help you, ask to speak to a supervisor. Sometimes, it is helpful to stress the inconvenience that the other passengers will experience (e.g., "When waiting more than fifteen minutes in a crowded area he will scream at the top of his lungs and will not stop for twenty minutes, which can be annoying to other passengers.").

• If there are two responsible persons traveling, you may wish to purchase walkie-talkies to communicate in the airport (in the event cell phones are off limits) so that one person may wait in line while the other is keeping the children happy elsewhere.

• Let the airlines know ahead of time if your child has food allergies or sensitivities. They may be able to accommodate his special diet. Always bring food items that your child can eat in case there is a flight delay or there has been a mix-up.

• Make sure your child is wearing clothes that are loose, comfortable, and easy to pull off and on if need be. Bring any medications or

pull-ups, baby wipes, assistive communication tool, diapers, preferred food and drink items, and books and toys the child likes.

• Allow yourself plenty of time to get to the airport. Everyone will
be calmer if there is a feeling of calmness rather than a hurried pace.

Addressing Other Issues Central to Home Life

There is not enough room in this book to discuss all the important areas
that parents may need to work on to make life easier at home. Those
listed here are important, but many books are available to help you with
others. Here are some suggestions.

Toilet training. This can be difficult for some, easy for others. Some children who have sensory processing issues and poor muscle control may not
"feel" when they have the need to urinate, or they may not have the necessary motor control. It can take a long time to toilet-train some people.
There are books specifically about toilet training that are good, and *Steps
to Independence* by Bruce Baker and Alan Brightman and *One on One* by
Marilyn Chassman have sections on toilet training as well as many other
areas you may wish to address. *Steps to Independence* explains how to
teach functional living skills to children at home, and *One on One* is the
best book I have seen for teaching skills to the less able child with autism.

Chores. Teaching a child to do chores not only gives him independence,
but also makes the statement to siblings that everyone contributes to the
household. Both books mentioned above have ideas for you to try.

Desensitizing. Some children with sensory processing issues have a terrible time getting their hair cut, their teeth checked by the dentist, wearing a hat, and so on. Teaching a child to get used to an item or sound
little by little is helpful. Anyone who has a practical knowledge of ABA
can devise a system. *One on One* by Marilyn Chassman has a good sec-

tion about how to teach your child to tolerate stimuli that are difficult for him.

Behavior plans. These are an important part of making life easier at home and teaching a child responsibility for his actions. Again, these are ABA techniques and *Steps to Independence* by Baker and Brightman has a section on them.

Social skills training. Children with an ASD need to be taught social skills in order to participate in activities with other children. In chapter 5, different ways of teaching these skills and helpful resources are discussed.

Safety training. Many children with ASDs do not have any notion of safety and this needs to be taught to keep your child safe. *Dangerous Encounters: Avoiding Perilous Situations with Autism* by Bill Davis and Wendy Goldband Schunick has some good suggestions for all types of safety issues at home and in the community. The Autism Society of America website (www.autism-society.org) has a useful section entitled "Safety in the Home" that explains how you can make your home a safer environment for your child.

Other issues. For some of the above concerns mentioned and other issues, you may wish to consult *Overcoming Austism: Finding the Answers, Strategies, and Hope That Can Transform a Child's Life* by Lynn Kern Koegel, Ph.D., and Claire LaZebnik.

Adolescent Issues in ASDs

Some adolescent issues will be discussed in chapter 7 on education, and the reader may wish to consult that chapter as well. Jerry and Mary Newport, Luke Jackson, Clare Sainsbury, and Liane Willey, all authors with ASDs, have written about their teenage years and how their ASD affected them in contrast to their neurotypical peers. Parents should read some of these accounts. They will give you information you can share with your child's teacher. See the Resources section.

Puberty and Hygiene

Puberty is usually an awkward time, even for neurotypical people. Bodies are changing, hormones are raging, moods are swinging. All children nearing adolescence need to have an understanding of what is going on in their bodies. Children with ASDs need even more information and input from parents at this time. Things to keep in mind:

- Boys usually start puberty around age eleven and it may last until age seventeen. They start producing testosterone, which leads to changes in the body such as hair growth on the face and legs and under the arms, developing muscles, growth spurts, deepening of the voice, growth of penis and testicles, and development of the Adam's apple. Boys need to be told about how their bodies are changing, about erections and "wet dreams" that can happen while they are sleeping, and that ejaculation can happen when their penis is rubbed, or they may be perplexed and wonder what is wrong with them.

• Girls generally start puberty before boys, beginning sometimes as young as nine years old. In girls, overall body shape starts to change as breasts and hips begin to develop, the menstrual cycle commences at some point, and hair begins to grow on legs and pubic area and under arms. It is important that girls are told about the menstrual cycle before their first period, so they are not confused and upset and think there is something physically wrong. They will also need to be told who are the appropriate people to discuss this with (parents, a teacher, a girlfriend) and that it is not necessarily a lunchtime conversation topic in a mixed group.

• Seizures may appear during puberty for one in four individuals with ASDs, possibly due to the increase of hormonal changes in the body. Sometimes the seizures are associated with convulsions and are noticeable, but for some they are very minor and may not be detected by simple observation. You may wish to keep an eye out for the signs that indicate seizure activity. These signs are: little or no academic gain in contrast to doing well during the childhood years; losing some gains academically or behaviorally; and showing behavior problems such as severe tantrums, self-injury, or aggression. You may wish to discuss any such changes with a knowledgeable professional.

• Hygiene is an area that needs to be addressed at this time. Puberty brings the onset of sweat, and some teenagers will develop acne as a result of intensified amounts of oil in their glands. Good habits need to be developed. Daily face-washing and the application of deodorant are good places to start. Boys need to be told about shaving facial hair. Girls will need to learn how to use feminine hygiene products.

• Teaching about puberty depends on the level of understanding your child demonstrates. Some will need things explained and pictures shown a few times; others will need to be motored many times through the various aspects mentioned above. If your child learns very slowly, an early start will be helpful in the long run.

A helpful book for teaching adolescents about these issues is *Taking Care of Myself: A Hygiene, Puberty and Personal Curriculum for Young People with Autism* by Mary Wrobel.

Sexuality

Sexuality is a topic that many of us would rather skip talking about, even with our neurotypical children. However, sexual feelings are natural and everyone has them, regardless of their level of ability. Children become adolescents and then young adults. Some individuals with ASDs want intimacy and to get married; some do not. Many want friends and to date; some may not. But as adults, it is up to them to choose, and it is up to us as parents to help them develop the social skills they will need and teach them about self-esteem and self-respect and about relationships and sex.

Even if your young adult is not interested in relationships or intimacy or sex, this subject needs to be addressed. Sadly, people who have intellectual disabilities are at a high risk of sexual abuse and of contacting HIV/AIDS. Even if your child does not have intellectual disabilities, the very nature of ASDs makes it difficult for someone with the condition to read the social cues and understand appropriate versus inappropriate behavior. These cues need to be taught. There are different ways to teach them, depending on the person's level of ability. It may take a lot of time and effort on your part, but it will be well worth it. You will not always be around for your child; he needs to learn these things from you. This is the time, while he is still living at home, to be teaching your child about appropriate behavior. Even if as an adult he chooses not to have a sexual relationship, he needs to know what is appropriate and inappropriate behavior toward him, about giving or withholding consent, how to say no to others, and how to let others know if he needs help or support. He needs to learn to be able to tell a responsible person about any inappropriate behavior that someone might be doing to him. It is imperative for your child's safety that he be able to identify appropriate places on his body where people can touch him. Not only does your adolescent need to understand about behaviors, he needs to understand what is behind them. Here are some books and videos to help you:

- *Autism-Asperger's and Sexuality: Puberty and Beyond* by Jerry and Mary Newport. This book is a wonderful resource for the more able teenager and young adult, although parental guidance is recommended. The publishers suggest photocopying certain sections of the book to give to your child to read. In this way you can give him the information he is ready to handle. Jerry and Mary Newport are a married couple who both have Asperger's and share their experience and advice about puberty and sexuality.

- *Sexuality:Your Sons and Daughters with Intellectual Disabilities* by Karin Melberg Schwier and Dave Hingsburger. This is a good resource for the parents of less able children, although some ideas could be incorporated for the more able. It covers a topic parents may have a difficult time addressing and therefore sometimes forget about, but it is a very necessary part of our teenagers and young adults that we would do well not to ignore. Even though this book is not written specifically with individuals with autism in mind, many concepts and strategies can be adapted.

- *Circles* is a commonly used program (on video) for teaching appropriate social and sexual behaviors to people with developmental disabilities. It is an expensive video system and would be a good thing for a parent group or resource center to buy. *Circles I* covers social and sexual distance, different levels of intimacy, understanding choice, appropriate behaviors, and relationship boundaries. *Circles II* covers how to recognize and avoid threatening or abusive situations. *Circles III* explains about communicable diseases and the difference between casual and intimate contact. Devised by Marilyn P. Champagne and Leslie W. Walker-Hirsch, the *Circles* videos are published by James Stanfield Publishing (www.stanfield.com/sexed).

Here are some concepts that every adolescent needs to learn:

Modesty—private versus public. If your child has not mastered the concept of modesty, now is the time to teach him. He needs to learn the appropriate place for private acts (such as dressing or being naked). If he does not understand through an explanation of the concept, then perhaps visual icons will help. Pick an icon or color to represent public and one to represent private (do not confuse him by using smiley and sad faces). Put the private icon on his underwear drawer and his bedroom and bathroom doors, and the public icon on the doors to the rest of the rooms and going outside. If he gets dressed in a place other than the bathroom or his bedroom, or if he runs around the house with no clothes on or in his underwear, now is a good time to teach him what is appropriate to wear in public and in private. Perhaps you don't really mind at home, but think of when he will be living with others and how inappropriate it will be then. He needs to learn now, or he won't understand what the fuss is about years down the line. If he comes out with no clothes on, you can remind him by showing him to his room or bathroom with the appropriate icon, and pairing it with the icon on his clothes drawer. Also, your child needs to learn about using the toilet on his own with the door closed.

For some children, social stories will be effective in teaching about what behaviors are to be done in private and which ones are okay in public. This concept of private versus public is crucial to the child's learning about the body parts that are okay for others to touch, and the parts that are private and should only be touched with his permission.

Masturbation. This is one of those activities that needs to be explained as okay to do, but in private. Your adolescent needs to understand that it is a normal behavior, but only in private. Many individuals with ASDs practice self-stimulatory behavior, and masturbation is the ultimate such behavior, so a parent needs to accept the inevitable and make sure it is done in an appropriate place. If your son starts touching himself in public, he needs to be told that that is a private area, not to be touched in public. If your child is masturbating at school, then a plan should be put into place. Communication on this issue should occur between home and school. One way to handle this is to tell the student it is inappropriate at school and that he can have private time at home. Then the student should be allowed that private time once he is home.

Teaching to say or communicate NO. Some children with ASDs are compliant and have learned through years of special education to follow instructions and rules of behavior. However, for safety reasons, now that your child is becoming a young adult, he needs to learn to say "no" even to you and people of authority. One way to do this is to offer him a choice between two things (e.g., a bar of chocolate or a carrot). When he states his preference, give him the wrong one—and teach him to say, "No, I want the . . ." This needs to be generalized to all kinds of subjects. Then you can make a list of situations to say "no" in, some serious and some funny to make it fun (e.g., a stranger asks you to get in the car; your dad wants you to eat worms). You can also teach him to say "go away" by invading your child's space when you know he doesn't want you there (e.g., when he has closed the door to his room and is watching TV). Stand very close to where he is sitting, and when he does avoidance behavior (pushing you away, moving to another spot), prompt him to push you and say "Go away." When you are teaching the concepts of "no" and "go away" you must respect his right to choose, but do not confuse him by asking instead of telling in a situation where he really has no choice (e.g., "Do you want to get ready to go out now?" instead of "Time to get ready to go out."). You can, however, create choices (e.g., "Time to get ready to go out. Do you want to wear your blue jacket or your red sweater?") that he really has.

Relationship boundaries. This can be a difficult concept to teach. First your child needs to learn about the various relationships (husband, wife, sibling, aunt, colleague, close friend, neighbor, shopkeeper, and so on.). Next comes the concept of appropriate types of conversations and behaviors. One way to teach this is through a "circle of friends." Draw a dot in the middle of a big piece of paper, with ever-increasing circles surrounding it. Each circle defines the acceptable behavior of people in that circle. The circle closest to the dot represents behaviors of people you are extremely close to, and when first introducing the concept write "close hug" in this circle, then in the next circle "big hug," and so on with "handshake," "wave," and so on. "Stranger" will be the largest circle farthest out. Hang this up in your child's room and add the people (by name or picture) he knows to the different circles, discussing the concepts at his level. Then, when he meets new people, you can add them to the circle.

Grooming and Dressing

In the teenage years, how you are dressed and how you present yourself are extremely important. Luke Jackson and Jerry and Mary Newport in their respective books talk about the importance of looking right. Jerry and Mary say that right from the first day at school it is important to not look like a misfit. ASD teenagers need help in this area. Reading parts of Jackson's *Freaks, Geeks and Asperger Syndrome* and the Newport's *Autism-Asperger's and Sexuality* and *Your Life Is Not a Label* can be very helpful to the teenager. The different aspects that need to be taught to your child are: what matches and what doesn't; what's "in" and what's "out"; and the importance of basic hygiene and cleanliness.

Parents, your teenager needs your support here. First impressions are crucial. Jerry Newport talks about the importance of looking right to avoid bullying, in addition to making friends. If you have no other teenager in the house, get a friend's teenager to tell you and your child what is hot and what is not. Often the brand name is important. If you have a very small clothing budget, it is better to buy the right thing from a secondhand store than the wrong thing new. Find out what the current hairstyles are and teach your teenager how to have that look. See if your teenage fashion adviser can go shopping with you and your child to help with getting the right look.

Teenage Emotions

With raging hormones come feelings that your child may not be familiar with. Jerry and Mary Newport, Luke Jackson, Clare Sainsbury, and Liane Willey all describe how their ASD affected their teenage years in contrast to their neurotypical peers. Reading about their experiences will help you understand about the thinking processes of many people with ASDs, and give you ideas on how to help your child get through this crossroad in his life.

Teenagers with ASDs may physically be maturing at the same rate as their teenage peers, but emotionally they tend to mature much later. Early adolescence is when most young people seek more independence from their parents, strive even more for approval from their peers, and try to fit in with the crowd. Teenagers start showing an interest in romance, dating, and perhaps getting physical with members of the opposite sex. Thus, while their peers are interested in romance and start testing the system, the teenager with an ASD may continue to stick to the rules and value high grades.

The young person with an ASD who as a child had difficulty with meltdowns and aggression may calm down at puberty. However, adolescence is often a time when tantrums appear or reappear. Usually these are due to frustration, which is a normal feeling to have when you have an ASD and don't understand the social cues and changes in your non-ASD peers. Another change is that usually in primary schools the children are in the same classroom with the same teacher for most of the day. In secondary school the teenager has to deal not only with different teachers, but also with moving around to different classes. These issues are discussed in chapter 7.

There is a risk of depression during these years as it becomes apparent to the teenager with an ASD how different he is from his peers. As he becomes more interested in socializing, he may be teased and scorned by others due to his lack of required skills. Your child may be experiencing feelings of anxiety, depression, or the "blues" that will go unrecognized if he is not encouraged to talk about his thoughts with you. Your child needs to know that these feelings are normal and how to recognize and identify the different feelings he is having. For those less able, picture icons or simple drawings of happy and sad faces can initially help the nonverbal person to communicate how they feel.

Research has shown that there is a higher incidence of depression or manic depression in families with a child with an ASD, perhaps due to a biological predisposition. It is important that a person with an ASD who is depressed be treated by a professional knowledgeable about the condition.

Tony Attwood has outlined some strategies for communicating about emotions and learning about friendship in *Asperger's Syndrome: A Guide for Parents and Professionals*, and Patricia Romanowski Bashe and Barbara L. Kirby in *The Oasis Guide* also offer advice on adolescent issues. See also the Resources section.

Bullying

Bullying is a significant problem in secondary school, and for this reason I have written about it in chapter 7 on education, which the reader may wish to consult. However, a few suggestions are in order here for parents.

There are a number of things that can be done about bullying. Luke Jackson suggests in his book that if bullying occurs from the teacher, the student should go up the hierarchical ladder to the head of the grade, the principal, or another teacher he trusts.

If it is fellow students who are doing the bullying, the parents may need to step in and sort it out, but Luke suggests seeing the teacher or an authority figure in private. For a parent to speak to the bullies themselves will only aggravate the situation as soon as the parent is gone. This situation has to be dealt with seriously but discreetly.

Bullying is very upsetting for the victim and should not be treated as a fact of life that everyone deals with, because in reality it is only people who are different who are bullied. Teenagers need to learn what is responsible behavior and how to be tolerant of others. If they don't learn this in school, where will they learn it?

As a parent, you can request that the school teach social skills to your child as part of his educational provision. You can also try to teach the social skills to your child that will make him understand more about neurotypical teenagers and the behaviors and conversation that they expect from your child. There are resources in the back of this book for you to consult.

Luke Jackson also mentions that learning tae kwon do helped him in many ways, including impressing his would-be tormentors. It not only helped him with his motor skills, it boosted his confidence and made him feel better about himself.

Social Skills and Dating Skills

Even if your teenager prefers to spend a lot of time alone, he will need some social skills to get by in life. In chapter 5, strategies for teaching social skills are described. In chapter 8, ideas for actual situations or places for socializing are discussed. Again, social skills should also be taught at school and adressed in the student's IEP, but dating may be a subject you want to discuss at home.

For the able teens and young adults who are interested in dating, Jerry and Mary Newport offer many words of wisdom in their book *Autism-Asperger's and Sexuality*. Have your teenager read certain sections (this can be done by photocopying the section in question, which is authorized by the book's publisher for this specific purpose), then you can discuss them with him and provide any support he needs. Luke Jackson's book is a good resource for the early teen years.

Siblings

It's not always easy to be a sibling, but having a brother or sister with an ASD has added challenges. These challenges can have both positive and negative effects on a sibling. Parents need to be aware of the sibling's feelings in order to develop strategies of support to help him adjust. Some helpful resources for siblings are listed in the Resources section.

On the positive side, many siblings develop a maturity and sense of responsibility greater than that of their peers, take pride in the accomplishments of their brother or sister, and develop a strong sense of loyalty. Siblings of ASD children are usually more tolerant of the differences in people, and show compassion for others with special needs.

On the down side, many siblings feel resentment at the extra attention the child with autism receives, and some feel guilt over their own good health. They may also feel saddled with what they perceive as parental expectations for them to be high achievers. Many siblings feel

FOOD FOR THOUGHT

"One way to help our young men is to help them learn a few stock social scenarios. Support groups should have practice sessions in introductions. Family members can go on 'dates' with their daughter or son with autism. The practice of any social activity is a good training ground."

—Jerry and Mary Newport,
Autism-Asperger's and Sexuality

anxiety about how to interact with their brother or sister. Often there is a feeling of resentment at having to take on extra household chores, coupled with restrictions in social activities.

Living with a Brother or Sister with an ASD

Because of the behavioral characteristics inherent to autism, living with a brother or sister with an ASD is not easy. It is hard to foster a relationship with a sibling who does not show any interest in being your playmate. After a while the sibling stops making attempts to interact with the brother or sister. It is hard to harbor tender feelings toward someone who invades your personal space and tears your favorite art project off the wall, or twirls the tail right off one of your favorite stuffed animals. And how can a sibling feel comfortable inviting friends over, knowing her older brother with an ASD may come running down the stairs with no clothes on at any moment? Some of the behaviors exhibited by children with ASDs would be typical of a younger child's behavior, but it is hard for a sibling as time goes on and the behaviors continue (or are replaced with other, more interesting ones) to feel anything but resentment.

My Brother Jeremy

BY REBECCA SICILE-KIRA, TWELVE YEARS OLD

Jeremy is my older brother. He is fifteen years old and has autism. He likes to watch TV, spin tops, twirl toys, and play computer games. He also likes to go for car rides and go swimming at the pool and the beach. His favorite foods are french fries, cheese, pasta, rice, salad, strawberries, cookies, and chocolate. He is in ninth grade. He has some friends that he hangs out with at school. He also goes to school dances with one of his aides.

I like playing games with my brother a lot. I'm usually busy, but when I am free I try to play with him. We play games on the computer as well as board games. Some of the games we play are babyish, so they can get really boring after a while. One of my good friends, Rozlin, plays with my brother, too. She plays with him when she comes over, and at the Boys and Girls Club.

Sometimes I get mad at my brother. If I don't lock the door to my room while I'm not in, he will mess up my whole room! He is constantly playing with my toys. If he sees one of my toys lying around, he will pick it up and twirl it, until he finds something else to twirl. After a while that gets very annoying. I also can't leave my toys out because he might break them. It's not often that he breaks my toys, but when he does I get really mad.

Now that Jeremy is learning how to type, he is able to communicate more with us. I like this because now we can ask him a question and get an answer. Unlike when he couldn't type and we couldn't ask him anything. Sometimes he types something about me or to me. I like this because when he says something about me, it is usually something nice. I do not mind that he is autistic too much. He has gotten better at many different things. He does not hit as much as he used to. He is also a lot more patient. Even though he is autistic, I like having him as my brother.

Concerns of the Siblings

Some of the concerns siblings feel are about the ASD itself. They wonder what autism is, if they can catch it, and if their brother or sister will get better or not. Many feel that the parents spend more time with their brother or sister, and thus feel that the child with an ASD is loved more. They can be resentful of the special treatment the other child receives and of the extra burden and responsibility they feel they have. As they get older, siblings are more and more concerned about the reactions of their friends.

How Parents Can Help a Sibling Adjust

Several different factors affect how a sibling adjusts, including the family size, the severity of the brother or sister's impairment, the age of the sibling at the time of the diagnosis, as well as the gender and age of the sibling, and their place in the birth order. An older sister may well feel responsible for a younger sibling with an ASD and try to "mother" or take care of him. On the other hand, a younger sibling may find herself caring at times for an older brother, in contrast to the traditional roles that she may be observing in other families. This can lead to feelings of resentment. All in all, the parents' attitudes and expectations have a strong bearing on how a sibling adjusts.

There is much a parent can do to help a sibling adjust and experience more positive than negative effects. Here are some tips:

- Keep the lines of communication open. Knowing that they can ask questions and talk about their feelings is the most important thing for siblings. Let them know their feelings are normal.

- Remind siblings that just because you give more of your time and attention to the child with an ASD, it does not mean that you also give him more of your love. Let them know you love them just as much and that they are just as important. They need to hear it.

• Make sure that siblings have a private, autism-free zone to call their own. Install locks to make sure they have a secure place to keep their precious objects. Siblings need to feel they are safe and have privacy.

• Set out consequences for the child with an ASD if he wrecks or ruins siblings' belongings.

• Teach siblings how to play or interact with their brother who has an ASD. When they learn the skills of getting his attention and getting a response from him, they will be able to interact with him on his level and that will make them feel good about him.

• Make time on a regular basis to spend with each of your children alone. It doesn't have to be a long period of time—a fifteen-minute breakfast alone can be beneficial for parent and child. Schedule a special outing every once in a while.

• Do what you can to try to get the behaviors of the child with an ASD under control.

• Make sure siblings have some time when they can have friends over and spend time with them without having to always include their brother or sister with an ASD.

• It may be helpful for siblings to meet or talk to children in the same situation. Check with your local organizations to see if a support group for siblings exists in your area. If not, see if there is any interest, and start your own with other families. The Sibshop information online at www.pyramidautismcenter.com/sibshop and the book *Sibshops: Workshops for Siblings for Children with Special Needs* by Donald J. Meyer and Patricia F. Vadasy will help you do this.

How to Keep Your Marriage or Significant Relationship Intact

Many couples look forward to having children, and all parents know the effects those little bundles of joy can have on your relationship with each other. It is put on the back burner as the new addition to the family takes center stage. When children enter the picture, the couple may realize that they don't see eye to eye on everything, and there are squabbles about child-rearing: how the children will be disciplined, what the appropriate bedtime is, how much TV the children can watch, what constitutes an acceptable diet, and the importance of table manners. Add to the mix the household division of labor (who does what), plus the monotonous day-to-day routine of running a household, and often the relationship starts to resemble two partners of a company gone bad rather than the romantic liaison it once was.

The same is true when a couple has a child with an ASD. However, more ingredients are added to the pot: the emotional turmoil of the grief cycle when a diagnosis is pronounced; the lack of support from the community; the waiting for information from professionals; the incredible demands brought on by the behaviors characteristic of ASDs; and the struggle to find and obtain an appropriate education, as well as other essential services. For many, as the child gets older, the demands of caring for him do not lessen as they do with neurotypical children, and the difficulty of finding someone to care for those older children with challenging behaviors so you can have some time alone sometimes becomes a challenge in itself.

This is a lot for any couple to survive, no matter how strong. However, this is the life you have now, so it is up to you, the couple, to do what you can to keep your relationship or marriage afloat. Here are a few basic suggestions:

Arrange for scheduled time alone on a regular basis. The first step in being a parent, whether an ASD is a factor or not, is to find someone to watch your children on a regular basis, even if only for an hour or so

FOOD FOR THOUGHT

"Anything you read about autism almost always says that the parents' marriage suffers more than anything. A lot of people separate. Men especially seem to have trouble. I think men suddenly feel they are not the head of the family anymore. . . . If I was going to believe in what I was doing, and allow my wife to take hold of her growth and help my son, then I was going to have to step out of traditional roles and complement her."

—Bill Davis,
Breaking Autism's Barriers

to have time together. Even when the children are not all-consuming, it is easy enough to fall into the trap of never having free time alone. Use this time to do something that you always enjoyed doing together before you had children. Granted, it is not always easy to find someone to care for your child. Your concern should be for your child and the carer's safety. You will need to tell any person helping you about the behaviors your child has and what they should do about them. Here are some tips:

- You know your extended family. Can you ask them to watch your child?

- Do you belong to a church or community group? You may find some volunteers who may wish to help you.

- How well do you know your neighbors? Are they likely to know someone?

- You may be eligible for respite services from a federal, state, or local agency (see chapter 4).

• Call the local university and ask them to put a notice up that you would like to hire a college student.

• If you need to pay for the respite and do not have deep pockets, apply for and use any available benefits. If all else fails, barter a service in return. Perhaps you can exchange hours with another couple needing a few hours off.

For more tips on finding and hiring respite workers, see "Tutors, Babysitters, and Respite Providers," chapter 8 (pages 251–62).

Discuss and decide what the division of responsibility and work will be. There is a lot more to be done when you have a child with an ASD. It is rare to find a partnership that naturally absorbs the extra work and stress without one of the partners feeling as if the burden has been placed on them. Usually, one person jumps right in and takes over (usually the mother). This will lead to burnout, and even more disengagement on the part of the other partner. Sometimes, when one parent is working to support the family and the other is the homemaker, the extra burden falls on the homemaker, while the breadwinner tends to be around less and less, as the workplace starts to seem more fun than the home environment at the moment.

Find someone to talk to. Sometimes, talking to other couples in the same situation can be helpful. Just being with another couple who know what the two of you are living every day can make you feel better. Perhaps you can help each other out by sharing information or tips, or just meet up to relax among understanding grown-ups. You can meet other couples through your local support groups.

Go to couples' counseling. If you are having a difficult time and feel that your relationship is severely suffering and heading the wrong way, couples' counseling can be helpful. Don't wait till things are so bad you are talking divorce. And if your partner refuses to go, then go alone. Contact your physician for a referral. Try and find a counselor who has experience with ASDs. Ask your local support group for the names of any professionals they may know.

How to Provide for Your Child for When You Are Gone

Thinking about what will happen to our children when we are gone is not always pleasant and something we'd rather not have to think about. But the reality is, no one lives forever, and provision needs to be made. No matter the ability or needs of the child, there are always challenges you know they will face. Whether your child is still a toddler or approaching middle age, a plan needs to be created.

Many people procrastinate when it comes to this all-important area in regard to our children. Parents are so busy just trying to deal with the present. And having to take the first step toward making these plans is acknowledging that one day you won't be around, and that is a painful thought. However, making plans is empowering because you are planting the seeds for your child's future, and you can rest assured that no matter what happens, you will have helped him as much as possible, even when you are gone. Would you want the future of your child to be decided by strangers because you hadn't made plans?

Ten Steps for Future Care Planning

Bart Stevens, ChLAP, AzCLDP, has been providing estate planning services since 1972. Since 1993, he has exclusively been assisting families in planning for the future care of their loved one with a disability. A nationally recognized authority and speaker, Bart is also the author of *The ABCs of Special Needs Planning Made Easy*.

In order to prepare a plan in a simple step-by-step procedure without feeling overwhelmed by the process, Bart Stevens recommends that families commit to knowing the following ten life planning steps. If these steps are followed with the assistance of a qualified special needs planner, the family will create a comprehensive plan that addresses the lifestyle, legal, government benefits, financial, and care needs of the person.

Regardless of the age or severity of the disability, creating a plan is critically important now.

1. *Prepare a life plan.* Decide what you want regarding residential needs, employment, education, social activities, medical and dental care, religion, and final arrangements.

2. *Write informational and instructional directives.* Put your hopes and desires in a written document. Include information regarding care providers and assistants, attending physicians, dentists, medicine, functioning abilities, types of activities enjoyed, daily living skills, and rights and values. Make a videotape during daily activities such as bathing, dressing, eating, and recreation. A commentary accompanying the video is also useful.

3. *Decide on a type of supervision.* Guardianship and conservatorship are legal appointments requiring court-ordered mandates. Individuals or institutions manage the estate of people judged incapable (not necessarily incompetent) of caring for their own affairs. Guardians and conservators are also responsible for the care and decisions made on behalf of people who are unable to care for themselves. In some states, guardians assist people and conservators manage the estate of individuals. Many parents who have children with disabilities do not realize that when their children reach eighteen, parents no longer have legal authority. They must petition the courts for appointment as a legal guardian. Choose conservators/guardians for today and tomorrow. Select capable individuals in the event you become unable to make decisions in the future.

4. *Determine the cost.* Make a list of current and anticipated monthly expenses. When you have established this amount, decide on a reasonable return on your investments, and calculate how much will be needed to provide enough funds to support your child's lifestyle. Don't forget to include disability income, Social Security, and so on.

5. *Find resources.* Possible resources to fund your plan include government benefits, family assistance, inheritances, savings, life insurance, and investments.

6. *Prepare legal documents.* Choose a qualified attorney, paralegal, or certified legal document preparer to assist in preparing wills, trusts, powers of attorney, guardianships, living wills, and other necessary documents.

7. *Consider a "special needs trust."* A special needs trust holds assets for the benefit of people with disabilities and uses the income to provide for their supplemental needs. If drafted properly, assets are not considered income, so people do not jeopardize their Supplemental Security Income or Medicaid. Also, they don't have to repay Medicaid for services received. Appoint a trustee and successor trustees (individuals or corporate entities, such as banks). There are various types of special needs trusts. Make sure the person preparing your documents understands the differences and provides you with the right one.

8. *Use a life-plan binder.* Place all documents in a single binder and notify family/caregivers where they can find it.

9. *Hold a meeting.* Give copies of relevant documents and instructions to family/caregivers. Review everyone's responsibilities.

10. *Review your plan.* At least once a year, review and update the plan. Modify legal documents as necessary.

Once you have decided to prepare a plan, find someone to help you or hire a professional planner. Referral sources are available through governmental agencies, organizations, or local support groups. "Who will care when you are no longer there?" is an overwhelming concern that people with disabilities and their families must address. Solutions are available. The next step is up to you.

Bart Stevens's book, *The ABCs of Special Needs Planning Made Easy*, is a simple, step-by-step, comprehensive guide to help families and professionals plan for the future care, supervision, security, and quality of life of a person with special needs. For more information on special needs planning, you can call Bart Stevens Special Needs Planning (888-447-2525), send an e-mail (info@bssnp.com), or visit the website (www.bssnp.com).

Another good resource for parents is the ARC of America website (www.thearc.org) and the group's *Special Needs Planning Handbook*. It is not designed to be a "do-it-yourself" guide, but it does help parents determine what should be in a plan and how to locate qualified professionals and resources to finalize it.

7

Education

It would be nice to think that things had changed since my school days, but, in discussions, teenagers still at school today described the same problems and issues as people in their thirties and forties (many of these school problems, incidentally, were described in Hans Asperger's original paper in 1944). In the 80s and 90s awareness and research into Asperger's syndrome increased dramatically, but it is still taking considerable time for this new knowledge to reach teachers and others "on the ground."

—CLARE SAINSBURY, *Martian in the Playground*

I really hated to do it, but I had to file for due process. I did not want to go through the cost in time, energy, stress, and money we didn't have. But there comes a time when you have to take a stand. My son was regressing, and there was abuse and neglect occurring in the classroom, which had been documented.

The severely handicapped class he was in was being taught by an untrained substitute teacher, and there were different untrained school aides in there every other week. They were barely providing babysitting services, let alone a safe environment or an appropriate education. Meetings with the school district's director of special education just supplied us and other parents with unkept promises. The advocate we had hired said she had done all she could.

We removed my son from school, started a home program, hired a lawyer, and filed for due process. We were spending all our savings, and I was doing nothing else but teaching our son, overseeing the other tutors, making educational materials, and taking data. But I knew I was ethically and legally right, and that I could prove it. At home, Jeremy gained back his lost skills and learned new ones.

We wanted to avoid going to fair hearing, so we attempted mediation. The school district came to the bargaining table with no alternative or compromise for us to consider, and was chastised by the mediator for wasting everyone's time. We were obliged to proceed to fair hearing. On the first day of the hearing, the new director of special education (the old one had gone) agreed that the school district would refund us the money we had spent educating our son at home, and agreed to provide an appropriate program for him, including training for staff, stating that none of this should ever have happened.

A Few Facts about the Special Education System

If you are an older parent or a professional who has been in the trenches for a while, this chapter will ring a few bells. If you are a parent of a newly diagnosed child, a member of the general public, or a new teacher straight out of college, you may be surprised by what you are about to read. If you are in a position of power or hold the purse strings at the state or federal level, I hope that you will read carefully, and reflect long and hard about the state of education for children with ASDs in the U.S. today and the working conditions the educators are faced with.

The United States has arguably the best laws in terms of education and protecting the rights of people with disabilities. As the years go by, advances are being made, and in terms of education, students in need of special education services are so much better off today than their counterparts of thirty years ago.

Challenges, Expectations, and Demands

However, there is a crisis going on in early intervention programs and schools across the country. Nationwide, the number of children being diagnosed with ASDs is rising at an unbelievable rate. The settings may be different, but the challenge is the same: parents and professionals everywhere are grappling with the issue of how to educate an increasing number of children in the best possible manner. And more and more, as the struggle intensifies between the expectations of the parents and the budgetary policies of administrative officials, it is the frontline teaching staff who get caught in the crossfire, and the children who are the casualties.

Over the last few years, the expectations of the parents have increased drastically. This is due to an increase in the number of teaching methods and strategies known to be effective for children with ASDs, and the access to knowledge that parents now have thanks to the World Wide Web. Regardless of ability, parents expect their child to be treated with dignity and respect, and to be given the opportunity to learn, using the methods that are known to be effective. Parents believe that every child has the right to reach his or her potential, no matter his capability. And rightly so.

As the parents' knowledge base and expectations for their children have changed, so have the demands on the teaching staff, school administrators, and education budgets. As demands intensify, educators are requesting more support in terms of assistance and training in order to provide for these students, which, of course, translates into the need for more funding.

The large numbers of court cases attest to the tensions that exist between the school districts and parents. When communication breaks down between the two, large amounts of time and money are spent on litigation instead of programs and training.

When it comes to a challenge as all-encompassing as the education of our children, there are no easy solutions to suggest. Parents and educators alike know and live this crisis every day. But parents and educators should not be the only ones concerned. Today's children with ASDs will become adults. If they do not receive a proper and intensive early intervention, if the educational system does not provide adequate resources for the educators teaching them, as well as proper resources for preparing adolescents to transition into real adult life, society as a whole will suffer. Not only will the costs to support these individuals all their lives be greater than those of a proper education, but society will lose out on the valuable contributions they could have made.

Special Education and the Law

Basically, students in need of special education services (i.e., special class services, one-to-one school aides, assistive technology) are protected under the Individuals with Disabilities Education Act (IDEA). IDEA was originally created in 1975 and reauthorized in 1997. IDEA ensures that all individuals have access to a "free and appropriate education" (FAPE), thus requiring public schools to make education available to all children with disabilities. Until 1975, disabled children were often excluded from school. Since 1975, IDEA has protected and continues to protect the rights of hundreds of thousands of children with disabilities, including ASDs. At the time of this writing, IDEA is currently going through another reauthorization process.

IDEA is a federal act, and each state may provide more special education rights than provided by IDEA, but a state may not take away rights that are provided under this act. Much costly litigation takes place between parents and school districts over the interpretation of what is considered an "appropriate" education under the student's right to a "free and appropriate education."

In January 2002, the No Child Left Behind Act of 2001 (also called the NCLB Act) was enacted. This law specifically forbids schools and states from excluding students with disabilities from accountability systems, and all students must participate in tests that accurately gauge their progress. This is important because tests give parents and educators valuable information to target the areas in which the child needs help. Parents have a right to know, even for the most cognitively challenged, what their child is learning and if the teaching strategies being used are effective or not with their child.

To stay up to date on changes to the law, parents and educators can stay informed on special education and funding facts and concerns by checking the U.S. Department of Education website (www.ed.gov) and your state department of education.

Funding Facts and Concerns

When IDEA was created twenty-nine years ago, 40 percent of the funding for educating special education students was supposed to be provided by the federal government. To date, the annual appropriations from Congress for IDEA have only been around 14 percent. Therein lies the crux of the matter: local school districts are mandated to provide a "free and appropriate education," yet they are not receiving funds that were promised when the federal law was originally created. This creates much tension at the local level as special education encroaches on the general education budget.

Reports released in the summer of 2003 by the Center for the Special Education Finance show that students with autism have the highest per pupil expenditure for special education services ($11,543). Also interesting to note was the disparity between the states (the thirty-nine that participated) in the amount spent per special education student. The figures ranged from a low of $2,889 (in Oklahoma) per special education student to a high of $12,899 (in New York) for the 1998–99 school year.

Obviously, funding is a major issue when it comes to providing for special education students.

Personnel Facts and Concerns

The most important aspect of any educational program is the frontline educational staff teaching the children. Recent studies and presentations released by the Center on Personnel Studies in Special Education (COPSSE) show that:

• There is a high turnover rate in special education teachers. Thirteen percent of special education teachers depart each year, which is ten times the rate of general education teachers. The available data suggests that there is a critical shortage of special education teachers willing to work at the salaries offered, under the working conditions that exist in the classrooms. The shortage of special education teachers is chronic and long-term, and 10 percent of all teachers are uncertified. ("Teacher Education: What Difference Does It Make?" April 2003)

• Work environment factors such as low salaries, poor atmosphere, lack of administrative support, and role-definition problems lead to stress and low levels of job satisfaction and commitment. These, in turn, can lead to withdrawal and eventually attrition. Teachers who were younger and inexperienced, and those who were uncertified, had higher rates of attrition, as did those with higher test scores. ("Special Education Teacher Retention and Attrition: A Critical Analysis of the Literature," Bonnie S. Billingsley)

• In the 1900s and 2000–02, the role of paraprofessionals (i.e., school or instructional aides) evolved into one with a high level of responsibility including decision making regarding adaptations, providing behavioral supports, and interacting with team members including parents. The teachers' roles changed too, becoming more

FOOD FOR THOUGHT

It's a Team Approach

BY PATRICIA H. SNIDER

Effective programming for children diagnosed with an autism spectrum disorder requires a team approach. Whatever the amount of programming (twenty hours, twenty-five hours, and so on), a good one is based on applied behavior analysis and includes social skills and play skills. We believe that a highly structured classroom with at least three-to-one staffing is necessary to be able to provide both one-to-one and small group instruction. In addition, effective programming includes parent support activities such as clinics and periodic in-service. In order for the program to be effective, everyone in the child's environment must understand and provide "therapy." Hence, parents, school, and independent providers, such as regional centers, must act as a team.

But it's expensive! Yes, an effective program is *very* expensive. Two extremely important team members are the state and federal governments. It is crucial that the federal government fund its share of our mandated special education programs as it promised. Then it is equally important that the state government fund an additional fair share. This way, local school districts will not be put in the position of paying for special education–mandated costs from the general education budget dollars, as is currently the case. If everyone is in the boat rowing in the same direction, the boat goes forward. Otherwise the boat goes in circles. We need a team!

Patricia H. Snider, M.Ed., Ed. S., is the director of pupil services, Del Mar Union School District in California. She has been in education for thirty-nine years, teaching both general and special education, and, for the past fifteen years, as an administrator in the field of special education.

like managers and instructional team leaders. ("Paraprofessionals," Terri Wallace)

• Federal provisions require that all paraprofessionals be adequately prepared for their roles and responsibilities. The 1997 Amendments to IDEA require training and supervision for paraprofessionals who assist in the provision of special education services. Despite these laws, many local and state agencies do not provide significant pre-service or in-service training. ("Paraprofessionals," Terri Wallace)

• Special education administrators face the increasingly difficult task of recruiting, retaining, and developing the professional skills of special education personnel. Skilled administrators are sorely needed to steer special education in the right direction. However, in the past ten years, the preparation and licensure of special education administrators has not received much attention. Also, states vary on how they endorse and certify special education administrators (or avoid doing so). ("Special Education Administration at a Cross-roads: Availability, Licensure, and Preparation of Special Education Administrators," Carl Lashley and Mary Lynn Boscardin)

Most special education administrators are (or should be) familiar with an important 2001 study by the National Research Council's Committee on Educational Interventions for Children with Autism; the book describing the study, *Educating Children with Autism* by Catherine Lord and James P. McGee, is available online from the National Academies Press (www.nap.edu/catalog/10017.html) and the usual on-line bookstores. Parents and frontline teaching staff would benefit from it as well.

The study created a framework for evaluating the scientific evidence concerning the effects and features of early intervention and school programs designed for children up to age eight. The authors conclude (among other things) that one of the weakest elements of effective programming for children with ASD and their families is personnel preparation. They also state that teachers are faced with a huge task and outline recommendations for educating children with ASDs properly and for giving personnel the training and tools to do so. This report has been cited by due process hearing officers and the courts in terms of appropriate services.

Conclusion

Obviously, each individual state would be better off in terms of funding special education if the federal government would follow through on its promise to provide 40 percent of the funding of IDEA. However, for this to really help, the states, when receiving these monies, would need to put them into the special education budget, and not (as has happened at least in one state . . .) put it in another purse.

Money helps, but it is not the cure for all ills. Suggestions for retaining qualified personnel have been made by many and include: keeping class sizes and caseloads smaller, providing a higher salaries for special education teachers, providing some secretarial help to manage the paperwork, offering graduate-level courses paid for by the school district, clearly defining job descriptions, and providing opportunities for shared decision making.

Ensuring that instructional aides or paraprofessionals are adequately trained and making sure their roles are clearly defined has also been suggested, as has providing information to regular education as well as special education personnel.

As school administrators are the leaders and decision makers when it comes to funding and training, the preparation and licensing of these professionals needs to be carefully examined to ensure that quality candidates are supported in their quest to move upward in the system.

As one of the wealthiest (and supposedly more civilized) countries in the world, we owe it to our future generations to leave the educational system all the better for having been a part of the process—whether educator, administrator, parent, or simply just the taxpayer.

Taking Responsibility

Everyone needs to take responsibility in an emotionally intelligent way. Parents need to take responsibility for not accepting less than an appropriate education for their child, while supporting the educational staff whenever possible and having good communication with all concerned.

Teaching staff need to accept responsibility by stating their needs to their superiors and refusing to provide services without the proper training and specialist support, as well as asking parents for information that can help them understand the child's learning style.

And finally, special education administrators and the principal need to take responsibility for leading the way by listening to what the frontline teaching staff are telling them, understanding the educational needs of the child, and making some effective changes. With the increasing numbers of children being diagnosed with ASDs today, this challenge is not going away any day soon.

As parents, educators, and administrators, we are responsible for the future of all individuals with ASDs. It is our responsibility to work together to ensure the best preparation for the future of these children. They are counting on us and we must not let them down. As neurotypicals, we should be able to handle the pressure, communicate effectively, empathize with, and understand each other well enough to work together. Aren't we the flexible, socially cognizant ones?

How to Get the Educational Provision Your Child Needs

Although this section is intended primarily for parents, educators may find it interesting reading.

In chapter 5, various types of therapies and teaching methods were discussed. To determine which of these methods—and exactly what program—best meet the educational needs of a given child, information-gathering must take place. Different professionals will do assessments, but as parents spend the most time with their child, they can learn a lot about his abilities and learning styles just by observing him. Regardless of whether your child is a baby or school aged, you will need to form your own opinion based on your observations of your child in his daily life.

The observations you note about your child's abilities, challenges, and learning styles will clarify which educational strategies and therapies could be useful for your child. Significantly, they can also help you in your quest for the right educational program. Once you know about your child, you can look at what is on offer (and what is not!) and decide if they will meet his needs. And if you believe that what is available is not appropriate for him, your documented observations will help you get others (teachers, school district administrators) to agree with you that another educational program or therapy is needed for your child.

Determining What Your Child's Educational Needs Are

To start with, I recommend you read the following for more information on this subject:

- *Negotiating the Special Education Maze: A Guide for Parents and Teachers* by Winifred Anderson, Stephen Chitwood, and Deidre Hayden is an excellent user-friendly book that has good advice on becoming an educational advocate for your child. The authors explain how to make observations and collect information, and suggest what questions to ask when visiting prospective schools and classrooms. They also supply useful charts and questionnaires to use as guidelines to gather information. Teachers may find the book helpful as well.

- *Wrightslaw: From Emotions to Advocacy: The Special Education Survival Guide* by Peter W. D. Wright and Pamela Darr Wright gives good, simple advice on how to become an advocate for your child and obtain the education he needs.

• Another good book is *How Your Child Is Smart: A Life-Changing Approach to Learning* by Dawna Markova and Anne Powell. This book is helpful in determining your child's learning style—auditory, visual, or kinesthetic.

• For a short but interesting read, see "Learning Styles and Autism" by Stephen M. Edelson, Ph.D., at www.autism.org/styles.html.

Observing and Recording Your Child's Abilities

This kind of information is invaluable when thinking about your child's needs, and what kind of educational program would serve him best. Yet planning an appropriate program for a child requires documented and specific facts about the child, not just impressions and concerns. Parents need to learn to observe their child, to organize the information they glean, and to make sense of it.

Anderson, Chitwood, and Hayden give suggestions for recording observations on how the child acts in different environments, and how he relates to objects and people. These observations need only take five to ten minutes at a time. A good way to do this is to step back from your role in the family and watch your child, and see how he does without your help. For example, can your one-year-old sit himself up without your help? Does he know and respond to his own name? If your child is five, does he understand the rules of games and does he follow them?

Different developmental areas. Once you have written down your observations (e.g., "Sam can eat with a fork"; "Debra can do long division unaided and correctly"), you can organize them into the different developmental areas they pertain to. These areas are: senses and perception, movement, self-concept and independence, communication, thinking skills, and social relationships. Your child will have different abilities in the different developmental areas. Knowing about these different areas will be helpful for you in identifying problems in your child.

In regard to young children from birth to five, check with your child's pediatrician. A good resource is "The ABC's of Child Development" on the PBS website (www.pbs.org/wholechild/abc) or for a baby's monthly milestones see the Baby Builders website (www.babybuilders .net). If you do a search on "developmental milestones" on the National Institutes of Health website (www.nih.gov), you will have access to information about speech and language milestones. For school-age children, your child's teacher should be a good source of information as to what is considered normal development.

Your child's learning style. Children are different from each other, and so is their learning style. Think about yourself. Do you learn better by hearing information or by seeing it? Do you work best in a neat environment or a messy one? Do you work long and hard, or do you take frequent breaks?

Now think about your child and what you have learned from observing him. Observe him some more if you are not sure, thinking about how he learned to do the things he does. Does he like watching videos and has he learned some phrases from the programs he watches? Does he copy an action he sees someone else do? Does your child do homework better alone or in the company of friends? Does he do his homework in a quiet environment or a noisy one? Sharing this kind of information with those who will be or are teaching your child will enable them to create the best possible setting for him.

Getting Early Intervention and Special Education for Your Child

Perhaps you are the parents of a preschool child, or you have an older child who is experiencing difficulties. It may be that you are a teacher who has concerns about a child in your class. A child may have been identified as having special educational needs as a baby or toddler before entering the school system, when he starts school, or when he starts encountering difficulties as he gets older. Sometimes the teacher has concerns; sometimes the parents; or perhaps a young person is having anxieties about their own ability to progress or difficulties in certain areas.

It is not my intention to give legal advice, or an in-depth explanation of how the system works, as each person's situation is different, and every state is different as well. Parents should be aware of their rights and responsibilities. Teachers as well should know their rights, and need to inform themselves about how IDEA is implemented in their state. There are wonderful resources available, for both parents and schools, which are listed in this chapter and at the end of this book. Every state has a federally mandated "protection and advocacy" agency that can provide information and protection on the rights of persons with developmental disabilities through legally based advocacy. To find the one in your area, go to the Autism Society of America (ASA) website (www.autism-society.org) and click on "Resources."

Basically, every child under the age of three and at risk of developing a substantial disability if early interventions are not provided is eligible

The Meek Shall Inherit the Earth, but Only the Bold Will Get a Decent Education for Their Child with Autism

This chapter may be difficult reading for those who are used to abiding by authority and professional opinion. I mean no disrespect, but after living in three different countries with my son, I can tell you that one must be polite, but not be meek, when it comes to getting the education your child needs. If you do not fight for your child, who will?

The status quo will not change unless parents become proactive, learn about their rights and responsibilities, and convince the special education administrators that they know what the effective teaching strategies are for their child with an ASD, and that they won't go away until they get them, regardless of the school or ability level of the child.

Be careful of the words of assurance from people in positions of power. Get promises in writing. If people don't call when they are supposed to, keep calling until you get them on the phone. Document everything. Be polite, but be insistent. And most of all, be brave.

for early intervention. Your physician should be able to point you toward the resources in your area and any assessments your child may need. However, if your physician says, "Wait, your child will catch up," and yet you feel that something is amiss, do not hesitate to go see another doctor for a second opinion.

The names of the different programs vary by state, but you can check with your state's Department of Health, Department of Developmental Disability, or Department of Education about early intervention in your area. If you are having trouble finding out where to turn for help with your child, look on the website of the Federal Interagency Coordinating Council (www.fed-icc.org) and click on the link to resources and other links to find the agencies that can help you in your state. There are helpful links on the ASA website as well.

If your child is eligible for early intervention, an individualized family service plan will be drawn up including the infant's present levels of development and a statement of outcomes to be expected, among other things.

Once a child is eligible for preschool services, the educational system takes over. An Individual Education Program (IEP) is developed that sets out ways of helping the child with his areas of difficulties, and goals and objectives are developed. IEP team meetings take place annually to review the child's progress and placement, but may take place more often. The IEP team is made up of the child's teacher; a general education teacher (if that is not his regular teacher); the parents; any professionals providing services such as speech and language, occupational therapy, or adapted physical education; and a special education administrator. Tips on preparing for the IEP meeting are discussed later in this chapter.

If a parent has concerns about a child's progress, she should first discuss matters with the teacher. If the concerns have already been discussed with the teacher, and nothing has been resolved, you could approach the special education administrator or ask for an IEP team meeting.

Advocating for Your Child throughout the Special Education Process

It may be that you are one of those lucky individuals living in a school district that is truly knowledgeable about autism spectrum disorders and what works best for these students and that provides good training to its staff. Perhaps you have a wonderful early intensive program with trained staff and appropriate supervision. Or perhaps your older child with an ASD is fully included at your neighborhood school with specialist support, teachers who are knowledgeable and have the support they need to help your child, and not a bully in sight.

However, you are probably one of the many who are obliged to persuade their school district administrator about what is best for their child. If you have other children, you may already have experience with the educational system. However, when you have a child with special educational needs, you are entering unfamiliar territory and you need to learn a new set of navigating skills.

For a few years I wrote and gave workshops with Merryn Affleck, president of the North County Chapter of the Autism Society of America in San Diego. Our workshops were about developing the skills to become an advocate for your child, and creating a good working relationship with your child's school. Whatever your situation might be, as a parent you will need to follow these suggestions derived from our workshops to ensure that your child is getting the program and educational services he needs.

Get to know how your child learns. For a pre–school-age child, observe how he interacts with people and objects. Does your child imitate others? Does he try to do new things with different toys? Does he appear curious about his environment? For older children, look at what your child's track record says about his learning style. For example, does he learn new concepts only with one-on-one instruction? Is he able to focus with twenty-nine other students in the classroom? Does he need a communication device? Does he learn by imitating others? For how long can he successfully be integrated into a mainstream school with support? What has worked in the past for your child and what hasn't? What has worked for other children like yours?

Learn about the educational strategies that work for ASDs. Join local autism groups, look at resources on the Internet, read books, talk to other parents and professionals. Read chapter 5 for a general overview on treatments and therapies, and read the section for teachers later in this chapter (beginning on page 213), as well as chapter 6 on family life. You will find plenty of information about educational strategies and what research has to say about the various techniques, plus resources to find out more. ASDs are a spectrum; all children are different. Find out about which particular teaching methods and strategies have been proven to be most effective with children like your child.

Learn about IDEA and "No Child Left Behind" and what these acts say about the school's duties and parents' duties with regard to the education of children. Live by the motto "Always be prepared." You and your child are consumers of the education system and have certain rights as well as responsibilities. As a consumer you need to be informed as to what those are. You need to be as astute on the law as your school district is. As mentioned earlier, there are resources to help you. Every parent should contact their state's protection and advocacy agency (visit the ASA website at www.autism-society.org to find your state's agency).

Learn about your local school district. School districts vary on what kinds of programs or specialist support they have given in the past and are geared toward providing. There are regional differences, and some are better about hearing the needs of the child versus the budgetary constraints. Again, it is up to you to think outside the box. Don't depend on the district giving your child what he needs; more often than not you will have to ask for it. Remember, your child's IEP should be about meeting his educational needs, not what the school district is used to providing. Find out from other parents what your school district's track record is for children with autism spectrum disorders.

Familiarize yourself with the different types of school options. Your child has the right to a free and appropriate education in the least restrictive environment. Depending on where you live, your child, and his needs, there are different options, including: full inclusion in his neighborhood school, resource units, learning centers, special education classes in neighborhood schools, regional classes, classes for severely handicapped children, learning-disabled classes, residential placement, homeschooling, and private schools.

Visit different schools and different types of classrooms. Before making a decision regarding your child's educational program, and what you think would be best for your child, visit the different options that are in your area. Keep in mind, however, that the class you are seeing now may not look the same the following year, and the teacher whose class you are visiting may not be there when your child is going to be a student there. There are many factors to consider when making a decision about your preference. Regardless of the type of classroom, there are many aspects to be considered. At any school, the appropriate questions to ask would include:

- How many children are in a class?

- What is the ratio of staff to children?

- Do the staff have appropriate skills and access to training to help your child?

- Are there any specialist resources (such as a behavioral consultant)?

- What kind of experience do the school and the teacher have with children with ASDs?

- What teaching methods and strategies specific to ASDs are the staff trained in?

- Is the school prepared to fit their systems around the child rather than being concerned about how a child will fit into the school system? For example, if your child is fully included, is there a "safe" place for her to go if she is feeling overwhelmed and stressed? Can school rules about eating in the dining hall be bent so that vulnerable children and their friends can eat together and have a lunch-club in an empty classroom?

It is critical to ask specific questions about the teacher's experience with and knowledge of ASDs. Flexibility is also important. A teacher may not have much knowledge about ASDs, but may be flexible about the needs of your child and willing to learn what is necessary to make this a positive experience for your child.

Do not be comforted by a good ratio of staff to children in a special education class unless you know that the teaching aides or support staff can demonstrate a functional knowledge of teaching methods proven to be effective with children with autism. Even the best teacher cannot be effective if she has untrained staff.

As autism is a spectrum, the staff may have had experience with a different ability level from that of your child or a different severity of autism. You want to make sure the staff have a working knowledge of your child's type of difficulties or ensure that specialist support will be provided by someone with that level of knowledge. Some children with autism require a one-on-one aide, and you will need to consider whether or not you feel it is necessary. Again, this person will require training.

Develop good relationships. Develop and maintain good relationships with everyone you meet. If your child is already in school, make sure you have open lines of communication with the school staff. There should be a good flow of information going in each direction to make sure that you are all on the same page when it comes to behavior plans, toilet training, and homework. Often the frontline staff have their hands tied. By working together you may be able to get resources for your child or the classroom.

Learn about intensive behavioral therapy. (See pages 94–99) This has been shown to be the most effective treatment for young children. Some districts are providing this for students with ASDs. If you think this is what is best for your child and want to find out more, contact the local chapter of the Autism Society of America and ask to be put in contact with parents who have experience with this in your area. Contacting other parents can be very informative.

Keep good records. Make sure you have copies of any assessments, reports, individual education plans, and statements. Keep all assessments and reports in chronological order; they will be easier to find. Make sure you get copies of any assessments the school district has requested on your child's behalf.

Keep good notes of any phone calls, meetings, and conversations about your child. Keeping a notebook for this purpose is a good idea. Sometimes it is easy to forget suggestions professionals may make that are helpful, or when someone at school has told you something they are doing for your child, so writing notes (including names, professional positions, and dates) is very helpful. This is also a good way to jog people's memories about timelines and follow through on actions that need to be taken. It is also an ideal place to note attempts that you make to contact individuals who are having a hard time getting back to you. It's helpful to keep each contact on a separate page. This makes it easier to refer to in any meetings or letters, as well as to organize as evidence in any potential due process.

Do not be afraid to ask questions. If you don't understand certain expressions or jargon, or what someone said, ask for an explanation. If you are unclear about who is supposed to be doing what when, ask specific questions. This is especially true in something as important as a statement. Make sure the wording is specific. For example, what does "help on a regular basis" mean? Does that mean once a year, once a month, or once a week? How small is a "small group"? If you are told that a particular professional will monitor a program, the question begs to be asked, who is devising the program, carrying it out, and how often? Sometimes the wording is vague in order to allow flexibility. However, it should be specific enough so you know who is responsible for what, and how often it should happen.

Do not feel intimidated by the professionals. Remember, you are the expert on your child. Never feel intimidated or that your input is less valuable than that of the teaching staff, other professionals, or the school district. If you feel intimidated, learn more about your child, his disability and abilities. Knowledge is power. Remember that you can consent in whole or only in part to team decisions made. You can delineate in writing that which you do not agree to.

Keep focused on your goal: a free and appropriate education in the least restrictive environment for your child. Although you do want to develop good relationships, remember that this is not about whether people are "nice" or trying to do what they can. Either your child is getting an appropriate program (meaning staff are knowledgeable and trained or given the specialist support they need if necessary) and is showing progress, or he is not, and that is the crux of the matter.

Monitor your child's progress and educational program. Education is a continual process, including review and assessment: you review what is supposed to be happening, and you assess its effectiveness. Parents of neurotypical children monitor their children's progress all the time. Parents of children receiving special educational services may need to be more vigilant. There are a variety of ways to achieve this. Base your monitoring method on your relationships with your child's teachers, therapists, and school administrators.

Develop good relationships in the community. Being on the local school board or advisory committee of the school or district your child is in is an excellent way to meet other parents and to network with the professionals. I encourage those of you out there with extra energy and time on your hands to get elected. This is where decisions are made regarding local school issues. Our children need to be represented. You can have a positive impact on your community.

The Individualized Education Program (IEP)

If your child is receiving special education services, an Individualized Education Program must be developed at a meeting with at least the parent or parents, the child's teacher, and a school district administrator. At time of writing, this meeting must take place at least once a year.

The IEP document is very important, as it establishes what services your child will receive and the goals and objectives for the coming year. For more information read *How Well Does Your IEP Measure Up?* by Diane Twatchman-Cullen and Jennifer Twatchman-Reilly; it's a great resource for helping to prepare an IEP. *Better IEPs* by Barbara D. Bateman and Mary Anne Linden is another good book.

It may be that you and the other members of the IEP team meeting are in agreement about your child and his educational needs. Sometimes, however, this is not the case. Remember that team meetings are not meant to be battlegrounds. If you are not in agreement after listening to the other members of the team, then state your position. If you cannot agree with the team, then you must agree to disagree. Once you start "losing it" in front of staff and make insulting and degrading comments in front of others, you have most likely already lost the battle. If you have concerns that a team may have differing opinions, it's a good idea to ask permission to tape-record the meeting (you will need to check your state's required notice time and the district may tape-record the meeting as well). This saves a lot of "he said, she said" if ever there were to be mediation or due process.

FOOD FOR THOUGHT

Parents and Educators as Partners

BY ELLEN LEGARE

Remember when kids went to school to get an education and parents reinforced learning by helping (but not too much) with homework? Like it or not, times have changed; and so must we. We must recognize that children may go to "toddler school" or preschool and although parents are a child's first teacher, they may share the educational experience with a variety of professionals.

Educators educate and parents parent; but somewhere along the line these two groups come together to form a "team" to provide an appropriate program for kids with special needs. Both are educated, experienced, and want the best for kids.

Team meetings get personal. Discussions may range from where and how the child sleeps and eats at home to the level of training a teacher may have. How can meetings between educators and parents be successful?

Try a few of these ideas:

- Stick to the facts and don't try to interpret

- Don't be quick to judge

- Listen to each other

- Be honest

- Be respectful

- Stay organized

- Discuss the present—not the past

- Recognize barriers

- Collaborate

- Communicate in a nonthreatening manner

- Question each other

- Explore all the possibilities

It takes time and energy to build a relationship, to trust in another person, and when concerns and issues become barriers it is even more difficult to reach an agreement. Don't limit the team meetings to discussing the goals and objectives without recognizing that each team member brings individual expertise as well as their own perspective. Do remember that each perspective is just that—their own view. Listen respectfully and move on to address the issues and concerns that brought the team together.

Meetings between parents and educators should be considered "works in progress" and dynamic. Listen and learn; you may be glad that you took the time to do so.

Ellen LeGare is a special education advisor (and a parent) with over twenty years' experience building relationships with educational teams. An active member of parent associations such as PTA, CAC, and EFRC (Exceptional Family Resource Center), Ellen has been trained in alternative dispute resolution and mediation methods.

Eighteen Tips for Getting Quality Special Education Services for Your Child

The following eighteen tips were written by Ellen S. Goldblatt and Dale Mentink, senior attorneys at Protection & Advocacy, Inc. (PAI), a private nonprofit organization that advocates for the rights of Californians with disabilities. Each state is mandated by federal law to have an advocacy agency to protect the rights of people with disabilities, including those with developmental disabilities. Go to the Autism Society of America website (www.autism-society.org) to find the one in your state.

BEFORE THE IEP MEETING

1. *Request needed assessments in writing or get independent assessments.* Your child can be assessed in any area of suspected disability and for any services needed for him to benefit from school. For example, assessments may be done of reading or math levels, on the modifications needed to fully include your child, for therapy services (OT, PT, speech, mental health), and to identify assistive technology like a communication device. If you disagree with the school district's assessment, you can obtain an independent assessment at public expense. Always request assessments in writing. An assessment plan must come in fifteen days. Once you sign the plan, the assessment must be completed and the IEP meeting held in fifty days (with some exceptions).

2. *Ask to obtain assessment reports one week before an IEP meeting.* Whether you or the school district requested the assessments, ask the school *early on* to provide you with copies of the written assessment reports *a week before* the IEP meeting. This is very important so that you can read the reports, discuss them, and plan for the meeting.

3. *Plan for the meeting with a friend or advocate.* In planning for your child's IEP, you may want to contact a local advocacy organization or parent advocacy group. (All states have a protection and advocacy agency and, depending on where you live, there may be other advocacy resources or attorneys who specialize in special education law.) Or buddy up with another family and assist each other to plan for IEPs.

4. *Review any assessment reports with this person.* Identify your aims for the meeting, and think about what your child accomplished last year and what you hope they will learn next year. Identify the special difficulties or strengths of your child that

you want to bring to the school's attention. If you are seeking full inclusion or increased integration, identify how your child interacts with nondisabled children outside of school and what makes it successful.

5. *Consider full inclusion or increased integration.* The law says that to the maximum extent appropriate, as decided by the IEP team, children with disabilities shall be educated in their neighborhood schools and attend regular classes (with supplemental aids and services). These placements are called "full inclusion." Today many researchers and parents believe all children with disabilities can and should be fully included. You should definitely consider before the IEP meeting whether you want your child fully included or simply want to increase her integration opportunities in classroom and/or extracurricular activities (clubs, field trips, etc.) at her school.

6. *Make a list of the points you want to raise at the IEP meeting.* However well you plan, you may get nervous or distracted at a meeting with several professionals. Thus, it is good to make a list of points and questions in advance so you won't forget. You can check off points as they are discussed and jot down the answers to your questions.

AT THE IEP MEETING

7. *Bring a friend, advocate, and/or a person who knows your child.* You can invite anyone you want to your child's IEP. It is always a good idea to have someone with you. If there is a day-care operator, grandparent, tutor, behavior specialist, or other person who knows your child and her learning style, it can be helpful to bring them to the meeting.

8. *Don't be afraid to ask questions, and make sure you understand any "jargon."* Schools are required to explain all findings and

recommendations in easily understandable language. District staff use the same terms every day and may forget that the world doesn't know what they mean. Some parents don't ask questions because they feel it makes them appear unintelligent or unsophisticated. The fact is that the most intelligent and sophisticated parents often ask the most questions.

9. *Discuss the present level of your child's performance.* Discuss reports, assessments, and your own and the teacher's observations of your child's performance; record his abilities and issues.

10. *Develop annual goals and short-term objectives.* Review progress on prior goals, then formulate new goals and objectives. If you want your child to have greater integration or full inclusion, then you should request objectives that include interaction with nondisabled students (e.g., "Molly will learn to take turns by playing a game with nondisabled peers").

11. *Identify full inclusion or integration opportunities and the supports needed for success.* The district must provide supplementary aids and services to accommodate the special education needs of students with disabilities in integrated settings, including, for example, a trained aid, use of a tape recorder, an inclusion specialist to help the regular education teacher modify curriculum, or a behavioral plan to address disruptive behaviors.

12. *Describe the placement for your child and identify specifically the supports and related services needed.* All related services, such as speech therapy, should be identified, including frequency and duration; for example: twice a week for one hour. The parameters of the placement should be stated clearly (e.g., "Karen will be fully included in second grade with a full-time aid and five hours a week of a full-inclusion specialist" or "John will attend a special day class for communicatively handicapped students with mainstreaming for science, chorus, and all regular

school activities"). You do not have the right to require the district to provide its services from a particular teacher in a particular classroom. Specific placement options should, however, be discussed at the IEP.

13. *Sign the IEP only if you are satisfied.* You do not need to sign the IEP at the meeting—you can take it home to discuss it with others and think about it. You can consent to only part of the IEP so those services you agree with can begin. If you sign the IEP and later change your mind, you may withdraw your consent by writing to the special education administrator. If you and the district disagree on services, the last agreed-upon IEP remains in effect while a due process hearing is held. This is called "stay-put."

AFTER THE IEP MEETING

14. *Meet your child's teacher(s) at the beginning of the year—be a classroom volunteer if possible and/or participate in school activities.* Parents have different amounts of time and money. Analyze your situation and then contact the teacher or school to determine how you could be of assistance. If you work during the day you may be able to help prepare materials in the evening in your home. Not only will you become more familiar with the school and its staff, but your child will feel special.

15. *Support your child in developing friendships with her classmates.* Assist your child in calling friends outside of school and to make playdates. Having friendships with nondisabled and disabled children will help your child be part of community.

16. *Monitor your child's progress.* You may want to arrange for a regular communication system with your child's teacher, such as a notebook that goes back and forth to school. Note projected target dates for your child to master particular skills

and ask the teacher to let you know of his progress. Monitor to ensure that supplementary aids and services are actually provided.

IF THINGS DON'T WORK OUT

17. *You can file a compliance complaint if the school district does not follow the law or fails to provide services required in a signed IEP.* You have, as a recourse, filing a compliance complaint when you believe the district has violated a part of special education law or procedure. The complaint is investigated by the district or the state Department of Education, which then issues a written determination of whether the district was or is "out of compliance." Check with your local advocacy agency for more information.

18. *You can file for a due process hearing if you and the school district cannot agree on the special education services appropriate for your child.* When you and the district disagree about your child's eligibility, placement, program needs, integration, or related services, either of you may request a due process hearing. At the hearing both parties present evidence to an independent hearing officer (hired by the state). The hearing officer will decide on the facts and the law and issue a written decision. Check with your local advocacy agency for more information.

Other Tips to Keep in Mind during the IEP Process

• The Individual Educational Program (IEP) is not the "end all"; rather, it is the beginning of ensuring a suitable education for your child. Maintaining the IEP is a continual process, just like education. As a parent, you may need to monitor the plan that is being implemented.

• Risk-taking is an integral part of life. Many people are timid by nature and do not like to risk the ire of those in power by questioning authority or professionals. However, you are the expert on your child. What is it that you want for your child—what do you think he needs to learn and how does he learn best? If you are not in agreement with what others think is best for your child, you need to think about what the risk is of not speaking up. Think about what you would do if you were not afraid, then do it. Do you want to spend the rest of your life thinking, "What if I had said . . . ?"

• Parents who have a child with a disability have more stress than other parents. Dealing with the systems that are in place to "help" your child often creates even more stress than the child himself does. These feelings will overpower you (remember the grief cycle?) from time to time. You will find that you take your frustration out on the wrong targets, usually the systems and people who are actually there to help you. Learn to recognize when you are not in control of your emotions or your stress level is high.

Become More Knowledgeable about the Law

You are going to be your child's advocate in the education system for some time. Empower yourself with knowledge about your rights. Here are some books and organizations that have useful information:

• Know your rights regarding protection and advocacy. If you are in need of advice your local protection and advocacy agency can help you with advice, or recommend an advocate. Every state has some sort of protection and advocacy agency. Find out what publications they have available; these are free and available online. To find out your state's agency, look on the Autism Society of America website (www.autism-society.org).

- *Autism: Asserting Your Child's Rights to a Special Education* by attorney David A. Sherman will be released when IDEA is reauthorized by Congress; in the meantime, Sherman's previous book, *Autism: Asserting Your Child's Special Education Rights,* is helpful and specific to autism. Sherman's website (www.aboutautism law.com) is informative and has links for more on education and the law.

- *Wrightslaw: Special Education Law* by Peter W. D. Wright and Pamela Darr Wright is an informative and helpful book for those who want to read and understand about the laws that pertain to special education. For more information, see the Wrights' website (www.wrightslaw.com).

- *Educating Children with Autism* by the National Research Council (sponsored by the Department of Education). The book is filled with recommendations that you can use to obtain an appropriate program. It is often cited by due process hearing officers and the courts. Quote the recommendations in the book to help secure appropriate services. It is not easy to read for a layman, but well worth the time and effort. Available online from the National Academies Press (www.nap.edu/catalog/10017.html) and other bookstores.

- The Council of Parent Attorneys and Advocates (COPAA) (www.copaa.net) is an independent, nonprofit organization of attorneys, advocates, and parents, whose primary mission is to secure educational services for children with disabilities. You can write to them (321 Pennsylvania Ave., SE, Washington, DC 20003-3027); phone (202-544-2210); or send an e-mail (copaa@copaa.net).

- The American Bar Association (www.abanet.org) is where to go to find out more about attorneys. Write (750 N. Lake Shore Drive, Chicago, IL 60611); phone (312-988-5000); or send an e-mail (ask-aba@abanet.org).

- U.S. Department of Education (www.ed.gov/nclb) is a good place to find out about the No Children Left Behind Act.

- IDEA Practices (http://www.ideapractices.org/law/index.php) gives information about IDEA. At the time of publishing, only The Individuals with Disabilities Education Act Amendments of 1997 Public Law 105-17, IDEA 1997, as well as the final IDEA '97 regulations released in March 1999 are available. There is currently a reauthorization of IDEA under way, and the reader will need to find out more about the resulting regulations.

Become More Knowledgeable about Attorneys and Advocates

Hopefully, you will never need an advocate or an attorney. But if you do, there are some things you should know. If you cannot afford to hire an attorney or advocate, there are usually advocates available through your protection and advocacy agency. Also, if you want to hire someone but have little discretionary income, they can give you the names of individuals who work on a sliding scale. Here are some tips you should keep in mind when looking for someone to represent your child.

First, know the difference between an attorney and an advocate:

- An attorney has passed a state bar exam and holds an active State Bar card.

- Fees paid to an attorney may be reimbursed in the event that you should win a due process. Advocate fees are not.

Before hiring an attorney or advocate, talk to parents who have used his services and ask:

- Are they happy with the results? Do they feel they obtained what their child needs and should have under the law?

• What style does the professional have? Look at what your needs are and analyze the type of person you wish to represent you. For example, is he warm and fuzzy or is he a hired gun? You need to feel comfortable with the person. Speaking from experience, at this point in the game you are looking for someone to be effective in getting what your child needs. If you need hand-holding, go see a therapist.

Find out more about the attorney or advocate by talking to them over the phone, or if they are very busy and in much demand, ask their office staff to get back to you about any questions you may have, such as:

• What percentage of cases handled by the professional are resolved in mediation? This will tell you about their ability to negotiate and how successful they are in avoiding going to fair hearing.

• How many cases have they handled that are similar to yours, or in your school district, and what is their success rate for those cases? This person may have much experience, but it could be more with learning disabled children and in another school district.

• What are the hourly rates, what estimate is there for this kind of case, how much is the retainer, and how is billing handled?

If you are leaning toward hiring an advocate, you need to ask these questions:

• Does the advocate have an attorney to refer you to if necessary? This is important, because if you are unable to come to agreement with the school district and decide to file for due process, you will most likely need an attorney, and your advocate will be able to hand the case over easily to one. Also, if the advocate has any legal questions she is unsure of, she has someone to check with who will guide her.

- How much training has she had in special education law, and how much experience with your type of situation and your school district?

- Is the advocate a member of the Council of Parent Attorneys and Advocates (COPAA) (www.copaa.net), and does she attend conferences regularly to keep up with the changes in law?

If your state department of education publishes due process cases online, then you can do a search of the history of the potential attorney or advocate you are leaning toward hiring to see their history with that agency.

Keep in mind that once an attorney or advocate has done their thing for you, and the IEP has been worked out and signed, you will be the one left to do the monitoring. You will need to do some relationship building with the school staff.

Educators: Teaching the Child or Adolescent with an ASD

Whether you teach a special or general education class, or in a resource center, you will have students with autism spectrum disorders in your class. This section is written particularly for those who work in education; however, parents will find this section informative as well. Some resources are mentioned here, many more are listed in the back.

As indicated earlier in this book, the incidence of ASDs is rising and they are not going away. Perhaps you already have a lot of practical experience or knowledge of the best teaching strategies for children with autism, and you work for a school district that is supportive of your need and desire for specialist support or access to knowledge in order for you to use strategies proven to be effective with children with ASDs. If so, hurrah!

However, not all school districts or schools give the same level of ac-

FOOD FOR THOUGHT

Be Precise

"For any classroom assistants or teachers reading this, then please, please try to realize that instinctively knowing where to go or who to talk to, and what to do next just isn't possible for a kid on the autism spectrum. If a teacher says 'now get out your books and turn to page 10' and doesn't say 'and now start answering those questions,' then the AS kid is not likely to know, so to tell them off for doing no work that lesson is unfair."

—Luke Jackson, *Freaks,*
Geeks and Asperger Syndrome

cess to autism expertise or specialist support. Young teachers fresh out of college may not be aware of the politics of education, and some administrators will convince them they know enough to run a class and teach the children with little or no behavioral support or autism-specific training. There are also teachers who do not understand that students with ASDs are differently wired; who don't understand that they need to learn specific strategies to be effective with students with ASDs; or who have difficulty being flexible enough to accommodate the needs of these students. Nonetheless, most educators, by the nature of their chosen field, recognize that you can never stop learning or have too much knowledge.

The Basics Everyone Working at Any School Needs to Know

Making assumptions must be avoided. Remember, every child is different, and every child deserves the same respect, whether they are nonverbal and severely handicapped by their autism or very able with idiosyncratic behaviors. Just because someone is unable to talk doesn't mean he doesn't understand what is going on around him. And just because someone is verbal doesn't mean he understands more than the literal sense of what you are saying. Assumptions about a child's intelligence cannot be made because of his lack of communication or social skills.

ASDs are unlike any other disability. Some children with ASDs do not have imitation skills. Imitation is how most people learn. Many children with mental retardation or learning disabilities have imitation skills and are social. They may pick up social behaviors and language "naturally" by being put in a class of their peers. This is not true for the most part for children with ASDs. Many have a good academic understanding of social skills but are not able to apply them. They need to be taught how to apply, in everyday situations, the social skills that most of us take for granted. The challenges that people with ASDs have are due in part to different wiring in the brain. They are not just being "difficult." Obviously, there are different ability levels in children with ASDs, but regardless, all have problems with social skills, communication, and understanding more than the literal meaning of words.

ASD-specific training is necessary. It does not matter how many years you have been teaching developmentally delayed children, or how many children with ASDs you have seen in your class, you need to learn more. It is only in the last decade that the results of effective teaching methodologies and strategies are being seen and recognized. Currently these strategies are still being developed or refined or built upon. Your special education administrator and school district needs to be convinced of the need for specialist training and support. This is true no matter what type of school you are working in, no matter the level of disability or ability.

Teaching assistants and all staff working with the child need to be trained. A person who does not have the skills to do the job properly will not be an effective person to have around. Giving people the right skills to do their jobs will make them effective, confident, and provide

A Teacher's Quest for Integration

BY KARLA ZICK-CURRY

"They are able because they think they are able." —Virgil

Two days before school started, I got copies of nine Individual Education Programs (IEPs) from the district secretary. I began reading through the IEPs, speech and language reports, and psychological reports. I began to wonder, how am I going to effectively teach nine students with only two paraprofessionals and myself? I knew that two days of contemplating this question would only cause even more questions to arise, so I decided to focus on the empty classroom that awaited and the endless new employee meetings that I was required to attend.

The bell rang two days later at nine A.M., and I was about to meet the nine students that were assigned to my classroom. One by one each student entered the classroom either independently or with assistance. As I looked around in a daze, I noticed two feet sticking out from underneath the big blue beanbag that sits in the corner of the room. That must be Kyle, I thought. This was the first of Kyle's many responses to situations that mimicked what I ultimately wished I could do, but I am not diagnosed with autism.

This was Kyle's second year in the district program and, like most students with autism, he came with quite a reputation. I tried to focus on the facts: Kyle was a male, twelve years old, and diagnosed with autism. Eventually, Kyle moved from under the beanbag to on top of the beanbag. I took it as a cue that he was ready for some sort of interaction. I got down on his level, introduced myself, and tried to connect in one way or another. He looked at me with these big green eyes, smiled, and proceeded to attentively look around the room.

Two days had passed, and I was coming to terms with the fact that I was working for a system that supported exclusion, isolation, and the segregation of students with disabilities. I did not think any of my students belonged in my special day class, but I just could not figure out why Kyle was placed in my classroom. He did not have a physical or medical condition, which unfortunately seems to be an automatic referral to the district program. I was not seeing any of the behaviors that I had read about in the psychological reports or heard about from other staff. Knowing what I did about autism, I believed that Kyle was dealing with the change in teachers and programs better than my staff were—or even myself, for that matter. He seemed to be content in just going with the flow.

On the third day, I was ready to throw in the towel. I was tired, frustrated, understaffed, and trying to figure out how I was going to develop an effective and integrative program with the bare minimum of support from the district. I had nine students who had never been integrated into regular education classrooms, general education teachers who had never taught students with multiple disabilities, and two paraprofessionals who thought I was crazy for even mentioning such an idea.

Instead of taking a warm bath or drinking a much-needed cold beer, I decided to thumb through previous student assessments, observations, and recommendations. According to the district, the one thing these students had in common was that their overall developmental delays impacted each student's ability to progress in a general education curriculum, and that he or she would benefit from a program that had a functional curriculum. I was once again reminded that placement is often based on disability rather than the child's needs.

After the first week, Kyle was starting to communicate what seemed to be boredom and the need for attention by running out of the classroom or hitting staff. While Kyle was reaching out for attention, I was trying to meet the basic needs of my other eight students. It was taking three hours to just feed and change the students. I was beginning to feel like a highly qualified babysitter. I expressed my concerns to the district. A few phone calls were made by the administration, and I was "graciously" given a temporary paraprofessional for two weeks.

Over the weeks, Kyle started to have good days and bad days. His teeth were starting to come in so a completely new set of behaviors began to surface. Kyle refused to go anywhere but my classroom and the baseball field. Red flags began to pop up in regard to integrating Kyle this school year. I knew that Kyle would be able to learn and progress in a general education classroom, but did I have the right tools, accommodations, and supports needed to successfully integrate Kyle?

The federal law mandates free and appropriate public education for all children with disabilities in a least restrictive environment (a general education classroom) with appropriate supports and services. I was beginning to realize that it was entirely up to me to find the additional supports for my students. The supports provided by the district were just enough to meet the basic needs of the students. I was frustrated with the fact that I was going to have to rely on volunteers and peer tutors to implement the law, but if that's what I had to do in order for my students to progress in a natural environment, then I would find a way to make it happen.

I was fortunate to have a change in staffing and receive two new paraprofessionals who believed in the students and my overall mission of integration. I also had an amazing support system at home and at the university that really helped put things into perspective and remind me to take one day at a time. I began to focus on what I did have and what resources I could draw upon to help make my goal of integration a reality. After numerous conversations with general education teachers and phone calls to community agencies, things were starting to happen. With the support of two amazing paraprofessionals, a community volunteer, the site principal, a handful of general education teachers, an intern, and peer tutors, I was able to integrate my students into general education classes.

Kyle was the only student that I was waiting to integrate. I wanted to get everyone else settled in their new classes so I could focus on Kyle's integration program. He was starting to show interest in the school environment. For example, one day he followed me to the copy room, waited for me to make copies, and walked with me back to the classroom. A few days later, he followed a classmate to art class and sat outside the door.

I knew it was time for Kyle to make his way outside of my classroom, but I needed to find a teacher and classroom environment that would support Kyle's sensory and security needs. Mr. Sullivan, a science teacher and my inside connection to the general education world, once again helped me find another incredible general education teacher. In just a few days, Kyle was set to attend a first period language arts class with the support of a paraprofessional.

I think my paraprofessional and I were more anxious than Kyle was on the walk over to the classroom. Our goal for the first day was to get him to the classroom, have him sit in his seat, and then stay in the room as long as possible. Once again, Kyle surpassed our expectations. He stayed seated the entire class period, picked up a pencil and started to scribble on a piece of paper that a peer gave him, participated in the class activity by choosing a color for the kimono, and did not once try to run out of the classroom. Kyle was happier than I had ever seen him. I am not sure if it was the natural environment of a general education classroom or the three pretty girls that came to sit with him at his table.

To this day, Kyle has played an integral part in the development of his school program. His unique view of the world is something that I admire and most of all respect. We have both learned to take one day at a time and deal with the fact that life is filled with challenges and rewards.

Regardless of the labels assigned to them, my students continue to grow as individuals and are an essential part of the school campus. Since good teaching means different things to different people, I am thankful to the parents, professors, and colleagues who have positive visions for people with disabilities, thus helping to shape my idea of what good teaching truly is—all students learning together in a natural and inclusive environment.

Karla Zick-Curry is a teacher, advocate, and friend of students with multiple disabilities. She is currently working on her master's degree in Special Education at California State University–Northridge.

---

more job satisfaction, which makes for a low employee turnover rate. And that is always a good thing.

Peers need to be informed about disabilities and taught tolerance. Peers need to be given information so that they understand why people are different and why they act the way they do. This is true for all disabilities, not just ASDs. However, autism is an "invisible" disability, as you can't see it and the person may act neurotypical in most ways. Peers need to be told that they will benefit from having students with differences like their classmates. If there is concern about "labeling" on the part of the parent or the student, it is possible to talk about the issues without naming the disability. For example, peers could learn about how "social communication" is a challenge for some. Just as the student with an ASD is learning new appropriate ways of behaving, the peers need to learn to be more accepting of the differences in others. If they don't learn this at school while they are young, how will they learn to be tolerant and responsible members of society? A good resource is the book *My Friend with Autism* by Beverly Bishop.

Peer tutors are a great resource. Often schools include peer tutors to help teach the child. This is a wonderful idea; however, for this to be successful, the peer tutors need to be appropriately trained. Peers may be used to developmentally disabled individuals who are social but not used to the lack of automatic social interaction and apparent lack of emotion shown by some children with autism and may be discouraged. For peer tutors to be successful, they need to have an understanding about autism and some knowledge in helpful prompting strategies.

The principal sets the tone. Tolerance and flexibility are key words that should be practiced in every school toward any student who is "different." Principals should show by their own actions and attitude that bullying by other students will not be accepted and that staff are expected to be flexible to meet the needs of these children.

Communicating with parents is very important. Keeping lines of communication open with the parents can help alleviate a lot of stress at both ends. Many parents are willing to follow any suggestions you may have to help their child. Any behavior plan should be explained to parents so they can enforce them at home as well. Parents, out of necessity, have become more and more knowledgeable about their children's dis-

Wanted: Emotionally Intelligent Principals

Leadership is what drives performance in all organizations, including schools. In 2000, the Hay Group was commissioned by the Department for Education and Employment in the United Kingdom to analyze the effectiveness of different leadership styles. They studied forty-two schools and discovered which leadership styles resulted in high academic achievement. In 69 percent of the high-performing schools, the principal used four or more leadership styles depending on what was needed, whereas in two-thirds of the low-performing schools, the principal showed only one or two leadership styles, usually the dissonant ones of "command and control." In other words, when principals were flexible in their leadership style depending on the situation (a key element in emotionally intelligent leadership), the working climate among teachers was most positive, and translated into better performances by the children.

abilities and can give you information on ASDs and their children that can be useful to you.

MUST-READS FOR TEACHING STAFF, PRINCIPALS, SPECIAL EDUCATION ADMINISTRATORS . . .

• An essential text for anyone working in education is *Freaks, Geeks and Asperger Syndrome: A User Guide to Adolescence* by Luke Jackson. It describes what it is like to be a child or teenager with an ASD, from one person's perspective, attending a school where the staff and other students have no understanding of this "invisible disability." There are specific examples of how someone who is academically very capable can only understand the literal meaning of words unless taught otherwise, and needs to be taught social skills to be able to act normally in a neurotypical world. This book also shows us, sadly, how youngsters with ASDs are routinely bullied by their peers as well as misunderstood by unknowledgeable teaching staff. This alone should put the book at the top of all school educators' and principals' reading lists.

• Another good book is *Asperger Syndrome and Adolescence: Practical Solutions for School Success* by Brenda Smith Myles and Diane Adreon. This has a detailed discussion of strategies and supports necessary to ensure a successful school experience for students with AS at the middle and high school levels.

• Useful as well is *Access and Inclusion for Children with Autistic Spectrum Disorders: Let Me In* by Matthew Hesmondhalgh and Christine Breakey. The authors describe the challenges they faced in setting up a resource unit at a mainstream secondary school. Besides teaching the regular school curriculum, they also taught additional life skills in the community, and some students participated in a work placement scheme.

• An interesting article on the web for parents and teachers about inclusion and transition to middle school is "Strategies for Surviving Middle School with an Included Child with Autism" by Ann Palmer (www.teacch.com/survmidd.htm).

Specific Challenges by Students with an ASD

Bullying. Bullying is a major problem for students with ASDs. It is apparent in elementary school, but becomes a significant problem in secondary school. Bullying, which can range from verbal taunts to actual physical encounters, is very upsetting to the victims and should not be treated as a fact of life.

Jerry and Mary Newport, Luke Jackson, Clare Sainsbury, and Liane Willey, all authors with ASDs, discuss bullying in their respective books at some length. Luke Jackson writes about how he was chased and pinched, shoved, and hit many times. He also describes having personal school items such as rulers and pencils taken from him, having his lunch grabbed and stepped on, and doors being slammed in his face. More distressing are his stories about teachers making fun of his difficulties and calling him names such as "thick" or "dopey" in front of the class.

Bullying occurs for a number of reasons. It can happen simply because the teenager with an ASD appears different to the neurotypical teens because of his dress and grooming. Often it is because as the other teenagers start to question authority, the ASD teen is still in the mentality of following the rules and thus seems to be "nerdy." Sometimes bullying is due to the misinterpreted behavior of the ASD teen. Many children with ASDs have monotone voices, and sound rude or as if they are mimicking the person they are speaking to, which makes it appear as if they are poking fun. Many children with autism have mindblindness; they do not understand that others have different thoughts from theirs, and so are unable to anticipate what others may say or do, which creates problems in social behavior and communication. As mentioned before, some of the bullying comes from teachers who are uninformed about ASDs. It is hard for teachers and other students to comprehend that someone who is verbally astute and gets good grades for his work is unable to pick up all the nonverbal cues most people take for granted.

A teenager with an ASD may give the appearance of being "sneaky" or "manipulative" because of some of his body language when stressed (avoiding eye contact, shifting from foot to foot, speaking in a flat voice). The teen with an ASD, usually a stickler for rules, may correct another student or tell off a child who is breaking a rule, thus enraging the teacher, who does not realize that he has no sense of hierarchy, only a sense of what is right. If a person with an ASD has good language skills, others tend to forget that his comprehension of the language is different—that he only has a literal understanding of language, which can lead to trouble.

FOOD FOR THOUGHT

"Another reason I think I have been bullied in the past and am prone to being picked on is that I just don't want to 'run with the pack.' I never have and never will. I don't see any point in pretending that I like things when I don't. I think this is one of the reasons why other people don't want to make friends with me or hang around with me."

—Luke Jackson,
Freaks, Geeks and Asperger Syndrome

An Asperger Dictionary of Everyday Expressions by Ian Stuart-Hamilton can help those with Asperger's Syndrome who "take things literally" to understand the meaning of expressions the rest of us use. The guide provides explanations of over five thousand idiomatic expressions plus a guide to their politeness level. Parents and teachers will find this a helpful tool to help teach and explain social communication.

Neurotypical peers need to be told about ASDs and how they manifest themselves. It needs to be made clear that bullying will not be tolerated. Having an ASD is like having an invisible disability. If a student is having difficulties with bullying, his teachers and classmates need to be educated about ASDs and how they affect people.

Sensory processing issues. Most people with an ASD suffer from sensory processing issues, which is part of the reason why they have difficulty with transitions and need schedules so they can anticipate what is going to happen next. They may easily experience sensory overload, which can lead to meltdowns. Sensory processing can affect learning, as some students have challenges in their auditory processing, some in visual, and some in both. This is also important in understanding how the

FOOD FOR THOUGHT

The Educational Environment

"There are many things that people with 'autism' often seek to avoid: external control, disorder, chaos, noise, bright light, touch, involvement, being affected emotionally, being looked at or made to look. Unfortunately, most educational environments are all about the very things that are the strongest sources of aversion."

—Donna Williams,
Autism: An Inside-Out Approach

learning material should be presented to the student. For more information, see "Teaching Tips from Temple Grandin" on pages 228–29.

Social situations. Social situations are usually a challenging area for a child or teen with an ASD. If a child or teenager with an ASD prefers to spend time alone, parents and teachers need to respect that. However, some social skills are called for, because we all live in society and have to deal with people at one time or another. All children, no matter the age or ability level, need to learn some social skills. School resembles a mini society and it is one of the first places where people learn how to interact with other people. In the next section some strategies and resources will be discussed.

Safety. Most children with an ASD have no notion of safety. This is an area often overlooked yet vitally important, and can range from not understanding the dangers of traffic or fire to not understanding the possibility of personal danger from strangers or aggressive individuals. More attention is being paid to teaching emergency responders about autism, which is a positive move; resources addressing this issue are listed on pages 264–65. However, the child needs to learn some safety notions, and educators as well as parents must work with the child on these.

Transitions. Transitions are another challenging area for students with ASDs. Whether transitioning from one school to another, one teacher to another, or one classroom to another, it needs to be prepared for. Another change is that usually in primary schools the children are in the same classroom with the same teacher for most of the day. In secondary school the teenager has to deal not only with different teachers, but also with moving around to different classes. For some individuals with spatial difficulties, this is an added stress. Picture or word schedules can help in this area.

The section "For Problems with Finding Your Way Around" on pages 299–300 gives suggestions for how to enable students to move around from class to class. Transition from one school to another needs to be carefully prepared. One way of doing this is through social stories (see pages 107–8); another way is through creating a scrapbook with pictures and descriptions of what will happen so the student can go over it (such as in the tips for traveling, on pages 152–55). Teachers who are going to have the student in their class need to be prepared. Information can be given to them about the student, and the student could have a picture and a description of the teacher for his scrapbook.

Adolescent issues. Adolescence is a difficult time of life for most people. Hormone levels start flaring, the body changes in weird yet wonderful ways, and teenagers are in a state of flux. Puberty, hygiene, sexuality, dating, and social skills are areas that create special challenges for the adolescent with an ASD. Adolescent issues are discussed at length in the previous chapter (starting on page 156), which should be consulted by teaching staff as these areas affect school life.

In elementary school, the student usually had one principal teacher, and that teacher had to be able to recognize the warning signs of a possible meltdown, and how to defuse it. However, in secondary school there are many different teachers. If the teachers do not all recognize when a student is nearing meltdown, then more tantrums and unfortunate incidents may occur.

Arranging for a quiet place where the student can go to calm down if he feels overloaded, stressed, or confused is very helpful. School staff should seek advice from experts knowledgeable about ASDs and put effective strategies in place as a preventative measure, rather than waiting for a major incident or crisis to occur.

Learning More about Educational Strategies

How does a teacher go about learning more? If you are not getting adequate information about ASD-specific training and conferences from your school district, there is still hope; resources are out there. Look on the Autism Society of America website (www.autism-society.org) and check out the local chapters in your area. Become a member and get on their mailing list. Read their newsletters and find out about workshops and conferences and when they are being held. Contact the organizations or companies that offer information and training on certain techniques you want to know about (such as PECS, ABA, social relationships).

Presented here is a condensed version of effective educational strategies. This is by no means an exhaustive list, but rather suggestions based on what is known to be most effective and practical. For more information on certain techniques, look at chapter 5 as well as the Resources section.

Applied Behavior Analysis (ABA). Regardless of what kind of school you work at or ASD ability level you teach, all teaching staff should have a working knowledge of ABA. It is the cornerstone of all effective teaching techniques for people with ASDs and, for that matter, all students.

Teaching Tips from Temple Grandin

As mentioned earlier, Temple Grandin is a woman with autism who has a successful international career designing livestock equipment, and she is a world-renowned speaker on the condition. The following is her advice on what can help people with ASDs to learn, based on what was effective for her and information she has accumulated over the years about what has worked for others:

• Intensive and early intervention is very important.

• Having the right kind of teacher is more important than what kind of program you are doing. The teacher needs to be structured and clear in what is being requested and what the correct response is.

• Talents and special interests can be used to motivate a child to work and learn, and as he reaches adulthood it can be transitioned into a line of work. For example, if a child likes trains and is studying math, ask him to calculate how long it takes to go from New York to Boston by train.

• Some people cannot process visual and auditory input at the same time. Their sensory processing system cannot process visual and auditory input simultaneously. These individuals should only be given either an auditory or a visual task.

• Having rooms that are quiet and have low distracters is important. Carpeting on the floor is good for noise absorption. Fluorescent lighting is terrible for many people with autism. Having a lamp at each desk with an incandescent lightbulb is better.

• Children who are echolalic and repeat commercials or jingles do so because they are hearing it in the same tone each time and that makes it easier for them to learn. Be thrilled the child is echolalic. You can teach this person by using flashcards with both the picture and the word on the card, and saying the word in the same tone to begin with. When the child has learned the word in one tone, then teach it using a different tone. Teach nouns first. For verbs and other words, illustrate the action by modeling (e.g., jump while saying "jump," or make a plane take off from the desk to teach "up" and also visually show the word going up) or by having the word look like the action (e.g., write falling as if it were falling).

• Some people with auditory processing issues cannot "hear" consonants, and therefore cannot reproduce them verbally. Overemphasizing consonants when teaching words is necessary for them to hear and reproduce them.

• Some individuals respond better if words or sentences are sung to them. People with sensitive hearing will respond better to being spoken to in a low whisper.

• Laptops and the new flat-monitor computers are better for people who have visual processing problems, as some individuals are distracted by the flicker of the screen.

• For people who like to rock, sitting on a therapy ball or a T-stool (made from two pieces of wood nailed together like a T), which the person balances on, can be helpful.

Most people think of O. Ivan Lovaas when they think of ABA, but while Lovaas developed a particular intensive teaching program for young children, ABA has been around for many years and is useful in all contexts. In fact, twenty-five years ago, before Lovaas was known to the world at large, the author was trained to use some aspects of ABA, such as task analysis, prompting, shaping, and rewarding, in order to teach developmentally disabled adolescents at a state hospital.

ABA techniques can be used with all types of students, not just those with ASDs. For example, plans can be drawn up for unruly students to teach them appropriate behaviors, and students with cognitive disabilities can have academic skills broken down into smaller teachable steps. So ABA is a good general method that all teaching staff could learn that would be useful in all aspects of their work, regardless of the student population they are teaching.

Specifically, ABA techniques such as task analysis and discrete trial teaching can be adapted to teach academic skills, life skills, communication, anger management, and so on. Many of the effective techniques for students with ASDs (such as PECS, social skills training, and TEACCH) are based on or use some behavior principles. If you know basic ABA, you will be more effective in applying these other strategies and with practice will be able to adapt techniques and curriculum for all types of children.

Keep in mind that students with autism do not intuitively generalize. Skills that are learned in one environment may need to be retaught in another. This is important to remember when changing schools, teachers, or aides. It is best to change one variable at a time (such as a new classroom teacher, but the same aide) than to change all at once.

Some good books to teach general practical ABA techniques are *Steps to Independence* by Bruce Baker and Alan Brightman, and *One on One* by Marilyn Chassman. To learn basic discrete trial teaching read *Teaching Developmentally Disabled Children: The ME Book* by O. Ivar Lovaas.

Behavior plans. Behavior plans that are clear, precise, fair, and written down are necessary to address inappropriate behaviors and replace them with appropriate ones. Bad behavior will not just go away. Students with autism need a systematic way of understanding how to behave appropriately. Consistency is necessary for behavior plans to be effective. They can be drawn up to encourage or eliminate specific behaviors, once the behaviors have been analyzed and the antecedents identified. It is important that anyone working with a student knows what the behavior plans are in order for them to be effective.

One last word about ABA and behavior plans: Many people are under the impression that ABA turns people into little robots or that it does not take into account people's feelings and emotions. That is just not true. For example, if you have a student who is kicking the back of someone's chair in the classroom every day, you will analyze why he is kicking the chair, and then you will teach him an alternative appropriate behavior. Perhaps he is kicking the chair because he can't stand the sound of the squeak every time the student moves. He needs to learn to appropriately tell someone, and then the squeak will be fixed. However, if it is discovered that chair-kicking is one of many behaviors he is exhibiting because he has anger management issues, you will use ABA techniques and teach him to express his anger in an appropriate manner. The student will have counseling sessions about why he is angry and what can be done about it. But he still needs to learn in a clear, concise, on-the-spot way which behavior has to stop and what can replace it.

Picture exchange communication system (PECS). For nonverbal children, PECS is very useful. It immediately teaches the child a basic system of communication, and it can convey many academic concepts too. This method is wonderful for small children, but even nonverbal adults who have never developed a communication system can learn to use it. See pages 101–2 for contact and resource information.

Schedules. Schedules and structure are necessary for students with ASDs. Clarity and precision are the key words. Schedules can be pictures or words, simple or complex, depending on the student's need. A good book about schedules is *Activity Schedules for Children with Autism: Teaching Independent Behavior* by Lynn E. McClannahan and Patricia J. Krantz.

TEACCH. Certain elements of TEACCH, such as schedules, are very effective and can be adapted for use at many different ability levels in all environments. However, classrooms that use only TEACCH techniques appear to be about making it easier for the teacher to teach a certain number of children, and appear to be lacking in offering social situations or opportunities for teaching communication. See pages 133–34 for more about it.

Social skills training. Because of the impairment of social skills that people with ASDs have, it is very important to teach these. Social skills are used in every aspect of life and are necessary to be able to function even basically in society. People with ASDs don't pick up these skills by rubbing elbows with their peers. They need to be taught systematically. For a more able autistic child included in mainstream classes, this is an area where a lot of support will be needed. Teaching the student some social skills can help him avoid some of the bullying he may be prone to as a result of not knowing what neurotypicals expect in terms of behavior. Again, strategies can be geared toward various ability levels. Social stories can be developed with the student. Social skills groups teach social skills by breaking them down and providing practice in a safe environment. Forming a "circle of friends" has been found to be effective. See chapter 5 for a more complete description of the different methods.

A good book for teaching the more able child is *Incorporating Social Goals in the Classroom: A Guide for Teachers and Parents of Children with High-Functioning Autism and Asperger Syndrome* by Rebecca A. Moyes.

Self-esteem training. Working on self-esteem is a necessary component of education for children and adolescents with ASDs. They need to learn about ASDs, the challenges as well as the strengths. An interesting book with good worksheets is *I Am Special* by Peter Vermeulen.

Safety training. This is an area that often falls through the cracks and should be addressed. Whether it is knowing to look both ways before crossing the street or who to approach if you are lost at the mall, or recognizing certain dangerous situations or what to do in a fire, safety needs to be taught. A book that has some useful strategies is *Dangerous Encounters: Avoiding Perilous Situations with Autism* by Bill Davis and Wendy Goldband Schunick.

Preparing for Life after High School: Transitions to College or Work

Just as for any other student, plans have to be made for the future. During adolescence, the student and parents should begin to think about the future. It is useful to have discussions with the student, family members, and other people who have gotten to know your teenager over the years to get input and ideas. Of course, the most important aspect to consider is what your student's likes and dislikes are. Temple Grandin suggests taking a good look at any interests and obsessions he may have and seeing if they can develop into a skill that can be useful and enjoyable for after school.

Some other areas to be explored besides the student's interests include what he is capable of doing and what level of support he needs for his life as an adult in terms of living arrangements and finance. Does your teenager want to go to college, get vocational training, or go right into employment? Does he have a support system of friends in the community?

Regardless of the ability level of the individual, the person's own choice should be taken into account. Obviously for the less able and nonverbal it is harder to get an idea of his wishes. Sometimes the opinions or ideas of people that know him in different aspects of his life can help in making choices through Person Centered Planning. The person at the focus of planning, and those who love the person and know him well, are the primary authorities on the person's life direction. In Person Centered Planning, questions are asked about who the person is, and what community opportunities will enable this person to pursue his or her interests in a positive way. Some of the techniques used are: Individual Service Design, Lifestyle Planning, Personal Futures Planning, MAPS, PATH, and Essential Lifestyle Planning. For more information, see these two web pages:

- www.reachoflouisville.com/person-centered/whatisperson.htm

- www.inclusion.com/PI-PERSON.C.PLANNING.html

More on the Politics of Education

For six years I served in a voluntary capacity on a state-mandated community advisory committee made up of parents, educators, and administrators. For two of those years I sat on the executive board. Our mandate was to give input and advice to the special education directors and school superintendents of the fourteen member school districts, who were obliged by law to listen to, but not necessarily to follow, our recommendations.

One of our most important tasks was to draft a list of priorities for special education in the districts for the coming year. The administrators would look at the priorities and address these areas of concern, then report back to the community advisory committee about what they had done to address those concerns.

One year, a major concern drafted into a priority was about the exodus of qualified special education staff. Our suggestion was that each school district develop and implement strategies to attract and retain competent staff. At the end of the year, we sent a questionnaire to the directors of special education to ask them what strategies they had come up with. One special education director actually wrote back to say that he had done nothing, because staff left because of the parents. This reply begged the question, "What are the parents doing that makes staff leave?" Here are some possible answers:

• *The parents were expecting their child to learn.* For some reason, there appears to be an assumption by some school administrators about severely handicapped children: as long as the child is happy and loved, and goes home with his nose clean and his pants dry, the school has done its job. Often, good teachers who want to teach this population recognize when there is a lack of support from above and leave to go to work in a more supportive environment (possibly a neighboring school district).

• *The parents were expecting that staff would demonstrate a knowledge of teaching methods and behavioral strategies that were proven to be effective with that child.* Often teachers' aides are thrown into classrooms with insufficient (if any) training or knowledge. This is detrimental to the child and the teacher who is running the class, and also to the teacher's aide herself. If people do not have the skills to effectively do their job, they will eventually be unhappy and leave.

• *The parents were expecting that the general education teacher would be given some information about their child and his learning methods.* Inclusion will not work if support is not given to help the teacher. Teachers need to be given the tools and training to do their job; they cannot be expected to be knowledgeable in all strategies simply through osmosis.

Many school administrators like to play the game of convincing the staff that the parents are too demanding. People in a position of power will convince staff that yes, they can do the job, they don't need specialist support or to learn new educational strategies. Then the parent is put in the uncomfortable position of explaining why the teacher (or other school professional) is not able to provide for the child's educational needs. The administrators pit the parents and the teachers against one another, when in reality they should be partners. If you are the only proactive parent in that class, then you also get the reputation of wanting "special treatment" for your child. However, the way the process works, you can only address your child's program, not the whole class. In essence, by requesting that a staff member be properly trained, you are helping the whole class, and smart teachers will recognize this.

IDEA requires that a transition plan should form part of the first annual review after the child's fourteenth birthday, and any subsequent annual review. The purpose of the plan is to gather information from the parents, as well as a variety of individuals at the school and different agencies, in order to plan for the teenager's transition to adult life.

Transition services need to be planned, and these are intended to be a coordinated set of activities for a student to move from school to postschool activities. These transition services need to be developed and written up as an Individualized Transition Plan (ITP), which is a part of the IEP, or it can be a separate (but agreed upon by the team) document. Because the goal is to transition to adult life, interagency collaboration with whatever local services exist is an important part of the transition IEP. Agencies that may be involved include the Social Security Administration (SSA) and the local Department of Rehabilitation.

A good way for a more able teenager to get some ideas is to do volunteer work or have a part-time job during the summer or on weekends. Parents can help by giving chores to their child to teach a sense of responsibility (no matter the ability level).

An interesting study by Michelle L. Nuehring and Patricia L. Sitlington was published in the Fall 2003 edition of the *Journal of Disability Policy Studies*. Besides making an analysis of the professional literature on transition, the authors followed three high school students with autism who had been educated in a classroom for students with autism and who had received community-based job training. The students picked different adult vocational service providers (i.e., places of employment that provide job training) to attend after graduation, and even though they had received the same education, the students' transition experiences were quite different from one another. Nuehring and Sitlington suggested several ways to improve the process of transition:

- provide more education to high school teachers regarding the transition process

- provide more education for adult vocational service providers about the characteristics of individual disabilities

- align programming between schools and adult vocational providers

- include more assessment of the student's strength, weakness, and preferences in the transition process

- increase communication among all involved: the student, the family, the school, and the adult vocational service provider

Although the researchers followed only three teenagers, their observations seem to reflect what is often heard over and over again in different school districts: it's all about planning, communication, and training!

It is important to remember that (as you may have learned coming this far in the educational system) the process does not always go as smoothly as one would expect, so parents and educators need to work closely together to ensure a somewhat successful transition. Having made it thus far as a parent or an educator, you have many skills at your disposal to use in helping the process along.

Good places to go for more information on transitions:

• *Developing Talents: Careers for Individuals with Asperger Syndrome and High Functioning Autism* by Temple Grandin and Kate Duffy

• "Life after High School"—this article, on the Autism Society of America website (www.autism=society.org), has good suggestions for the steps to take in transition planning

• *Life Beyond the Classroom: Transition Strategies for Young People with Disabilities* by Paul Wehman

• *Community-Based Curriculum: Instructional Strategies for Students with Severe Handicaps* by Mary A. Falvey

• *Asperger Syndrome Employment Workbook* by Roger N. Meyer (a person with Asperger's)

• "The Individual Transition Plan: An Overview"—this article, edited by Kristin Stanberry, is on the Schwab Learning website (www.schwablearning.org/articles.asp?r=782)

Successful people who have an ASD such as Temple Grandin, Stephen Shore, and Liane Willey, have good, useful advice to share about what was helpful for getting them where they are today, and what strategies

FOOD FOR THOUGHT

"There is so much more to the life of an autistic than just being on SSI and safely tucked away at home, sheltered from the world. That is minimal existence, and I know from my conversations with people with autism and Asperger's that many of you want more than that out of life. You would like to make some money, hopefully doing something you enjoy. I'm here to tell you that it's possible to be gainfully employed, but to accomplish this, you need 1) an idea of what you would like to do, 2) some sense of the availability of jobs in that area, and 3) an appropriate education that will prepare you for working in that field."

—Mary Newport, "Education and Jobworthiness," in
Autism Asperger's Digest Magazine, Sept./Oct. 2002

they use to continue doing well. Even if the student you are planning for is not at the same level of ability, these stories give insight and ideas that may be helpful for those who are less able or cannot express themselves in the same way. In chapter 9, their advice, as well as some ideas about employment and college options, are discussed. Parents, educators, and others involved would do well to read that chapter when thinking about transition plans and the future.

8

Community Life

I . . . had trouble learning the rules to the games that other children played and I often played the wrong way, causing the other kids to avoid me as well or tease me. . . . My reactions to various situations were not quite what people expected . . . I knew that I did not act right but I was often at a loss to know what I was doing wrong.

—CLARE SAINSBURY, *Martian in the Playground*

MY son often goes shopping with college students who help him with his afternoon activities. We started off by teaching him appropriate behavior in stores, such as how to walk up and down the aisles without pulling the price tags off items. He then took an interest in finding his favorite food items and taking them off the shelves, so we taught him shopping skills. This included looking at a modified shopping list, finding the items he wanted to buy, waiting in line, and paying for them. One day my son and I were shopping and when we reached the checkout counter the relatively new cashier said, "Hi, Jeremy, how are you? Oh, are you his helper for today? Wait, he can empty the shopping cart himself." I laughed, feeling good that the cashier knew him, knew what he could do, and was looking out for him. It's a small thing, but it's these kinds of connections that make the place you live in a community.

Creating Ties in the Community

Most people go through life easily developing all sorts of relationships, from the casual relationship with the store owner or cashier to relationships with colleagues, classmates, and a partner for life. Like a garden, all relationships take a certain amount of tending to grow and maintain. And like gardens, the more intense the relationship, the more tending is involved. No matter the age or ability of a person, having relationships and ties in the community is vital. Though we all like to think of ourselves as independent, none of us is self-sufficient; we all rely on other people in one way or another.

The same holds true for people with autism. However, because of the very nature of ASDs, developing community ties can be mind-boggling. For those of an age and ability where they are on their own, it can be frustrating and seem unnecessary and illogical. For parents of children and the less able, it is another reminder of how their child does not fit in, and how society on the whole is geared toward the competitive neurotypical person. Creating relationships in the community can be hard work, but it is worth it and necessary.

Community ties are the threads in the fabric that binds society together. Whether your child is shopping at the grocery store or an active participant in the Boy Scouts, he is engaging in some form of social relationship. Adults with ASDs also have different levels of contacts in the community. By creating these ties, no matter how small, you are laying the foundations for being a part of the community you live in. This is important for many reasons, not the least of them being safety.

For an adult, community ties can provide a support network you can fall back on if you ever need assistance. For a parent, they can help create the foundation of the relationships your child will have as he gets older, and perhaps be there when he is an adult and you are no longer around.

How to Create Community Ties

Community ties can be developed at different times on different levels. Remember that a person has different relationship needs at different times of his life, but all people need friendships and feelings of security and safety. As people with ASDs are in the minority, it is still up to individuals with ASDs and/or their parents to educate others and create those connections. Here are some tips.

Identify what the needs and desires are. If you are an adult with an ASD, you need to think about what your comfort level is, and what you would like to do in the community. If you are a parent, you will need to identify your child's abilities, challenges, and interests, as well as what community skills he needs to learn to prepare him for adult life.

Identify what information or skill the person needs to develop that community relationship. If a person likes to go shopping but doesn't have the patience to wait in line, then he needs to learn the skill of waiting. A person who likes to go to the library to look at books will not be fostering good community relationships by taking all the books off the shelves and dumping them on the floor.

Identify what information people in the community need in order to facilitate building relationships. Perhaps the adult with an ASD does not need any special consideration; it all depends on the individual. For a child learning to shop, perhaps the cashier will need to call him by name and ask him for the money. A recreation leader will need to know about any behavior challenges, and how to handle them.

It's Getting Easier

Twenty-five years ago I worked with adults with severe autism and other developmental disabilities living in a state hospital. Some of these individuals were going to be deinstitutionalized and live in group homes. My task was to help them learn self-help and community living skills, including how to act in public. Along with other staff, I would take them out to restaurants and teach them safety skills such as how to cross the street. Currently, with my own son, I am faced again with trying to figure out how to find programs and activities that my son will enjoy, as well as finding ways to teach him community living skills. It is not an easy task, but definitely not the challenge that it was decades ago.

Everyday Life in the Community

Regardless of a person's age or ability, we all need to learn how to go about everyday life and be safe in today's society. Creating community ties is necessary for that to happen. Think of all the skills you use just to function every day and the skills you use to keep safe: shopping for food, stopping at the curb, ordering in a restaurant, asking for directions, going to the movies, having a friend over, locking your door. These are the skills everyone should learn. Children and adolescents with ASDs, and adults as well, all need to learn basic community skills. Some of them can be taught or addressed at school, but they still need to be generalized.

Safety Issues and Concerns

Safety is an area that everyone needs to learn about. Children with ASDs do not have some of the natural survival skills that neurotypicals do—many have no notion of safety—and these need to be taught systematically and thoroughly. Safety issues can mean anything from learning to stop at every curb and look for traffic, to knowing what to do if you are lost. *Dangerous Encounters: Avoiding Perilous Situations with Autism* by Bill Davis and Wendy Goldband Schunick is a good resource. Later in this chapter other resources for making law enforcers and others who work in the community more "autism aware" will also be discussed.

Community and Recreational Activities for Children and Adolescents

In reality, integration in community programs is not about *finding* the right fit, but about searching for possibilities and creating opportunities for involvement in existing programs or out in the community. It's really about *making* a good fit.

A person who is severely autistic, even if he has no aggressive behaviors, will not be able to participate in any community programs without a helper. In the end, this person may have an easier time, in that he will always have someone watching out for him and guiding him through the experience. A more able person may benefit more from the actual experience, but if he is not accompanied by an aide, he may be vulnerable to, at the very least, misunderstanding by the group leader; and at the very worst, bullying by his peers. This is why it is so important to choose activities carefully.

Every community offers opportunities for integration. Thanks to the American with Disabilities Act (ADA) no one can discriminate against a child or adult who wishes to participate in a community program, and in fact should try and accommodate the person as much as possible. That means that some places (such as our local Boys and Girls Club) may have a recreation leader or two specifically trained to help integrate your child. As always, their training may be general, and not ASD-specific, and so you may have to give them more information. Some places to look are your local parks and recreation department, community centers, recreation facilities, Boy and Girl Scouts, swimming pools, churches, libraries, and sports clubs.

Activities have many benefits to them besides integration. Luke Jackson, in his book *Freaks, Geeks and Asperger Syndrome,* writes about the benefits he derived from tae kwon do. Not only did he learn a new skill—it helped him improve his motor skills, increased his self-confidence and self-esteem, and made him feel safer when threatened by others.

There are also activities designed with individuals with disabilities in mind, or certain times designated at recreational facilities. To find out what is on offer in your area, contact your local parks and recreation department, your local community services department, your local ASA support group, other parents, and your child's school.

How to Find the Right Activity or Program

Depending on where you live, you may have few options or many. The most important thing is to make this a positive experience for your child, as well as for the activity leader and the other participants. The first thing to do is to look at your child and where his interests lie. Here are some questions to ask yourself.

What are your child's likes and dislikes? What makes him tick or motivates him? Does he like music? Computer games? Obviously, if the individual is verbal or able to communicate in some form, you will be able to ask him his opinion as to what he likes or doesn't like, what he would like to learn to do or participate in. Never assume that because you know this person you know what he wants to do. Sometimes we make assumptions, and we need to ask the right questions to know more.

What are your goals for your child with this activity? Are you looking for an opportunity for your child to socialize with others his own age? Are you looking for him to develop a hobby or learn how to play

Never Underestimate the Power of a Group of Parents . . .

BY SHIRLEY FETT

As my two sons with autism grew older, I began seeking opportunities for them in the community. More specifically, I searched for recreation programs that would, hopefully, afford them the chance to have some fun and experience some of the same things as other children their age. After a rather exhaustive search, I found there were a few programs available for all special needs children, staffed primarily by volunteers and untrained personnel. My children often did not like the scheduled activities, or their attention waned far sooner than "the group," so the end result was often tantrums, aggression, or increasing anxiety. The few slots available in these programs were always quickly filled.

In my quest for something "more" I was often told the following: "We **can't** enroll your sons because we don't have enough staff to supervise them. There are certain rules all of the children must follow. If they **can't** comply, then we **can't** accept them into the program." And on and on it went . . . I felt if I heard this one more time, I would explode!

As a board member of our local Autism Society of America (ASA) chapter, I posed the idea to them of starting our own summer camp for children with autism. There were camps for children with cancer, children with epilepsy, children with Down's syndrome . . . you get the picture. Why not a camp for children with autism? Armed with support from the local chapter and a couple of other parents equally committed to the project, we began to plan during the summer of 2001.

Being completely naïve about what we were about to do turned out to be our biggest asset. We decided we would create a camp specifically for children with autism, designed with their favorite activities, their interests, and with the appropriate duration of time for each. Every child would have a one-on-one aide who was experienced in working with persons with autism, as well as interaction with teenaged volunteers. We called this **Camp I CAN**—Camp Including Children with Autism Now.

Considering the total amount in the bank account of our ASA chapter at the time we began was roughly $20,000 and the estimated cost for this camp was $60,000, we had our work cut out for us. It took one year to develop the project. Through lots of hard work, collaboration with our local YMCA, and fundraising via grants and local events, we successfully raised the money. We began **Camp I CAN** in August of 2002 and enrolled eighty children ages six to twelve years. We had a waiting list the first year, so we worked harder, raised more money, and offered the camp to one hundred and fifteen children in 2003, including one week for teenagers. Still, we had a waiting list. **Camp I CAN** 2004 was just as popular.

What started as a simple idea, driven by the passion of parents, has already turned into a legacy in our community. In fact, this camp has become a model (and object of envy!) for other communities across the country.

"Never doubt that a small group of thoughtful, committed people can change the world. Indeed, it is the only thing that ever has."   —Margaret Mead

Go out there and change the world, even if it is just your little slice of it!

Shirley Fett is the mother of two boys with autism, a nurse practitioner, and President of the San Diego County Chapter of the Autism Society of America (SDASA). The SDASA website is www.sd-autism.org.

---

an instrument? Do you want to offer him the opportunity to strengthen an existing skill?

Does your child have gross and fine motor challenges? Some activities may not be a good choice for the individual with these challenges; however, some activities that appear challenging may be just the thing for him to enhance or improve those areas he may be clumsy in. A martial art such as tae kwon do may be a good choice.

Does your child easily imitate and learn by watching others? Does he need to be "motored through" an activity (physically prompted) many times, or can he learn with minimal prompting and by watching others? Choose activities where his learning can be adapted to the situation.

Does your child have behavior problems that may prevent him from participating in certain activities? To make a community experience a positive one for all involved, the child should not be a danger to others. Behaviors such as hitting and throwing tantrums do not necessarily mean that he should be excluded; however, a behavior plan should be in effect and working, which can then be transferred to the community program. Identify any problems, and look at how they affect him working in a particular activity. Then work on those behaviors. In addition, skills such as taking turns and waiting are usually a prerequisite for taking part in activities, and can be successfully taught at home.

What kind of sensory integration or processing issues does your child have? Some activities may seem appropriate, but may be taking place in a physical environment that is bothersome to the individual with autism. For example, if your child has a hard time with noise or bright lights, then a location with an "echo" to it or fluorescent lighting may make the activity difficult to participate in. Perhaps he will be able to get acclimatized to it; perhaps not. It all depends on the individual.

Does your child need a one-on-one aide to participate? Are you providing a person to go with your child, or will they have to manage? Who is going to provide the supports your child needs, and how will it be done?

How to Analyze the Different Options Available

Once you have short-listed some options depending on your child's desires, needs, and capabilities, going without your child to observe an activity or program in progress is the next step. Here are questions you should be asking yourself when observing.

What is the activity leader's style? Does the leader seem authoritative? Does he appear to make allowances for the different types of children? Is he patient? How would the leader's style mesh with your child's personality?

How many other participants are there? Is it a small group or a large group? Is that conducive for your child? Make sure you find out if that is the usual group number.

What is the physical environment like? Are the lights very bright? Is it noisy? Is the space large or small? Are there lots of distracting posters and artwork up on the walls? Do you think your child would be comfortable and able to participate here? Would your child need some desensitization to the environment?

How to Approach the Activity Leader and What to Tell Him

After observing, if you consider this activity to be a possible match with your child, talk to the leader and see how receptive he is to having your child in his program. Although by law your child cannot be excluded from participating, it will be a much more enjoyable experience if the leader is enthusiastic about your child joining in. You will need to gauge how much or how little to tell the activity leader at this point. The more able the child, the less you may want to say. If your child needs to have a shadow aide or helper with him, you will need to tell the leader. You should ask if you can bring your child to the activity on a trial basis, and arrange the most practical time for all of you.

At some point, you may need to give the activity leader more information. It all depends on your child, the activity, and the leader. You may have your own personal philosophy and comfort level about what to divulge. Obviously, if your child is severely affected by his autism, the leader and others in the group will need to have at least some basic information about him. When placing a more able child, the activity leader (and peers) need to be aware of how your child is different. Luke Jackson (author of *Freaks, Geeks and Asperger Syndrome*) and Clare Sainsbury (author of *Martian in the Playground*) talk at length in their books about the bullying and misunderstanding they were subject to, all because the teacher and their schoolmates had no knowledge of their condition.

Here are ideas for what you may want to talk about with the activity leader.

Talk about the positive attributes of your child. Any special gifts or interests your child may have that could pertain to the activity would be a good thing for the leader to know. Even if they do not pertain to the activity, they will be a point of contact and perhaps conversation.

Talk about the challenges of your child. If your child is a "runner" or bolts out of the door when he hears the fire drill bell because his hearing is very sensitive, the leader needs to know that. Does your child have any behavior challenges? The leader needs to know what to do in situations that might arise.

Explain about the ASD and how it affects your child. It is a personal decision whether a parent wants to identify their child in a group as having an ASD. My personal opinion is that as parents of children with ASDs, we should also be advocates and educate the public in a positive manner so that our children will be accepted everywhere. However, not all parents feel the same. Some parents who have very able children do not want to use any label. To each his own opinion. However, the important thing is that even if you do not use the word "autism" or "Asperger's," you need to explain the communication difficulties that may arise so that your child does not become the victim of misunderstanding on the part of the leader or the other participants. He may get enough of that at school, and this is supposed to be fun!

Make it clear what your goals are for your child. Are you expecting your child to participate 100 percent in every aspect of the activity? Is your child doing the activity to learn a skill or to learn how to be part of a small group?

Explain the shadow aide or helper's role. If your child will be accompanied by another person to assist his integration and participation, you need to explain. Offer to come in and talk to the other participants. Again, think of your child. It is important that he does not suffer bullying because of lack of knowledge on the part of others. It is always a good idea to talk about ASDs so people will become more accepting and knowledgeable. If you explain to the others about your child's challenges and interests, they will know why he may seem a bit different and will be more accepting. They may even find any special interests he has cool. A good resource for the parent is *My Friend with Autism* by Beverly Bishop. Beverly is a parent who wrote this book to help explain to peers and teachers at the school where her child is mainstreamed about autism. You may find it helpful.

How to Prepare the Child

Depending on his ability, there are different ways of doing this. Again, as discussed in earlier chapters, schedules of what is going to happen and social stories about the expected behavior are a good way of getting your child geared for the activity. Think of what works in helping him adjust in other areas, and use those strategies here.

Tutors, Babysitters, and Respite Providers

Before the start of every school year, I begin my search for any tutors or respite providers I may need. At first, I dreaded doing this. After all, hiring and supervising personnel were my least favorite responsibilities when I was a TV producer. And now, I am hiring people who will be responsible for most of what my son will learn, people who will be in our house and part of our home life.

I have been doing this for ten years, yet it is still hard when people have to quit as they move on to another city to go to graduate school, or they become teachers and aren't available. But these people never really leave us; they come back to visit on weekends and during the holidays, tell me their news, and take Jeremy and his sister, Rebecca, out for some fun. They have become part of our extended family, and most of them will always be a part of our family's life. Inadvertently, we have created a support system in every city we have lived in, meaning that even now we have people familiar with Jeremy and his needs in the different places we return to for visits. Most of the time, I have hired individuals with no prior training in autism or applied behavior analysis, and after their experience with Jeremy many of them have changed focus and gone on to become professionals in special education or ABA. It makes me proud of Jeremy, for he is contributing to society in a most valuable way.

Having Someone Working in Your Home

Some families with two working parents are used to having a babysitter or a nanny in their home on a regular basis during the children's growing years. However, few families are used to having a constant rotation

FOOD FOR THOUGHT

How We Prepared Our Son for the Library and Bookstore

My son loves looking at books. Going to the library and bookstore were activities he really wanted to participate in. However, although he had quickly mastered the concept of pulling books off the shelves at home to find the one he wanted, he had not mastered the concept of putting them back. He seemed to enjoy having thirty or more books all spread out on the floor. This may be appropriate behavior in one's bedroom, but certainly not in public. He also had, on occasion, ripped off the flaps of pop-up books. We decided that he needed to learn that it was not appropriate to rip books and that books should be returned to shelves. These behaviors were addressed and practiced at home before we allowed him to go into the community to look at books in public. Once he was able to put away books at home with minimal help, and had learned that ripping books would not be tolerated, we started taking him to the local library, and finally the bookstore. Any ripping of books or refusal to put away books and my son was immediately taken out of the library or bookstore. As he enjoys these environments, he has learned to treat books in a respectful manner in public.

of people in their home over a period of many years. If you have a child severely disabled by an ASD, two or more children with autism who are living at home, or you are running a home program, you will need more than the usual help and understanding provided by the occasional sitter, and perhaps for many more years. Hiring, supervising, and having other people in your home is not always as easy as it seems. You may sometimes feel, for example, as if your privacy is being invaded. However, if you choose the right people, and keep a positive attitude and a happy demeanor, you will grow to enjoy it.

For those readers contemplating working as a behavioral tutor or a respite provider in a family with a child who has an ASD, this section will give you clues as to what kind of questions you should ask the parents, how to know more about what you are taking on, and what possible challenges you should be aware of. Working for a family with a child with an ASD is not like a typical nanny, babysitter, or tutor position. It is hard for families to get used to having people work in their home, and it takes a long time for a child with an ASD to get used to you, and for you to understand them. If you are unsure after an initial interview, and the parents are interested in hiring you, ask them if you can come back one more time and spend time with them and the child before deciding. If you explain that you do not take your commitments lightly and want to make sure this is a good match for both of you, they will be happy to have you come back.

The most important thing to remember is that the person you hire is there to help your child, not be a counselor to you. Sometimes parents may start talking to their tutor or sitter about problems at school, how depressed they are, or how anxious they feel, and this is not appropriate. If you need to talk to someone about your feelings, you should visit a friend, another parent, or a counselor. Be sure to make your home a positive work environment for the people who are there to help your child.

How to Hire a Tutor or Respite Worker

If you are looking for a tutor, you will want someone who has experience in or is a good candidate for training in applied behavior analysis. However, in terms of your expectations and the issue of having another person in your home, many of the considerations will be the same as when you are looking for a babysitter or respite worker. These guidelines are here to give you a starting point and get you thinking about the many aspects inherent in hiring and keeping good people. The responses given to questions on pages 255–57 will help you in evaluating the strengths and weaknesses of potential candidates and how that person fits in with your needs.

Where to place an advertisement. Many people hire nannies and babysitters and respite workers through agencies. These individuals are usually specifically hired to take care of the children, not to be a housekeeper.

To hire people directly yourself, if there is a university or teacher training college in your area, those are good places to start. Find out from other parents what places work best to put up advertisements. Put ads in the newsletter of the local chapter of your autism support group, if there is one. If you are planning to have a supervisor oversee your home program, ask if they have any advice or guidelines for hiring tutors, and if they know of tutors who might be willing to work with your child.

An excellent resource for advertising for help online is through Jobtrak (www.jobtrak.com). A parent can place an ad at three different colleges or universities of their choice.

What to put in the ad. Take the time to write an ad that gives adequate information as to what type of person you are looking for. Some examples: "Looking for tutors to work with my son. Parent looking for three people who love children and are dependable and flexible, to teach my son, who has autism, using applied behavior analysis techniques. No experience necessary, training provided. Must be available 15 hours per week in 3-hour increments. Hourly rate to be discussed. Please email resume or call this number." Or, "Looking for trained behavioral tutors to work with my daughter with autism. Some weekend hours. Behavioral supervision provided. Pay depends on experience." Or, "Looking for a babysitter. Parent looking for dependable person who loves children and is flexible to provide after-school care for son with autism. Must be available from 3 to 6:30 p.m. Training provided. Pay depends on experience."

After stating the initial information of what you are looking for, take a few lines to describe your child and his personality, what he likes and enjoys. You want the person who responds to the ad to think of your child as a child, not a label.

Looking over a resume. You can learn a lot about the applicant simply by carefully reading the resume:

- Does he have work experience?

- Has he had job responsibilities before?

- Has he had a regular work schedule?

- Has he worked with children of the same age group as your child before?

- What has he been studying at college and what kind of work has he done?

Questions to ask on the phone. On the telephone, you may need to ask specific questions to draw the applicant out:

- Has she worked with children before? What age group?

- Has she ever babysat before or spent a lot of time around children?

- How many siblings does she have, and what is her position in her family?

- Why is she interested in working with your child?

- How long can she commit to working with your child?

- Can she provide any work references? If she has no work references, how about personal references?

- Is she willing to submit to fingerprinting (an administrative procedure)?

Questions to ask a person named as a work reference. You want to know if the candidate is reliable and easy to work with.

- How long did the applicant work for them?

- Is he dependable, reliable, and trustworthy?

- Was he on time or often late?

- Did he often call in sick?

- Was he good at working independently and as part of a team?

- Was he flexible and able to learn and do the job the way the employer wanted?

- Did he take constructive criticism well?

- Did he show a creative streak?

- What were his most positive attributes, and his least positive?

- Would they recommend him for the position you have in mind?

Face-to-face interview. After you have screened by phone the applicants you are interested in, it is time for the interview. Schedule it at a time convenient for you and your child. If possible, do it when someone else is home working with your son. First, interview the person face-to-face, asking her questions to find out more about what kind of person she is. For example:

- What did she like about the jobs she's had in the past?

- What does she hope to pursue as a career?

- What hobbies or other interests does she have?

- Why does she want this position with your child?

- How long can she commit for?

- What schedule constraints does she have?

- Does she have any questions for you?

Then bring your child into the room (without the other tutor) and see how he reacts to this other person, and how this person acts toward your child.

- Does the applicant try to make contact with your child?

- Does she appear respectful of your child?

- What kind of approach does she have?

- You know your child. Does it appear that he likes this person?

If you think this could be a match, go to the child's room with the applicant. Have her watch you or the other nanny or tutor play a game or do a puzzle with your child, and then ask if she would like to try. Watch how she gets on, then give her a few directives and see how she responds to that; if she is able to change what she is doing by listening to your suggestion? Again see if your child feels comfortable with this person. After she leaves, if your child is able to tell you, find out if he liked her.

If you are comfortable with this person, then call her to come back when a tutor or nanny is around to overlap. Spend some time again with your child and the applicant, then have the applicant spend some time alone with the other person and your child. This will provide the opportunity for the applicant to ask questions of a non-family-member who knows the child. It's not always easy to work for someone in their home, and you want to make sure she knows you can be trusted as an employer. Also, you will be able to get your tutor or nanny's point of view on the applicant, which is a good thing to have. They may have noticed some things you didn't. At the end of this time, talk with the person, and if you are interested in hiring her, find out if she is still interested in working with your child.

The applicant will have had two opportunities to meet your child and a chance to talk to someone in the position she will be filling. By now she should have a concrete idea of whether she really wants to work with your child.

How to Supervise and Keep Good People

Somehow, our house has acquired the reputation of being a good training ground for tutors and respite workers. I often get calls from special education administrators, parents, service providers that supervise home programs based on ABA, and social workers. They call asking if anyone currently working in our home or who has worked in our home is available for working elsewhere as well. This is mostly due to Jeremy and his pleasant personality, which is so endearing.

However, in asking people why they enjoy working for our family so much, the number one response after their love of Jeremy (and his sister, Rebecca) is: we are organized. This does not mean our house is particularly clean or neat, as we do not have the time it would take to earn the Good Housekeeping Award in our neighborhood. We do the minimum amount of cleaning so we will not be cited by the Health Department. Jeremy is particularly talented at "redecorating" the house ("Uh-oh, Jeremy's doing a 'Martha Stewart' again!"), and although we have attempted to teach him that he can only redecorate his own room, what he has learned is to redecorate when no one is watching.

Being "organized" in this case means that the wonderful people working in our home know what they are supposed to do, when they are supposed to do it, where everything is, and where to put it back. Here are some guidelines to make life easier for all of you:

• Make sure responsibilities are clear. Draft a contract that outlines your responsibilities toward the person you are hiring and their responsibilities toward your child and you. The contract should cover how much they are getting paid, how often they are getting paid, whether or not you are paying sick leave and holiday pay, when pay raises will be given, and, if they will be driving your child anywhere, what they will be compensated for using their car, or any insurance details if you are providing one.

• Make sure that the hours and times they are to be present are clear. Make sure they know they are responsible for those hours, and make it clear that if they need to make a change, they are responsible for communicating that to you as soon as possible. If there are several tutors, you may wish to make it their responsibility to find someone else to work their hours.

• Make a calendar and hang it in an easily accessible area so people can see special appointments or make changes in scheduling.

• Make sure appropriate notice is given if you have a change in schedule because of a doctor's appointments, or if your child is ill.

• If you expect some degree of flexibility on their part in terms of changes in work hours, be prepared to be flexible when necessary in regard to their schedule.

• Make sure you have everything they need to do their work, and that everything has a specific place so things are easily found.

• Have a communication book located near the phone or in the kitchen where notes to each other can be quickly jotted down if need be.

• In the home environment, it is important to remember the boundaries of the work relationship and keep them clear.

• Remember that they are there to help your child and not to be your counselor. Give them information that they need to know for working with your child, but do not overburden them with the emotional issues, school issues, or legal issues that are on your mind. Those are for you to handle and get help with from someone else. The people working with your child need to concentrate on your child and helping him learn, not think about your problems.

• If your tutor is working with your child at a school, clarify what their responsibility at the school is.

• Keep your rapport with the tutors respectful and professional. Never discuss any issues that are not their concern, such as any disagreements you may be having with the local school authority or another professional. Never speak negatively about other tutors or nannies who are currently working or have worked in your home.

• Make your expectations of the tutors or sitters clear.

• Do not expect them to do things you would not do yourself.

• Have high expectations of their job performance, but give them what they need to do their job well.

• Make sure any new babysitter or tutor feels comfortable enough with your child to be able to handle any behavioral situations that may come up, before sending them out in public with him.

• If you have any behavior plans for your child or if you are working on any particular behaviors, make sure everyone who helps or works with your child knows what to do and ensure that everyone is handling behaviors in the same manner. This will make life easier for everyone and be of great benefit to your child.

• Give people working with your child information about his likes and dislikes, as well as any other pertinent information. Having this written down somewhere is helpful. This makes tutors and nannies feel comfortable with your child, and they will know more about what they can use to motivate him. Your child will feel more comfortable with someone who knows about what is important to him.

• If you are running a home program, keep up to date and know what is being worked on. Give support when needed. When tutors are new and having problems with a behavior or noncompliance, or when new behaviors come up, they need to know you are knowledgeable enough to help them figure things out until they feel they can analyze it and handle the situation themselves.

• If you have any concerns or comments to make about what they are doing, talk to them privately. Explain to them your concern and ask if there is anything you can do to help. For example, think about why you have that concern and bring it up in a positive, constructive manner and not as a criticism. If you notice that one person always asks you for materials and never puts them away afterward, do not assume they think it is part of their responsibility to get them out and put them away. Or perhaps the needed items are not in a clearly designated area, and they do not want to root around in your things looking for them. Do not wait until you are frustrated and confront the person. After this has happened a few times, say something like, "Do you know where the items are located? It would be helpful to me if you could get the materials out and then put them away when you are done. Let me show you where they are." Perhaps they are not thinking, but perhaps you have not made it clear that you are expecting them to do that. If that is the case, make sure you make the responsibilities clear to them.

• Feedback is always appreciated. Show appreciation of the effort they put into their work by commenting favorably on progress your child has made related to work they are doing with him, or thank them for something you noticed they did that has been helpful to you.

• Showing appreciation on birthdays and holidays is always a good way to keep them feeling that they are important to the family.

• Holding a dinner party and inviting all the past and present tutors and sitters is a fun thing to do. Over the years, the nannies and tutors get to know each other, and it's nice to have this time to catch up with each other as well as get tips about college and jobs.

What the General Public Should Know about ASDs

Information for Retailers, Emergency Responders, Recreation Leaders, Day Care Providers, Law Enforcers, Bus Drivers, Designers of Public Spaces, Neighbors, Relatives, and Anyone Who Works with the Public

As ASDs become more and more common, it is important for you to have an understanding of these individuals as they are your neighbors, your clients, the person you may be called on to help one day. In order to help your fellow citizens and to avoid potentially dangerous situations, you need a basic understanding about autism spectrum disorders. You may not need to know everything in this book, but you can get a good introduction by reading the following sections:

• "Characteristics of Autism Spectrum Disorders" on pages 21–23

• "Why people with ASDs Act the Way They Do" on pages 45–51

• "The Myths about Autism Spectrum Disorders" on pages 2–6 will also be helpful in dispelling some of the false assumptions you may have.

Parents may want to use this section as a guideline on what information to convey to people who will encounter your child in the neighborhood and beyond.

- "Public Environments and Sensory Processing Issues" on pages 265–75 in this chapter

Once you have a general overview of what autism looks like and why, you will appreciate the concerns about safety in the community for people with ASDs. For some, it is as elementary as not having any notion of physical safety. They may take off in the middle of traffic to check out something interesting on the other side of the street, or to walk on the beautiful yellow meridian line in the street. For others, it may be not understanding about personal space and not recognizing when people are being "too friendly," or whom to approach when lost and needing directions. Many safety concerns and skills may be taught to some individuals with ASD, but for others they are extremely difficult.

Another concern is that if emergency responders are not knowledgeable about behaviors exhibited by some individuals, they may not know how to respond in the line of duty when faced with autism. For example, many children with autism do not reply to their name, nor do they follow directions, which can be a life-and-death situation in case of a fire, when the firefighter is trying to give instructions that need to be followed. Many people with autism do not like to be touched or do not tolerate loud noises, and they become tense. A very able person with autism or Asperger's may take everything literally, and does not understand expressions the rest of us take for granted. For example, the expression "spread eagle" means just that: a spread eagle; and the person will not understand that the peace officer is telling him to take a particular pose. The peace officer will need to tell him exactly what to do (i.e., "Stand against the car, and put your hands on the top of it"). A peace officer may be called because someone is reported to be peering into windows. Perhaps this person has autism and is staring at reflected light in the window, not looking inside, and has no idea what the fuss is about.

In the autism community, people are working hard at determining better ways of teaching safety issues to people with autism, as well as getting people to display stickers in their front windows explaining that someone with autism lives there and making sure people carry ID including the word "autism" and an explanation. Yet we really need the help of the community in keeping our children and teenagers, as well as adults with autism, safe. Being able to recognize some of these behaviors and how to deal with them is one way you can help. Here are three excellent sources of information on safety, for general use and for training emergency responders:

- Bill Davis and Wendy Goldband Schunick's book *Dangerous Encounters: Avoiding Perilous Situations with Autism* and Davis's video *Encountering Autism* are excellent training aids for emergency responders, retailers, group-homes and hospital staff, and others dealing with the general public.

    Website: www.discountlearning.com

- Dennis Debbaudt's book *Autism, Advocates, and Law Enforcement Professionals: Recognizing and Reducing Risk Situations for People with Autism Spectrum Disorders* and video *Autism Awareness Video for Law Enforcement* are informative.

    Websites: www.autismriskmanagement.com and http://police andautism.cjb.net/

- L.E.A.N. On Us: The Law Enforcement Awareness Campaign is an organization that provides emergency (or first) responders with information and resources that will allow them to better serve individuals within their communities affected by hidden disabilities such as ASDs, Alzheimer's, Tourette's, epilepsy, deafness, and mental illness.

L.E.A.N. On Us
P.O. Box 182338
Shelby Township, MI 48318-2338
     Website: www.leanonus.org

Public Environments and Sensory Processing Issues

In recent decades, we have seen more and more cases of asthma, hyper-activity, autism spectrum disorders, behavior problems, and allergies than ever before. Children are routinely given medication for hyperac-tivity and behavior problems.

In chapter 3, some of the behaviors of people with ASDs and what they could mean were discussed. Many of those behaviors can be in-dicative of allergies and problems with sensory integration. Every book by a person who has an ASD contains references to sensory processing difficulties, the sensitivity they have, and the pain they experience from overstimulation.

Fluorescent Lighting

Temple Grandin, Donna Williams, Stephen Shore, and Liane Holliday Willey all write about how terrible they find fluorescent lighting. But it is not only people with autism who are affected.

In her book *Is This Your Child's World? How You Can Fix the Schools and Homes That Are Making Your Children Sick,* Doris J. Rapp, M.D., discusses the subject. As would be expected, natural light-ing is best. Fluorescent lighting appears to be a major source of trouble for many people. A study of one classroom showed a decrease of hyper-activity by 33 percent when the fluorescent lighting was replaced by full-spectrum lighting. Germany banned fluorescent lighting in its schools and hospitals years ago, whereas in other countries such as the U.S., people seem to prefer the use of the drug Ritalin to counteract hyperactivity rather than looking at possible environmental factors that contribute to the disorder.

In his book *Health and Light*, Dr. John Ott discusses the possible health effects of different wavelengths of light. Dr. Ott videotaped students using time-lapse technology, and these videos demonstrated the increase in hyperactivity in some of them when fluorescent lights are used.

Sensory Integration Dysfunction

Sensory integration problems stem from the brain's inability to process correctly information received through our senses of taste, touch, smell, sight, and sound. People can be hyposensitive in some areas (meaning they fail to pick up cues) and hypersensitive in others (meaning that they are overly sensitive to stimulation of a sense).

When a person's senses are over- or understimulated, it affects their behavior as they try to compensate for a lack of stimulation or for over-stimulation. Some individuals with sensory integration problems are aware of these challenges; others are not. Once a person is aware, it is possible in some cases to learn to compensate in a positive way or to undergo desensitization over time. However, for many people, especially children, and people who are severely disabled by autism, it is difficult, as they are unknowingly put in situations where they have no control over their environment, which may lead to displays of inappropriate behaviors.

For an idea of what it is like to have sensory processing issues and live in today's man-made environment, read what some people with ASDs have to say:

I also found many noises and bright lights nearly impossible to bear. High frequencies and brassy, tin sounds clawed my nerves. Whistles, party noise-makers, flutes and trumpets and any close relative of those sounds disarmed my calm and made my world very uninviting. Bright lights, mid-day sun, reflected lights, fluorescent lights; each seemed to sear my eyes. Together the sharp sounds and bright lights were more than enough to overload my senses. My head would feel tight, my stomach would churn, and my pulse would run my heart ragged until I found a safety zone.

—LIANE HOLIDAY WILLEY, *Pretending to Be Normal*

It came as a kind of revelation, as well as a blessed relief, when I learned that my sensory problems weren't the result of my weakness or lack of character. When I was a teenager, I was aware that I did not fit in socially, but I was not aware that my method of visual thinking and my overly sensitive senses were the cause of my difficulties in relating to and interacting with other people.

—TEMPLE GRANDIN, *Thinking in Pictures*

Sensory integration dysfunction is not experienced only by people with ASDs. A. Jean Ayres, an occupational therapist, first described sensory integration dysfunction as the inability to process information received through the senses. Her two books, *Sensory Integration and the Child* and *Sensory Integration and Learning Disorders*, were not written with ASDs in mind. Neither was *The Out-of-Sync Child* by Carol Stock Kranowitz. Kranowitz discusses about how some children may be labeled as inattentive, clumsy, and oversensitive when they are really suffering from sensory integration dysfunction.

Creating People-Friendly Environments

Granted, there are some environments that people with sensitivities need to and should learn to tolerate for short periods of time. However, when designing an environment where people are expected to learn or work for long periods of time, or where people are going for medical treatment and are already not well, doesn't it make sense to look at environmental issues?

Dr. Rapp's book *Is This Your Child's World?* should be required reading for all school and hospital administrators responsible for having their buildings renovated or constructed. There are many toxins in ordinary classrooms that could easily be eliminated.

Here is some advice for designing environments:

My ideal educational environment would be one where the room had very little echo or reflective light, where the lighting was soft and glowing with upward projecting lighting. It would be one where the physical arrangements of things in the room was cognitively orderly and didn't alter and where everything in the room remained within routine-defined areas. It would be an environment where only what was necessary for learning was on display and there were no unnecessary decorations or potential distractions.

—DONNA WILLIAMS, *Autism: An Inside-Out Approach*

Imagining that one's senses are 1,000 times more sensitive than reality can help a person to design environmental accommodations for those on the autism spectrum. Considering each sense individually can assist with organization of both the issues caused by the sensitivity and the remedies for relief. In considering the sense of sight, a person with a vision hyperacuity might be bothered by the presence of fluorescent lights, because the lights cycle on and off 60 times per second in timing with the Hertz of alternating current. In such cases, a different form of illumination should be used. It is also possible that the humming from the ballast of a fluorescent lamp is irritating to individuals who are sensitive to sound.

—STEPHEN SHORE, *Beyond the Wall*

Sensory Processing Issues: Tips from Temple Grandin

Over two phone conversations, Temple shared the following important information about sensory processing and environments for people with ASDs.

All people with an autism spectrum disorder have sensory processing problems. Some of them may be auditory, some of them may be visual. Recently scientists have been able to map out the circuits in the brain for the separate visual and auditory areas, and they see that those corresponding areas are differently wired in people who have visual or auditory processing difficulties. Temple emphasizes that there are individual variations in the severity of the processing problems, and variations also depend on how tired the person is: the more tired the person is, the greater the risk of sensory overload. People with ASDs usually cannot multitask, as they usually can only fix on one sensory process at a time.

For each individual and for each sensory processing issue there is a balance to be found between adapting the environment to fit the need of the person, and adapting the person to the environment that already exists.

If you are a parent or caregiver of someone whom you suspect has sensory processing difficulties, but who is unable to communicate that to you, Temple suggests doing the "supermarket test." Take the person to the supermarket and see how he behaves, using the behaviors listed on pages 270–272 as a guideline.

The number one worst enemy for people with visual processing problems is fluorescent lighting. Some people with autism can see the flicker of sixty-cycle electricity. It has the same effect that being in a disco with strobe lighting has for neurotypical people. Unfortunately because of its low cost, fluorescent lighting is present everywhere.

For people with auditory processing issues, fire bells can be particularly painful. They are very loud and you do not know when they are going to go off.

Department stores and supermarkets are particularly challenging to people with sensory processing issues, not only because of fluorescent lighting but also because of the overstimulation provided by the colors, stripes, and mosaic patterns on the displays; the smells from perfumes, detergents, and cleaning products; and the noise level due to hard flooring.

So there are many questions that come to mind. For those individuals unable to communicate, how do you know what is creating the overload, and what can you do about it? Temple suggests observing the person's behavior.

Those with visual processing problems:

- use peripheral vision, with which they can see better (i.e., they look from the sides of their eyes and avoid looking directly at people or objects)

- flicker their fingers or other objects in front of their eyes

- avoid escalators in stores and appear afraid of them

- have difficulty negotiating stairs in places unfamiliar to them

If you have visual processing problems, here's what you can do (or help someone else who has them to do):

1. Go shopping earlier in the day when you are not tired.

2. For a temporary fix in areas that you cannot control, such as supermarkets, try wearing a hat with a brim, or a visor.

3. Wear colored lenses such as sunglasses or Irlen lenses. Some people with visual processing issues report that the lenses help not only with seeing, but with training the visual processing so that in some cases they need lighter and lighter lenses as time goes by. From

what Temple has heard from people who use colored lenses, the brownish, purplish, and pinkish lenses seem to work the best against fluorescent lighting.

Usually when a person in the family has sensory processing issues, a parent may have them too to a lesser degree, so for people unable to communicate, the parent could see what color works for them and start with that. Another way to see what is helpful is to try different-colored lightbulbs or transparencies to overlay on written work, and see how the person works, learns, or acts under those circumstances. Temple warns, however, that many sunglasses may be too dark to help with reading. She also reports that Blue Blockers sunglasses work well.

4. In areas you can control, such as your home, do not use fluorescent lightbulbs; use the old-fashioned incandescent kind.

5. Unfortunately, fluorescent lighting will not be replaced everywhere because of its low cost and efficiency. Schools that have students with ASDs should definitely remove these types of lights. In the meantime, for a quick fix for an individual workstation or desk, use a desk lamp with incandescent lightbulbs to offset the fluorescent lighting.

6. Use laptops or the newer flat-panel computer screens. The larger, older computer monitors have a flicker much like fluorescent lighting does.

Because laptops and flat screens are expensive, try finding a big company near you that frequently upgrades its equipment. Normally the used computers are donated or sent out to be broken up and recycled, and so you may find a sympathetic company happy to give you one of their throwaways.

Those with auditory processing problems:

- cover their ears or leave the room when loud noises go off

- cannot tolerate loud noises such as fire bells or school bells

- cannot talk on the phone in large places such as airports due to the echo and resonance of the noisy crowds

- move as far away as they can when there are too many people near them in the room talking

- cannot pronounce the consonants of words because they are unable to hear them properly (hearing tests do not measure auditory detail that they may not be hearing; the hearing threshold may appear normal, but in fact they may only be hearing vowels, so they cannot produce the sound of consonants)

If you have auditory processing problems, here's what you can do (or help someone else who has them to do):

1. Go to noisy places earlier in the day when you are not tired.

2. Get auditory training to help you tolerate the frequencies that may be causing discomfort.

3. For a temporary fix for supermarket shopping, wear earplugs, white-noise busters, or listen to music on a Walkman. Temple warns that although using ear plugs and noise cancellers are OK for getting through an experience such as a trip to the supermarket, they should not be used on a regular basis, as the auditory system needs to learn to get used to and tolerate some amount of the noise which is around in the everyday environment.

4. To get desensitized to the sound of fire bells, Temple suggests taping the sound of a fire bell and listening to it, controlling the volume and length of play. Every time you listen to it, the volume

can be adjusted as well as the playing time, yet always under the control of the person who is getting desensitized.

5. To ease the noise of scraping chairs on hard floors, pad the bottoms of the chair legs. You could use old tennis balls: make a slit and fit them onto the bottoms of the chair legs.

6. For soaking up sound, put carpeting on floors and also on the walls of rooms (or insulate the walls). A good cheap way to get carpets is to ask carpet stores for remnants as donations, or contact major hotels, which redecorate often, and see if you can get the carpet they are removing and throwing away. (You will have to clean it.)

7. To teach the consonants to a person who can't hear them well, emphasize them very strongly, putting the accent on them, so the person can hear them.

Some people with autism have body boundary issues. Most people can tell where they are in a space. Normally, a person can close his eyes standing in front of a wall, and put his hand on the wall, knowing where his hand ends and the wall begins. For those who have body boundary issues, they are unable to "feel" this. Temple says that lots of brushing, massage, and deep pressure can help people feel their body boundaries.

Many people with sensory processing difficulties seek relief from too much or too little stimulation by rocking their chair. A therapy ball can help, but to avoid the cost of a therapy ball (or to avoid a child playing on it and not concentrating), make a T-stool with two pieces of plywood. The person will have to rock slightly on it to keep their balance.

FOOD FOR THOUGHT

The Curse of the Fluorescent Light

Fluorescent lighting has got to be one of mankind's worst inventions. I always hated going shopping—after ten minutes I would become irritable, feel restless, and get a major headache. Once home, I would be so exhausted I would have to lie down. While shopping, my husband would ask me, "Are you hungry? Are you tired? Why are you so cranky all of a sudden?" I could never figure out why my mood would change so suddenly and how I could feel so physically bad so quickly. It was not until years later when I lived in France that I realized it was the fluorescent lighting that did it to me.

Most of the time in Paris I shopped at the wonderful food markets or local shops, but every once in a while it was necessary to go to a supermarket for sundry items. The small supermarket closest to our apartment had these horrendous fluorescent lights that you could actually see flicker and hear buzz. It was horrible. The checkout girl who worked there looked poorly and so depressed all the time. One day I asked her if she was OK, she looked so ill. She told me she had constant headaches and felt nauseous at work, and she thought it had to do with the lights.

Then all of a sudden it clicked. Looking at my past behavior patterns, I could see a connection between the kinds of stores that made me feel ill and the ones that didn't. I then started asking people around me and was surprised to find that many people suffer from the curse of the fluorescent light.

Once I realized what was causing my discomfort, I limited my outings to those kinds of stores and never planned a shopping day where I would hit more than one big shop (such as a Costco or Ralph's) in a day. My husband is now the designated supermarket and department store shopper in the family (he has a natural talent for this; at one time he worked in procurement). But mostly, we have taken our business elsewhere, avoiding major shops and spending money where people are more cognizant of making a comfortable working and shopping environment.

In the U.S., smoking is prohibited in most public places, and in some places even in restaurants and bars, and this was done to protect the workers behind the counters as well as the customers. And of course, new buildings have to be designed with easy access for people in wheelchairs. So how about a law banning the use of fluorescent lighting?

Think of all the checkout men and women and shelf stackers working in supermarkets. And what about the teachers and physicians who are obliged to spend long hours under those lights? Perhaps sensory integration dysfunction should be labeled a handicapping condition and no new buildings should be designed with fluorescent lighting. Then, perhaps, students will finally have a proper environment to learn in.

9

Adults Living and Working with Autism Spectrum Disorders

*Once you become an adult, usually at twenty-one at the most, nobody is oblig-
ated to take care of you anymore. After that, where you live and how you live,
more than anything else, depends on you and what you make of your abilities.*

*It will be easier for you if you prepare to accept an eventual change in
where you live before failing health or death of your parents forces this reality
on you. I am grateful to my parents for what they did but I have to say that
I live more independently and fully now that they are gone. I had no choice.*

—JERRY NEWPORT, *Your Life Is Not a Label*

*The problem of long-term care plagues all parents of people with cognitive
difficulties. People with cognitive disabilities are so vulnerable. . . . What
parents want for their children and what they get are two completely different things. The government offices and private agencies responsible for serving them make for a huge, complicated system. . . . Parents have mixed
feelings. They know what they want in a general way, but don't know how to
go about achieving it.*

—LINDA J. STENGLE, *Laying Community Foundations for Your Child with a Disability*

FOR a short while I worked as a case manager for one of California's re-gional centers, providing resources to individuals with developmental disabilities. Some of my older adult clients who required a lot of support were still living at home with elderly parents. When I visited them, I could feel the anxiety, hear the tremor in the parents' voices, sense their exhaustion, knowing they were concerned not only about today, but the future, when they would no longer be around to look out for their child.

Then I had Jeremy. Now he is fifteen, and I know that although he continues to learn, he will always need some level of support. He only has one sibling, and our relatives are spread out over the globe. The re-ality is that my husband and I are going to be like those aging parents, with few options for our adult child. We can't imagine him living alone or in a residential facility or group home, where he knows no one and where he will be at the mercy of others unknown to us or even find his "home" sold like a business and run by others. We want him to be sur-rounded by friends and people who love him, who can give him the sup-port and strategies he needs to continue to learn and find his niche. So with other parents we know in this area, we are exploring options that exist, and making plans for the future.

The Reality of Life as an Adult with an ASD

In chapter 7, we touched upon the need for preparation in high school for transitioning to the world of work or college. This chapter is written primarily for adults with ASDs and their families or caregivers, but edu-cators working with teenagers, prospective employers, and others work-ing with adults with ASDs will find a wealth of information as well. Those involved with transition planning from high school to real adult life would do well to read this for ideas and insight as well as resources for more information. (Those with ties to policy makers and purse string holders could highlight the parts of this chapter that discuss the lack of available services and the need for more funding, and send it on to them.)

Some adults with an ASD are able to live and get what they need with little or no assistance. Others, although able, will need support throughout the process. Even more will need support and supervision twenty-four hours a day for most of their lives. In this chapter, services and ideas for different ability levels will be covered.

More is known about adults with ASDs than ever before. Many of the more able people with ASDs have written personal accounts of what their lives are like, and how they overcame challenges to make living in a neurotypical world easier. Their suggestions will be helpful to many readers. New ideas about possible living and working solutions have been put forth recently that may be helpful for those needing more supports.

The federal and state governments have a responsibility to all its citizens. In the U.S., the American with Disabilities Act gives people with disabilities equal rights as others. However, although improvements have been made, equal access and opportunity is still "in progress." Not enough opportunity—or supports to benefit from an opportunity—is available. However, there is hope as parents, professionals, and organizations work together to improve the situation and generate alternative solutions and creative funding mechanisms.

The Challenges of the Individual

Over the last few years, more and more adults with an ASD have written books about living with autism or Asperger's. It is very inspiring to read the accounts of their lives and how they overcame some of their challenges. The skills they developed in order to survive in a neurotypical world can give ideas to others like them or to parents and educators to help prepare teenagers and young adults. However, the stark reality is that most people with ASDs, even those who are very able, do not enjoy the work and living environment that these authors do.

Why is that? First of all, these individuals are exceptional people, not only in their intelligence but in their determination and motivation to live a full life. These individuals have Asperger's or are on the very able end of the autism spectrum. Second, most of these individuals had strong, supportive mothers or fathers who were able to fight for what they thought their child needed while they were growing up, and who stood by them regardless of what label they had at the time for their difficulties. Thirdly, the parents raised them in such a way as to build a strong sense of self-esteem, and if they subsequently married, their spouse continued that support. These factors helped them to overcome the challenges they had and create a fulfilling life.

Unfortunately, all these factors do not always exist for most individuals. Even most neurotypical individuals do not have that drive and self-motivation to succeed against all odds. And not all parents have the knowledge, stamina, or conviction to go out and fight the powers that be for what their child needs as they grow up, and even less when they are young adults.

Options and Preferences

Some people on the more able end of the spectrum have found the college or university environment a comfortable place for them to learn and even work. Others have found that particular fields of work are more conducive than others. Dealing mainly with objects and data and less with people often appeals to those who have strong social impairments.

Many more will need help to find a job and coaching to keep it. Not only does the adult with an ASD need to develop strategies to be a good employee, employers need to know how to make the job a good match with the employee. Good coaches will be needed to help put strategies in place to help those with inappropriate behaviors learn to keep them in check in the workplace.

Still others will need extensive supports and may be in volunteer or day programs learning skills and behaviors necessary for appropriate job placement.

Adulthood

BY PETER GERHARDT, ED.D.

One way of understanding the development of comprehensive programs of intervention and support for adult learners with an ASD is to consider the difference between a disability and a handicap. A disability can be defined as a permanent reduction in the function of a particular body part or structure. A handicap, on the other hand, is defined by the challenges that the disability presents to the individual's participation in desired, life-relevant activities.

As such, any system of intervention or support first needs to identify the individual, environmental, instructional, and community conditions under which the disability of ASD may present an individual learner with less of a handicap.

Using this perspective, the adult with ASD becomes simply one target of potential intervention among a variety of targets (e.g., coworkers, cashiers, modifications to job requirements or the physical environment, the provision of community training, and support) designed to support increasingly greater levels of personal independence and competence. In this model, then, the goal is not to "fix" the adult learner with ASD but rather to simply view them as one of many potential targets for instruction, support, and growth, and in so doing, reduce the impact of potentially handicapping barriers while increasing the personal competence of all concerned.

Adulthood for learners with ASD needs to be understood as more than just a chronological state. For everyone, adulthood represents a time in one's life where there are increased levels of independence, choice, and personal control. Further, adulthood is generally recognized as a period of increased responsibility, commitment, and, more often than not, delayed gratification. It is during this time of life that we generally experience our greatest successes as well as some of our greatest difficulties. Adulthood, despite some popular perceptions, is a time of continued growth and learning and not a period of stagnation, and is, in many ways, the defining period of one's life. We may look back fondly on our childhood, but it is our accomplishments as adults for which we are generally most proud. Adulthood for the adult with ASD should be viewed as no different.

Peter Gerhardt, Ed.D., is the author and coauthor of articles and book chapters on the needs of adults with autism spectrum disorders, the school-to-work transition process as well as the analysis of intervention of problematic behavior. He has presented nationally and internationally on these topics. Peter has a private practice in Baltimore, MD.

The concept of self-determination is taking hold in more and more states by people with disabilities and their families. It is about allowing people with developmental disabilities to make their own choices and supporting them as needed. This philosophy, which is about recognizing people's abilities rather than their disabilities, necessitates changes in state policy and local agencies in how they provide support for individuals.

Regardless of the ability level of the individual, the person's own preferences should be taken into account, and there are ways of trying to figure out what is important to even the least communicative of individuals. This is at the heart of Person Centered Planning, an approach discussed in chapter 7 under the heading "Preparing for Life after High School" (pages 233–38).

The State of Adult Services Today

The United States has many laws that protect, and services that provide for, the developmentally disabled. Sadly, it is not enough for all in need today—or for the epidemic numbers of children with ASDs that will grow to be adults tomorrow.

In July 2001, the board of directors of the Autism Society of America (ASA) published "A Call to Action: Position Paper on the National Crisis in Adult Services for Individuals with Autism" (www.autismsociety.org/upload/images/AdultServices). The author, Dr. Ruth Sullivan, is herself a parent of an adult with autism and a professional who has created living and working options for adults with autism.

Her paper is an excellent source of information in regard to the history of services in the U.S., where we are today, and where we should be heading, as well as a call to arms for parents and professionals and the government to create what's needed.

Dr. Sullivan explains that although the Individuals with Disabilities Act (IDEA) mandates services and programs for all children with special educational needs, there are no mandated programs or services for people after they leave school. Although the majority of adult services for individuals with developmental disabilities are funded mainly by the Medicaid Home and Community-Based (HCB) waiver program, eligibility does not provide entitlement—unlike the mandatory services funded under IDEA. Unfortunately, many parents are shocked to realize, when their young adult is "aging" out of school, that although their child may be eligible for services, funding is only available for a limited number of eligible individuals.

This means that although a person may be deemed eligible for services, there is no requirement that it be provided. The number of people receiving services is determined by how much money is budgeted for those services and programs. Therefore, an eligible person could wait years to get into a particular program or to receive certain services.

There are some community agencies that serve people with ASDs; however, in 2001, there were only about twenty-five agencies providing specialized programs for these adults. These agencies experience high turnover in staff, because the inadequate Medicaid reimbursement does not allow for paying decent salaries.

Not only is staff turnover high, but there are very few, if any, college programs that train people about autism and strategies to work with adults with autism. Parents and professionals familiar with autism can attest to how difficult it is for staff to do their job—let alone how hard it is on the client with autism—if they have no training in the client's form of communication or behavioral strategies.

The cost of autism-specific services is very high. Few families can afford the cost, no insurance company will cover it, and providers have limited financial ability to develop more programs.

This means that currently, there is not enough of anything to go around, and it is not going to get solved overnight with a prayer and a wish.

What must be done. To alleviate the enormous residential need we are currently facing, Dr. Sullivan suggests that in-home support be provided for those parents who wish to have their adult children live with them for as long as possible. Small group homes, apartments with support staff, and access to home financing should be provided for those who choose to live in their own home.

People with autism would be more effectively employed if they had access to job coaches who were well-trained and knowledgeable about autism and could help them learn and maintain appropriate work-related behaviors. Taking the individual's interest into account when matching them to a job is also a key ingredient to successful employment, as it is for anyone.

The reality is, we cannot wait for the government to take action. Parents, professionals, and other organizations are taking the lead in many places and creating solutions: programs for adults regarding living arrangements and employment and college opportunities for those so inclined. These opportunities have been created out of frustration and need, which is a good example of taking a negative and turning it into a positive.

Some parents are joining together and creating group homes or nonprofit organizations to provide living arrangements.

In the past two years, more developmentally disabled individuals have become self-employed, which in turn pays for the supports they need in order to work in the position that has been created for them, based on their wishes.

Some undergraduate programs are creating supports specifically designed for college students with Asperger's or more able students with autism. At least one college is designing an integrated undergraduate program specifically for the more academically able with ASDs, and will provide necessary supports as well as opportunities to learn the skills a person may be lacking to be an independent adult.

As a group of parents or individuals with ASDs, if you have an idea, there are sure to be like-minded individuals and funding to help you get started. There is so much need that agencies and individuals are there to help you. It requires a lot of work and time, but it's better spent on creating a future than waiting for a spot that may never be available.

Where to Find Information and Possible Services

Meanwhile, it is apparent that regardless of the ability level of the person with an ASD, there are challenges and barriers to overcome in order to get the services that are needed. Although the type of need may be different, any person with an ASD who requires assistance, or their caregiver, should have access to information and advice. As mentioned earlier, there is not a federal mandate for services to be provided after the person leaves school. Every state provides differently, so you will need to find out what applies to your area. If you have made it this far, you are probably resourceful in terms of asking the right questions. Here are some suggestions of places to go for information:

- Apply for Supplemental Security Income (SSI). Adults considered disabled are eligible for SSI. Some states supplement the amount paid by the federal government. Contact the Social Security Administration (phone: 800-772-1213; website: www.ssa.gov) for more information.

• Contact your state's protection and advocacy agency to find out your rights and what you may be entitled to in your state. You can find your state's agency on the Autism Society of America website (www.autism-society.org) or the Administration of Developmental Disabilities website (www.acf.dhhs.gov/programs/add).

• Contact your State Council on Developmental Disabilities to find out about adult services by going to the Administration of Developmental Disabilities website (www.acf.dhhs.gov/programs/add).

• Look at the NICHCY website (www.nichcy.org) for your state's resources that might be of help including: transition services, vocational education services, the Client Assistance Program, housing, and more.

• Look at the Autism Society of America website (www.autism-society.org) for any additional information or helpful news in regard to adult services.

• To find out the contact information for the Statewide Independent Living Council (SILC) in your state, check out the Independent Living Research Utilization Project website (www.ilru.org).

• To find out the contact information for centers for independent living (CILs) in your state, see the National Council on Independent Living website (www.ncil.org).

• For more information about living arrangements, see the Arc-Link website (www.thearclink.org) and the Alternative Living Arrangements website (www.geocities.com/Heartland/woods/2869/alternatives.html).

• To find out about possible medical and Medicaid benefits, it is best to contact your state agencies; however, if you wish other information, contact the U.S. Department of Health and Human Services (www.hhs.gov).

Never Underestimate the Power of a Group of Parents

Although it should not be left up to volunteers or the parents to fill in the gaps in provision for adults with ASDs, the Berkshire Autistic Society (BAS) in the UK has taken an active role in doing so. Discouraged by the lack of available resources in Berkshire, the BAS has become proactive. Over the past few years, they have made the necessary contacts and set up a supported employment pilot project, organized police awareness sessions in collaboration with East Berkshire College, and provided information and emotional support through their helpline.

The Support into Employment Project is now in its final year with plans to become a fully functioning supported employment scheme for people with Asperger's syndrome. An integral part of the BAS scheme is to offer a number of work preparation courses with such partners as the East Berkshire College, as well as to continue to work with job centers and career services to provide employment advice and guidance. There are a few people currently supported in the workplace and some in the "Employability" course that BAS helped design at East Berkshire College.

In addition, BAS members are each sent an "awareness pack" to give to his or her employer's human resource department along with an offer to arrange a free employer awareness session for those hiring a person with an ASD. Links were also created with other service providers such as Mencap, Windsor & Maidenhead Social Services, the careers service, and local education providers.

Obviously, government should be doing more. Imagine the amount of energy and time that parents have put into creating provision while waiting for the local government to put into place what is needed. But think of the alternative: doing nothing and having no provision.

See the BAS website (www.autismberkshire.org.uk) for more information.

Suggested Reading for All

Recently, more able adults on the spectrum have written books or documents about their experiences and their suggestions to make life easier for others like them. Granted, many people with an ASD are not as able as these individuals, but the threads running through are very similar and can be applied to trying to understand the behaviors of others who are less able.

No one should consider planning a work or college program for an individual with an ASD without knowing what people with autism have to say, and these authors are a good place to start. (More are listed in the Resources section at the back of this book.) People with autism might find it helpful to read some of these as well.

ON THE INTERNET

- "Choosing the Right Job for People with Autism or Asperger's Syndrome" and "Making the Transition from the World of School into the World of Work," by Temple Grandin at Stephen M. Edelson's website for the Center for the Study of Autism (www.autism.org/contents)

- "Planning to Be Nerdy Where Nerdy Can Be Cool: College Planning for the High-Functioning Student with Autism" and "Planning and Self-Marketing for People on the Autistic Spectrum," by Lars Perner, a professor of marketing (www.larsperner.com)

- "Understanding College Students with Autism," from the *Chronicle of Higher Education* by Dawn Prince-Hughes (www.ohiou.edu/oupress/acquarticle2.htm)

- "Survival in the Workplace" (www.autismtoday.com/survivalwork.htm) and "A Slice of Life" (www.autismtoday.com/slicelife.htm) by Stephen Shore

- "A Survival Guide for People with Asperger Syndrome" by Marc Segar at the O.A.S.I.S. website (www.udel.edu/bkirby/asperger)

- "How to Understand People Who Are Different" by Brad Rand (www.isn.net/~jypsy/bradrand.htm)

- The website for University Students with Autism and Asperger's Syndrome (www.users.dircon.co.uk/~cns) is a great resource that includes first-person accounts and links to other websites

BOOKS

- *Aquamarine Blue 5: Personal Stories of College Students with Autism*, edited by Dawn Prince-Hughes

- *Beyond the Wall: Personal Experiences with Autism and Asperger's Syndrome* by Stephen Shore

- *Your Life Is Not a Label* by Jerry Newport

- *Pretending to Be Normal: Living with Asperger's Syndrome* by Liane Holliday Willey

- *Thinking in Pictures: And Other Reports from My Life with Autism* by Temple Grandin

- *Asperger Syndrome Employment Workbook* by Roger N. Meyer

- *Succeeding in College with Asperger Syndrome* by John Hapur, Maria Lawlor, and Michael Fitzgerald

- *Special Teaching in Higher Education: Successful Strategies for Access and Inclusion*, edited by Stuart Powell

- *Developing Talents: Careers for Individuals with Asperger Syndrome and High-Functioning Autism* by Temple Grandin and Kate Duffy

FOR PLANNING ANY COMMUNITY-BASED SERVICES FOR THE LESS ABLE

- "Lifetime Services for Individuals with Autism: A Working, Community-Integrated Model" by Ruth Christ Sullivan, Ph.D., et al. (http://trainland.tripod.com/ruthchrist.htm)

- *Laying Community Foundations for Your Child with a Disability* by Linda J. Stengle, M.H.S.

- *Autism through the Lifespan: The Eden Model* by David L. Holmes, Ed.D.

In the following sections, different employment, college, and living options are described, as well as coping strategies and practical tips based on the experiences of those with an ASD.

Employment and Careers

Jerry Newport has a great philosophy about work. He feels that no matter what job you have, you should do it well. In *Your Life Is Not a Label,* he gives many tips about work. He suggests that even entry-level jobs are important as they can teach you things that are necessary for all jobs, namely: how to follow instructions, how to be on time, how to dress appropriately, and how to work independently.

In his article "Survival in the Workplace," Stephen Shores talks about the various careers he attempted before finding the one that fit him, and what it was about the jobs that he found difficult. This kind of analysis is helpful in determining a good fit.

An excellent, practical book is *Developing Talents: Careers for Individuals with Asperger Syndrome and High Functioning Autism* by Temple Grandin and Kate Duffy. This book explains how to prepare for an interview, how to prioritize work commitments, and how to deal with sensory overload. There is an informative and detailed section on the best jobs for people on the spectrum.

A book that might be useful for the more able adult wanting to explore possible career choices is the *Asperger Syndrome Employment Workbook* by Roger N. Meyer, who has Asperger's. This practical workbook encourages readers to engage in an exploration of their employment history, and to identify the work they are best suited for by analyzing their needs, talents, and strengths.

Temple Grandin suggests developing your special interest or obsession into an employable skill. Even though your social skills may be lacking, you can impress someone with your talents, strengths, and abilities and be hired. People respect talent, and you can focus on selling your skills instead of your personality. Employers will have to understand your needs in order for a job or career to be successful, but having a special ability will convince someone that you are worth employing. Employers should be reminded of the positive attributes that most people with ASDs have, such as honesty and diligence, as well as the challenges you face.

Obviously, not everyone has the capabilities of Grandin or Newport; however, the concerns of finding a good fit, and a job that is interesting to the individual, are the same whether the person is more or less able.

Seeking Employment

Each state may propose different opportunities, or use different labels to describe what is available, so check to see what is available locally. Here is a glimpse at the usual options for finding and keeping a job:

- *Competitive employment.* These types of employment opportunities are usually good for people who can work at a job with some adjustments but who will not need support on a continual basis. People who have an employable skill will find it easier to find work. Networking through family members, friends, people from your

Employment Tips from Temple Grandin

In her book *Thinking in Pictures,* Temple Grandin gives some useful information about how she was able to transition from college to work. Here are a few of the points she makes:

• It is important to make a gradual transition from an educational setting to the world of work. Starting a job or career part time while still attending a class or two can make this possible.

• The freelance route has been a way that many people with an ASD have been able to exploit their talent area.

• Sometimes it is possible to get in trouble at a job by being technically correct but socially wrong. This happens to people with autism because they have a hard time being diplomatic and tactful. Temple learned by reading about international negotiations and using them as models.

• Temple has had many mentors. These mentors, whether at college or at work, helped her by teaching her the social aspects she needed to be successful, such as how to dress and be groomed appropriately and how to put together a portfolio showing off her talents, explaining to her the social nuances she did not understand, and helping others to understand her behaviors and actions.

church, or mentors you have had can perhaps lead to employment. If you are attending college, you may find a job through contacts made there: people who admire your abilities and know people who can use your talents. Local unemployment centers, the classifieds, and websites like www.monster.com are also places to look for openings.

- *Supported employment.* This provides assistance in areas where people with ASDs need help: job finding, job coaching, skills training, and employment advice and guidance. The goal is to place the person in a job in the community that fits in with their interests and abilities. These kinds of programs, regardless of the ability level of the person, provide each person with the training and support to maintain employment in the chosen career field.

- *Sheltered employment.* This is an option for those who will need security in a work environment where people are knowledgeable about ASDs. These jobs tend to be repetitious, and those who like structure and repetition may do well in them.

- *Self-employment.* This is a relatively new concept being considered as an option by some. Working as a freelancer in a particular area of interest is a possibility if the person has the discipline that self-employment requires. However, if the social aspect of marketing is difficult, this will work only if there is someone who can refer work to the individual. Mentors can be very helpful in this arena.

- *Self-employment for those who are less able.* This is an even newer concept. If done properly, even if the person needs constant supervision, the aide can become an employee of the self-employed person, thus lessening the need for government funds to provide assistance. This is a great concept as it provides a way for the individual to do something he is interested in doing and not be constrained by what "the system" has or doesn't have available for him. An article by Patricia Okahashi about self-employment for the less able is at www.vrri.org/rhb0401.htm, on the website of the Vocational and Rehabilitation Research Institute.

In her article on the web, "Choosing the Right Job for People with Autism or Asperger's Syndrome" (www.autism.org), Temple Grandin

FOOD FOR THOUGHT

"The bottom line is this: If you ever want the kind of job that buys you a house, a limo and anything close to that, you will have to do every job before that one as if it were the greatest job in the world. Just make believe, if you wind up cooking hamburgers, that every burger will have a photo of you on the wrapper, saying 'cooked by . . . ' Do every job to the best of your ability because you are proud of who you are and always do your best. If you do that, you will get the most out of your working days."

—Jerry Newport, *Your Life Is Not a Label*

has made lists of different types of jobs appropriate for different types of ASD people. Here are some of them:

- Visual thinkers: computer programming, commercial art, drafting, equipment design, small appliance and lawnmower repair, video game design, and the building trade.

- People who are good at mathematics, music, or facts: reference librarian, inventory control, accounting, taxi driver, computer programming, copyeditor, tuning pianos and other musical instruments, clerk and filing jobs, and statistician.

- People who are nonverbal or who have poor verbal skills: reshelving library books, copy shop, factory assembly jobs, restocking shelves, janitor jobs, cleaning and cooking in a fast-food restaurant, watering plants in large office buildings, data entry, and sorting at a recycling plant.

Practical tips and helpful hints are included in the "Helpful Strategies" section further along in this chapter.

Positive Aspects of Hiring Someone with an ASD

Prospective employers should know that there are positive benefits to hiring someone with an ASD. Honesty, dependability, loyalty, and diligence are traits that are can be found in abundance in the ASDs population.

College

There are different types of colleges: vocational or technical colleges, community colleges, and universities or four-year colleges. Vocational or technical colleges usually teach a skill in preparation for a specific job or employment goal. Community colleges are only two years, with students transferring to four-year colleges or universities to complete their education.

Many of the more able people with ASDs are successful at college. Some of the interests or obsessions they have can be pursued in a course of study. The challenge may well be translating that knowledge or degree into stable employment, but that is a challenge all students face. Some feel so comfortable at college that they develop their interests into a career on campus. Both Stephen Shores and Lars Perner in articles on the web describe college as being "heaven" either for themselves or for others they know on the spectrum.

Some students prefer community or local colleges as they can continue to stay at home. Dormitory living can be difficult unless the student has a private room. Living with unknown roommates in a rental unit also can be tricky. Community colleges usually offering two-year programs, however, can be a challenge if the student wishes to continue at a four-year college. The student will have to make sure to plan carefully what classes to take to make sure they apply. Also, if adjusting to different environments is a challenge or stressful, the student will be going through that step twice.

Getting Support for a Successful and Enjoyable College Experience

Colleges offer services and supports for students with special requirements. However, not all colleges are familiar with ASDs and your particular needs. Here are some suggestions for making college a rewarding experience:

- Give information about the ASD and how it affects you, the challenges you face, and what strategies can be used to help you to those you think may need to know.

- Find a sympathetic school counselor or mentor. This person can help in many ways, for example, by helping you find a group on campus that shares your special hobby or interest.

- Ask your school counselor or mentor which teachers would be more accepting of your difficulties and willing to make you comfortable with learning in their class.

- The same kinds of support that helped in secondary school will be of benefit at college, and telling your guidance counselor what those were is a good idea. For the visual learner, written schedules, lists, and visual aids for studying such as graphs, charts, and videos are helpful. For the auditory learner, tape-recording lectures or having a note-taker works well. Textbooks on tape can be another useful tool.

- Tests or exams can be modified to take into consideration any difficulties you may have with test taking.

Living Arrangements

At some point in time, you may be leaving the family home. As Jerry Newport points out in his book, it is better to start that transition while your parents are still well. That way, you will still have the support of people who love and care for you and whom you trust during the period of transition that you will be facing.

Obviously, living arrangements are a personal and family decision based on comfort level, needs, and budgets. If anything other than a totally independent situation is being considered, then it is important that the individual with an ASD and/or a family member look into the company that is providing or supervising the living arrangements. Make sure the company has a mission or philosophy that fits in with the needs of the prospective resident. ArcLink (www.thearclink.org), a nonprofit advocacy group, has a good website with helpful links and can help you understand the federal rules and regulations and how to identify and find what you need.

There are different options available, depending upon the adult's functional living skills, whether the person likes being alone or not, as well as available funding from the government or the adult and his or her family. Below are some of the more traditional options.

- *Residential facilities.* These are typically large facilities, usually for persons needing nursing care or a high level of supervision and care. Residents may spend time learning self-help and daily living skills, including housekeeping.

- *Supervised group homes.* Located in residential communities, these consist of several individuals who need supervision for daily life skills, and are staffed by trained personnel who assist the residents based on each individual's need. The residents are usually employed and go off to work every day.

• *Supervised apartments.* Individuals who need some assistance and supervision and who prefer living with fewer people usually choose this option. Often this type of living arrangement is a good transition to independent living.

• *Independent living.* This is a good option for those who are independent in their daily living skills but may still need support in, for example, decision-making areas such as money management. It is a good idea to have a good support system developed in the community in case of need.

Some less traditional options are becoming increasingly popular as families are becoming more and more discouraged by the lack of available options and are creating their own solutions. As states are investigating less-costly alternatives and encouraging self-determination, different funding options may be available. Contact your state agencies to find out more. Some of these living options are:

• *Home ownership with support.* The person with autism owns the home with financial help from either parents or government programs. Usually a neurotypical buddy will share the house, or college students will rent rooms. The necessary level of care is provided by an outside person paid for usually through a Medicaid waiver, or by one of the roommates in exchange for free lodging.

• *Co-ops.* Parents join together to create a family home for the individuals, and the families pitch in to run the house and provide some finances to pay respite caregivers, again utilizing available funding mechanisms.

• *Cohousing.* This is a type of collaborative housing made up of private dwellings, each with its own kitchen, living room, and so on, but it also includes shared facilities. These facilities could include a large dining room and kitchen, a lounge, recreation facilities, a laundry room, and a library. Usually, these communities are designed and managed by the residents, and they are intentional neighborhoods: the people are committed to living as a community; the physical design itself encourages that and facilitates social contact.

For more information, visit the Alternative Living Arrangements website (www.geocities.com/Heartland/Woods/2869/alternatives.html).

Housing Services

To find out about available housing services in your area, and to get on waiting lists, you need to contact local agencies in your area. If you are unsure of where to go for information, contact your state's protection and advocacy office, which you can find on the ASA website (www .autism-society.org).

Helpful Strategies for Work, College, and Everyday Living

Adults with ASDs face challenges in certain areas. For those who are not cognitively disabled, or who are on the mid to higher end of functioning ability, there are many strategies that can be put in place to help.

For Challenges with Social Communication and Contact

Getting and keeping a job or career, or signing up for and attending college, can be very difficult for people with ASDs. The social skills that are necessary to network, ask questions, and understand the true meaning (as opposed to the literal meaning) of what is being said, as well as to interpret nonverbal communication, are areas in which people with ASDs are lacking. However, there is much that can be done to overcome this obstacle:

• Much information can be accessed through the Internet now without dealing directly with another person. This can be a good way to make primary contact when trying to network for jobs.

• If possible, find mentors who admire your talent and know about your eccentricities and who can help you turn your talent into a career, or put you in touch with people who can help you find work or get through school.

• Decide who at work or college needs to know about your ASD and tell them how it affects you in the workplace. In his book *Beyond the Wall*, Stephen Shore has included a sample letter he helped develop for the Asperger's Association of New England. This letter, addressed to employers, explains the difficulties the person writing it has with reading nonverbal signs and understanding what it is like to be in someone else's shoes, and the situations that can result, as well as suggestions that would help the person.

• Practicing areas that you are not comfortable with, such as job interviews, discussion with teachers, or going on a date or outing with a peer, can be very helpful in relieving some of the anxiety.

For Problems with Finding Your Way Around

Many individuals with autism have difficulty going from one place to another, whether it's at school, on a college campus, or in shopping malls and big buildings. This can be a problem for getting to classes on time or accomplishing your job. What you can do:

• Go around the place you will be needing to learn how to navigate a few times before starting school or your job. It helps if you can have someone with you who is already familiar with the building. In some areas you may need to ask permission for access. If possible, walk the route from one place to another that you will have to take.

- Take pictures or draw the different landmarks that are on the path from one place to another. List on a piece of paper or dictate into a minirecorder the order of the landmarks, and where you need to turn or stop or take another direction.

- Make a small guidebook with the pictures and notes, including the times at which you must leave one place and go to the next.

- Draw a map if you think it will be helpful to you, of all the corridors or alleyways or streets and landmarks.

- Practice navigating through the areas you have mapped out. Using a bicycle can be a viable means of getting around large campuses or small towns.

For Daily Living

Keep in mind that the kind of strategies that help you with organizing your schoolwork or job will help you with your daily living skills. Perhaps you have already been using some of these while living at home. Some things that may be helpful are color-coding for files of paperwork and bills and schedules of your daily, weekly, and monthly activities and chores.

For example, some people find it helpful to do certain chores (laundry, vacuuming, food shopping) on certain days and have them marked on the calendar. Other responsibilities with a home that crop up less often, such as paying the bills, can be noted on the calendar to remind you when they need to be done.

For Sensory Perception Problems

Both Temple Grandin (*Thinking in Pictures*) and Liane Willey (*Pretending to Be Normal*) have much information to share about sensory difficulties. Getting an occupational therapist who has had sensory integration training to develop a program to help you in this area can be very useful. Look at chapter 5 for therapies that address sensory issues. Meanwhile, there are a few things you can do:

• Auditory sensitivity can be minimized for some through auditory integration training. Meanwhile, wearing earplugs may be helpful in curtailing your sensitivity to sound. Make sure you can still hear people talking to you, as well as emergency vehicles and signals such as fire bells. If it doesn't distract you from your work or studies, wear headphones and listen to music you enjoy at low volume. Temple cautions against using these strategies all the time, as some exposure to noise can help desensitize a person, and there is a need to get used to some everyday noise.

• For visual sensitivity, try wearing sunglasses, a hat with a brim, or a visor to minimize the amount of light reaching your eyes, making sure you can see well enough to safely continue with what you are doing.

• If you suffer from tactile sensitivity, tell those around you (at work, college, your living environment) that you do not like to be touched. Wear only fabrics that you like the feel of. If you enjoy deep pressure, there are weighted vests available. However, carrying a heavy backpack or shoulder bag or sewing pockets of little weights into your coat or sweater may work just as well and look better. Rub your skin with light or heavy pressure (depending on your preference) when you are alone, perhaps when getting dressed. If you feel the need to put things in your mouth, then chew gum.

• For those with olfactory sensitivity, put some of your favorite scent on a small piece of material, the inside of your elbow, or a cotton ball, so that you can smell this scent when others overwhelm you. If you can, tell those who are in close proximity to you all day long about your sensitivity and ask if they can refrain from wearing perfumes and other products with strong smells.

• If food sensitivity is an issue, think of the foods you can tolerate. Identify the restaurants or cafes that serve those foods. If invited to someone's home, you may wish to tell them you can eat only certain foods. If your food sensitivity is extreme and you are unlikely to find what you can eat in a restaurant or at someone's home, be prepared to make and carry your own foods when you are spending time outside your home.

Having a Social Life and Close Relationships

Leisure and Recreation Activities

Having a social life can sometimes be a challenge even for people who do not lack social skills. Some people are more gregarious than others, and those people tend to have more relationships and recreational activities. However, it must be remembered that it is not quantity but quality that counts.

For people with an ASD, building relationships and participating in recreational activities can be even more difficult because of the impairment of social interaction skills, and the lack of knowledge that most people in the leisure and community services have when it comes to ASDs. However, due to the increase in those being diagnosed with autism and Asperger's, people are at least becoming more aware of what they are. Rome was not built in a day, and even though laws protect your right to have access to leisure, recreational, and cultural activities in the community just like every other citizen, in reality people out there still suffer from a lack of knowledge.

One way you can help in this area is by spreading knowledge of ASDs. Contact your local ASA chapter and tell them if you think a particular agency or organization would benefit from training.

When looking for leisure activities, think about the talents, abilities, and interests that you have and find out if there is a local group that

FOOD FOR THOUGHT

"Many young adults meet each other at places that cultivate a common interest. These should not be 'negative' sites such as night-clubs, which are notoriously socially threatening environs for our people. Places like a bookstore that features poetry readings, health club, yoga club, running group, chess club, or any interest group are a good bet for our people, who have little problem expressing an interest in certain subjects. In these places, our extreme interest, which may not be appreciated ordinarily, might even come to be a social advantage."

—Jerry and Mary Newport,
Autism-Asperger's and Sexuality

meets around that subject. You may need to take any sensory-overload issues you have into consideration when looking at activities to join. Some activities may have more social pressure than you are ready to handle. Good places to start looking are local facilities such as leisure or sports centers, swimming pools, libraries, art galleries, and adult education classes. Other places where you may find groups are bowling alleys and bowling greens, cinemas, ice and roller skating rinks, gyms, and local sports clubs.

Depending on your ability level and the level of support needed there are different ways to access activities. You may be able to do it on your own, or with a parent or family member to start off with. If you need a high level of support and live in a residential facility, paid staff may accompany you. Sometimes there are autism-friendly volunteer organizations or befriending schemes in your area. Parents may already be providing a "circle of support" of family friends and caregivers who can help you access recreational activities.

Social and Internet Groups

If you wish to socialize with other adults with ASDs, some local autism chapters have social meetings and outings. Contact your local ASA chapter to find out more, as well as ASPEN (Asperger Syndrome Education Network) (www.aspennj.org), which has local chapters in some areas. Other organizations provide social outings, but are not necessarily ASD-specific.

The Internet has become a great resource for people with ASDs. Some people prefer to develop relationships this way and can communicate with others through the Internet at any time that is convenient to them. There are online support groups. If you do not have access to a computer at home, perhaps you can use one at your local library. There are websites for online support groups listed on the O.A.S.I.S. (Online Asperger Syndrome Information and Support) website: www.udel.edu/bkirby/asperger/.

Close Relationships

Many people with an ASD have close relationships and intimacy with others. Some get married and have children. There are difficulties that pose themselves, like in any marriage, and the areas of intimacy and responsiveness to the other are different for each person, depending on issues of sensory sensitivity and level of social exchanges that the partners are comfortable with. Reading some of the books by those with an ASD who are married, to either another person with an ASD or a neurotypical person, is useful. Some of the married authors worth reading are: Stephen Shore, Mary and Jerry Newport, Gisela and Christopher Slater-Walker, Liane Holliday Willey, Maxine Aston, and Donna Williams (see the Resources section for details).

Tips for All Who Know Someone with an ASD

Some people with ASDs manage well with little or no support. For others, social and communication issues, or perhaps learning disabilities, can get in the way of being as independent as possible.

The Challenges and What Can Help

Parents can help their children by instilling values and a sense of self-esteem and pride, encouraging them to see their individuality as something to be respected and appreciated, eccentricities and all. Parents can also help by creating networks of people who can be available for different areas of need for their adult child. Friends of the family or church members who have certain professional skills can help in their area of expertise. This is one way that community members can be helpful. Whether you are a plumber or an accountant, it would give peace of mind to a friend to know that you are willing to help if the need arises. Parents can also educate their child about safety, police, and emergency situations. (See chapter 8 for more about establishing community ties.)

Depression in Adults

Many adults with ASDs suffer at one time or another from depression or mental illness. This is not part and parcel of the ASD but can be exacerbated by the challenges they face in trying to find a place in our society. Friends and family members need to watch for signs that all is not well in order to get them the counseling or support they need.

Partners of Adults with ASDs

As ASDs become more and more recognized and diagnosed, many adults are realizing for the first time that they are autistic or have Asperger's. Sometimes this happens after the person is already married; it

FOOD FOR THOUGHT

Partners of Adults with ASDs

"If you are in an intimate relationship with someone who has Asperger Syndrome, you are one of the most important people in their lives. How you approach and cope with problems can make a difference to how he copes with many of the difficulties that having Asperger Syndrome can present him with. This is not to say that you will have to take responsibility for everything your partner does, but it is important that you are aware that there are some things that you will be naturally better at than he is."

—Maxine C. Aston,
The Other Half of Asperger Syndrome

may even be that being married her provoked getting the diagnosis. The spouse may have chosen her mate because he was calm and reliable, but after some years came to think of her husband as cold, unemotional, and unromantic, and realized that something was amiss.

Finding out that a partner has an ASD can provoke different feelings. One of them is anger at missing out on aspects of a marriage that you were looking forward to. Another feeling is relief that your partner is not trying to shut you out, he is just unable to give you the emotional response you need. Other feelings can be acceptance and understanding and letting go of the resentment you felt, because now you know he is not being thoughtless; he really does not get it. The positive aspects of having a spouse with an ASD include the fact that he will most likely always be loyal and honest.

Maxine C. Aston in *The Other Half of Asperger Syndrome* and Liane Holliday Willey in *Asperger Syndrome in the Family: Redefining Normal* describe the differences between the expectation of the spouse with Asperger's versus the more neurotypical one, and how it is important for each spouse to recognize the differences and understand where they come from. *An Asperger Marriage* by Gisela and Christopher Slater-Walker is very good, as it gives the point of view of both spouses.

Closing Comments

I am a person who is autistic.
What I want to say is that the hardest part of autism
is the communication.
Music is helpful.
I like that I can see colors in everything.
Help us by encouraging us.

—ANONYMOUS

One's first step in wisdom is to question everything—
and one's last is to come to terms with everything.

—GEORG CHRISTOPH LICHTENBERG (1742–99)

EMILY Perl Kingsley wrote a wonderful story in 1987 entitled "Welcome to Holland" in which she described how having a child with a disability is like planning a trip to Italy, but then landing unexpectedly in

Holland. The point of the story is that Holland may not be Italy, but it is still a nice place to be. Years later, Susan F. Rzucidlo wrote "Welcome to Beirut (Beginner's Guide to Autism)" about how having a child with an ASD is more like landing in Beirut with bombs dropping everywhere, with occasional ceasefires, but never knowing when the next enemy attack will begin, or where it will come from, or who the enemy really is. I sympathize.

AS a person close to someone with an ASD, your role is extremely important to him, even if he doesn't show it. Your main purpose will be to explain or translate to him the complexities of the neurotypical world and, in turn, to translate to the neurotypical world the eccentricities of the person with an ASD. You will be a sort of United Nations interpreter; a most important role to fill. Just as a stranger in a strange land needs to have customs explained to him, so will the individual with an ASD need explanations. And as the adopted country needs to have some understanding of the foreigner who has landed in their midst, so will the neurotypicals of our society need to learn from you about people with ASDs so as to be more accepting and tolerant of differences.

Parents need to do all they can to help their children, and as early as they can. Some will be "cured" or "recovered" thanks to interventions, and many will not be. The focus should be to teach them how to make sense of the world and give them the tools to function in it so that they can grow up to live independent, fulfilling lives.

As a parent you may have knowledge, but you will not always have control. You must learn to recognize that which you can change, and that which you cannot. And this advice holds true whether you are thinking about a behavior your child has or a policy your school district is sticking to. In some instances, the only thing you may be able to change is your attitude.

Professionals should recognize that autism includes the family. You may spend a few hours a day or month with this person, but for his loved ones, it is 24/7. You need to respect the fact that you may be an expert in your field, but while the person is growing up at home, the parent is still the expert on their child. Together you offer strong support and assistance to the person with autism.

Friends and extended family can lend support by learning about ASDs, and being open-minded. Do not judge the person with an ASD or the caregivers; realize that they may all be a bit overloaded. Continue to extend invitations and keep the lines of communication open. If you can help in any way, offer to do so. The offer will be appreciated even if it is not taken up.

The general public can be instrumental in how a person with an ASD or the caregivers feel in the community. Acceptance and a non-judgmental attitude toward those who act differently will do wonders to ease the stress. We are all part of the same community, and it does take a village to raise a child and make the place we live into a neighborhood.

SOME parents say that if it weren't for autism, they wouldn't have met the wonderful people they have come to know, that autism has given them a raison d'etre. As for me, I tend to believe that even without autism in my life, I would have met some wonderful people and become committed to some worthy cause. This is not to speak disparagingly of all the fantastic autism-related friends my family has made over the years. It is more a comment about the fact that I could do fine without having to deal with the individuals who don't "get it" or all the added stress of administrative paperwork, phone calls, and resource-searching one needs to do in order to get any assistance. I could still have a wonderful, rewarding life without autism.

What is certain, however, is that I have learned much about what is truly essential in life. I have learned how fortunate I am that my body and mind work in sync, and how much inner strength I possess. I have also learned literally to stop and smell the roses and to take pleasure in the simple moments of daily living between the bombs falling. I have learned that heightened senses can bring both pain and pleasure, and that passing the time of day by staring at dust particles in the sunlight, feeling the sand sift through your fingers, or your body floating weightless in a pool, doesn't seem so crazy after all. In fact, it's very relaxing. Try it sometime.

Appendix

SINCE 1967, the Autism Research Institute has been collecting parent ratings of the usefulness of the many interventions tried on their autistic children. The Parent Ratings of Behavioral Effects of Biomedical Interventions is a summary of the data from 21,500 parents who have completed questionnaires designed to collect such information. The Autism Treatment Evaluation Checklist (ATEC) is a form intended to measure the effects of a treatment on your child. Parents can fill this out before beginning any treatment and after a treatment to help rate its effectiveness. The filled-out form may be returned to the Autism Research Institute for free scoring and will be helpful in assessing the usefulness of interventions as perceived by parents.

PARENT RATINGS OF BEHAVIORAL EFFECTS OF BIOMEDICAL INTERVENTIONS
Autism Research Institute ● 4182 Adams Avenue ● San Diego, CA 92116

The parents of autistic children represent a vast and important reservoir of information on the benefits—and adverse effects—of the large variety of drugs and other interventions that have been tried with their children. Since 1967 the Autism Research Institute has been collecting parent ratings of the usefulness of the many interventions tried on their autistic children.

The following data have been collected from the more than 22,300 parents who have completed our questionnaires designed to collect such information. For the purposes of the present table, the parents responses on a six-point scale have been combined into three categories: "made worse" (ratings 1 and 2), "no effect" (ratings 3 and 4), and "made better" (ratings 5 and 6). The "Better:Worse" column gives the number of children who "Got Better" for each one who "Got Worse."

DRUGS	Got Worse[A]	No Effect	Got Better	Better: Worse	No. of Cases[B]	DRUGS	Got Worse[A]	No Effect	Got Better	Better: Worse	No. of Cases[B]
Aderall	39%	27%	35%	0.9:1	353	Klonapin[D]					
Amphetamine	47%	28%	25%	0.5:1	1186	Behavior	28%	35%	37%	1.3:1	169
Anafranil	32%	37%	31%	1.0:1	364	Seizures	38%	48%	14%	0.4:1	29
Antibiotics	31%	58%	11%	0.4:1	1668	Lithium	27%	43%	31%	1.2:1	395
						Luvox	30%	36%	35%	1.2:1	138
Antifungals[C]						Mellaril	28%	38%	33%	1.2:1	2040
Diflucan	7%	42%	51%	7.3:1	215	Mysoline[D]					
Nystatin	5%	48%	47%	9.5:1	791	Behavior	44%	41%	15%	0.3:1	133
Atarax	26%	53%	21%	0.8:1	453	Seizures	20%	58%	22%	1.1:1	59
Benadryl	24%	51%	25%	1.1:1	2573	Naltrexone	22%	45%	33%	1.5:1	207
Beta Blocker	18%	49%	33%	1.8:1	246	Paxil	29%	27%	43%	1.5:1	226
Buspar	26%	44%	30%	1.1:1	303	Phenergan	31%	44%	25%	0.8:1	249
Chloral						Phenobarb.[D]					
Hydrate	41%	37%	22%	0.5:1	390	Behavior	47%	37%	16%	0.3:1	1059
Clonidine	21%	31%	48%	2.3:1	1164	Seizures	17%	43%	41%	2.4:1	463
Clozapine	44%	40%	16%	0.4:1	89	Prolixin	33%	36%	31%	0.9:1	87
Cogentin	19%	53%	28%	1.5:1	153	Prozac	32%	32%	36%	1.1:1	1031
Cylert	45%	35%	20%	0.5:1	591	Risperidal	17%	29%	53%	3.1:1	471
Deanol	15%	55%	30%	2.0:1	197	Ritalin	45%	26%	29%	0.7:1	3650
						Secretin					
Depakene[D]						Intravenous	8%	44%	48%	5.7:1	250
Behavior	25%	44%	32%	1.3:1	901	Transderm.	10%	50%	40%	3.8:1	96
Seizures	12%	30%	58%	4.7:1	591	Stelazine	29%	44%	27%	1.0:1	417
Desipramine	37%	27%	37%	1.1:1	63	Tegretol[D]					
						Behavior	24%	45%	31%	1.3:1	1380
Dilantin[D]						Seizures	12%	33%	55%	4.5:1	740
Behavior	28%	49%	24%	0.9:1	1060	Thorazine	36%	40%	24%	0.7:1	902
Seizures	14%	36%	51%	3.8:1	383	Tofranil	30%	37%	33%	1.1:1	705
Felbatol	26%	46%	28%	1.1:1	39	Valium	35%	41%	24%	0.7:1	799
Fenfluramine	21%	51%	28%	1.4:1	455	Zarontin[D]					
Halcion	38%	31%	31%	0.8:1	45	Behavior	34%	44%	22%	0.6:1	131
Haldol	38%	27%	35%	0.9:1	1131	Seizures	20%	51%	29%	1.4:1	89
IVIG	11%	46%	43%	3.8:1	35	Zoloft	34%	32%	34%	1.0:1	240

A. "Worse" refers only to worse behavior. Drugs, but not nutrients, typically also cause physical problems if used long-term.
B. No. of cases is cumulative over several decades, so does not reflect current usage levels (e.g., Haldol is now seldom used).
C. Antifungal drugs are used only if autism is thought to be yeast-related.
D. Seizure drugs: top line behavior effects, bottom line effects on seizures
E. Calcium effects are not due to dairy-free diet; statistics are similar for milk drinkers and non-milk drinkers.

BIOMEDICAL/ NON-DRUG/ SUPPLEMENTS	Parent Ratings				
	Got Worse[A]	No Effect	Got Better	Better: Worse	No. of Cases[B]
Vitamin A	2%	58%	40%	20:1	398
Calcium[E]	2%	62%	36%	14:1	1084
Cod Liver Oil	3%	50%	46%	15:1	511
Colostrum	6%	57%	37%	6.0:1	213
Detox. (Chelation)	3%	27%	71%	27:1	153
Digestive Enzymes	4%	43%	53%	14:1	413
DMG	7%	51%	42%	5.7:1	4725
Fatty Acids	4%	45%	51%	14:1	379
5 HTP	10%	58%	32%	3.2:1	81
Folic Acid	4%	55%	41%	11:1	1188
Food Allergy Trtmnt	4%	37%	59%	13:1	362
Magnesium	6%	65%	29%	4.5:1	295
Melatonin[E]	9%	33%	58%	6.2:1	375
Pepcid	9%	60%	31%	3.3:1	75
SAMe	22%	54%	24%	1.1:1	37
St. Johns Wort	16%	62%	21%	1.3:1	61
TMG	15%	42%	43%	2.9:1	238
Transfer Factor	16%	54%	30%	1.9:1	50

BIOMEDICAL/ NON-DRUG/ SUPPLEMENTS	Parent Ratings				
	Got Worse[A]	No Effect	Got Better	Better: Worse	No. of Cases[B]
Vitamin B3	5%	54%	41%	8.7:1	526
Vit. B6 alone	8%	63%	30%	3.9:1	599
Vit. B6/Mag.	4%	49%	46%	10:1	5284
Vitamin C	2%	58%	39%	16:1	1408
Zinc	3%	53%	44%	16:1	931

SPECIAL DIETS

	Got Worse[A]	No Effect	Got Better	Better: Worse	No. of Cases[B]
Candida Diet	3%	45%	52%	17:1	641
Feingold Diet	2%	47%	50%	21:1	666
Gluten- /Casein- Free Diet	4%	33%	63%	16:1	933
Removed Chocolate	2%	49%	49%	30:1	1571
Removed Eggs	2%	60%	37%	16:1	949
Removed Milk Products/Dairy	2%	50%	48%	29:1	5159
Removed Sugar	2%	51%	47%	23:1	3486
Removed Wheat	2%	52%	46%	26:1	2842
Rotation Diet	3%	50%	47%	19:1	708

A. "Worse" refers only to worse behavior. Drugs, but not nutrients, typically also cause physical problems if used long-term.
B. No. of cases is cumulative over several decades, so does not reflect current usage levels (e.g., Haldol is now seldom used).
C. Antifungal drugs are used only if autism is thought to be yeast-related.
D. Seizure drugs: top line behavior effects, bottom line effects on seizures
E. Calcium effects are not due to dairy-free diet; statistics are similar for milk drinkers and non-milk drinkers.

Autism Treatment Evaluation Checklist (ATEC)
Bernard Rimland, Ph.D. and Stephen M. Edelson, Ph.D.
Autism Research Institute
4182 Adams Avenue, San Diego, CA 92116
fax: (619) 563-6840; www.autism.com/ari

For Office Use Only	
	Scorer
Can Vk.	
Study	I
Group	II
A	III
B	IV
C	Total

This form is intended to measure the effects of treatment. Free scoring of this form
is available on the Internet at: www.autism.com/atec

Name of Child _____ _____ ☐ Male

Age _____ ☐

Last   First   Female   Date of Birth _____

Please circle the letters to indicate how true each phrase is:

I. Speech/Language/Communication: [N] Not true   [S] Somewhat true   [V] Very true

N S V 1. Knows own name
N S V 2. Responds to 'No' or 'Stop'
N S V 3. Can follow some commands
N S V 4. Can use one word at a time (No!, Eat, Water, etc.)
N S V 5. Can use 2 words at a time (Don't want, Go home)
N S V 6. Can use 3 words at a time (Want more milk)
N S V 7. Knows 10 or more words
N S V 8. Can use sentences with 4 or more words
N S V 9. Explains what he/she wants
N S V 10. Asks meaningful questions
N S V 11. Speech tends to be meaningful/relevant
N S V 12. Often uses several successive sentences
N S V 13. Carries on fairly good conversation
N S V 14. Has normal ability to communicate for his/her age

II. Sociability: [N] Not descriptive   [S] Somewhat descriptive   [V] Very descriptive

N S V 1. Seems to be in a shell – you cannot reach him/her
N S V 2. Ignores other people
N S V 3. Pays little or no attention when addressed
N S V 4. Uncooperative and resistant
N S V 5. No eye contact
N S V 6. Prefers to be left alone
N S V 7. Shows no affection
N S V 8. Fails to greet parents
N S V 9. Avoids contact with others
N S V 10. Does not imitate
N S V 11. Dislikes being held/cuddled
N S V 12. Does not share or show
N S V 13. Does not wave 'bye bye'
N S V 14. Disagreeable/not compliant
N S V 15. Temper tantrums
N S V 16. Lacks friends/companions
N S V 17. Rarely smiles
N S V 18. Insensitive to other's feelings
N S V 19. Indifferent to being liked
N S V 20. Indifferent if parent(s) leave

III. Sensory/Cognitive Awareness: [N] Not descriptive   [S] Somewhat descriptive   [V] Very descriptive

N S V 1. Responds to own name
N S V 2. Responds to praise
N S V 3. Looks at people and animals
N S V 4. Looks at pictures (and T.V.)
N S V 5. Does drawing, coloring, art
N S V 6. Plays with toys appropriately
N S V 7. Appropriate facial expression
N S V 8. Understands stories on T.V.
N S V 9. Understands explanations
N S V 10. Aware of environment
N S V 11. Aware of danger
N S V 12. Shows imagination
N S V 13. Initiates activities
N S V 14. Dresses self
N S V 15. Curious, interested
N S V 16. Venturesome - explores
N S V 17. "Tuned in" — Not spacey
N S V 18. Looks where others are looking

IV. Health/Physical/Behavior: Use this code: [N] Not a Problem   [MI] Minor Problem   [MO] Moderate Problem   [S] Serious Problem

N MI MO S 1. Bed-wetting
N MI MO S 2. Wets pants/diapers
N MI MO S 3. Soils pants/diapers
N MI MO S 4. Diarrhea
N MI MO S 5. Constipation
N MI MO S 6. Sleep problems
N MI MO S 7. Eats too much/too little
N MI MO S 8. Extremely limited diet
N MI MO S 9. Hyperactive
N MI MO S 10. Lethargic
N MI MO S 11. Hits or injures self
N MI MO S 12. Hits or injures others
N MI MO S 13. Destructive
N MI MO S 14. Sound-sensitive
N MI MO S 15. Anxious/fearful
N MI MO S 16. Unhappy/crying
N MI MO S 17. Seizures
N MI MO S 18. Obsessive speech
N MI MO S 19. Rigid routines
N MI MO S 20. Shouts or screams
N MI MO S 21. Demands sameness
N MI MO S 22. Often agitated
N MI MO S 23. Not sensitive to pain
N MI MO S 24. "Hooked" or fixated on certain objects/topics
N MI MO S 25. Repetitive movements (stimming, rocking, etc.)

Resources

RESOURCES listed here are of two kinds: those that have been repeatedly mentioned in this book and merit being grouped here for easy access, and those that have not been mentioned at all but which are good additional resources. Many other excellent resources appear throughout the book.

ASD-Specific Organizations

Asperger Syndrome Education Network (ASPEN)
Website: www.aspennj.org
Provides support and information to families, individuals, and professionals, and has some local chapters.

Tony Attwood
Website: www.tonyattwood.com.au
Has great information on all things Asperger, as well as useful links.

Autism-Europe
Avenue E. Van Becelaere 26B, bte 21
B-1170 Brussels

Belgium

Phone: 01132 2-675-75-05; fax: 32(0)2-675-72-70

E-mail: president@autismeurope.org

Website: www.autismeurope.org

This European network groups nearly eighty parent associations in over thirty countries (of which fourteen are EU member states) whose main objective is to advance the rights of people with autism and their families and help improve their lives.

Autism Network International (ANI)

Website: http://ani.autistics.org/

A self-help and advocacy organization run by and for autistic people.

Autism Research Institute (ARI)

4182 Adams Avenue

San Diego, CA 92116

Phone: 619-281-7165; fax: 619-563-6840

Website: www.autismresearchinstitute.com

Besides conducting research, the ARI publishes the quarterly *Autism Research Review International,* which reviews the latest autism research. Bernard Rimland is the institute's director.

Autism Society of America (ASA)

7910 Woodmont Avenue, Suite 300

Bethesda, MD 20814-3067

Phone: 301-657-0881 or 800-3AUTISM (800-328-8476)

Website: www.autism-society.org

The largest autism organization in the U.S., the ASA has many local chapters, which are great sources of information. To find the one nearest you, look on the national website.

Center for the Study of Autism (CSA)

P.O. Box 4538

Salem, OR 97302

Website: www.autism.org

The CSA, directed by Stephen M. Edelson, Ph.D., provides information about autism to parents and professionals and conducts research on the efficacy of various therapeutic interventions. Much of the research is in collaboration with the Autism Research Institute.

Cure Autism Now Foundation (CAN)

5455 Wilshire Boulevard, Suite 715
Los Angeles, CA 90036
Phone: 323-549-0500 or 888-8AUTISM (888-828-8476); fax: 323-549-0547
Website: www.canfoundation.org
CAN is an organization of parents, clinicians, and leading scientists committed to accelerating the pace of biomedical research in autism through research, education, and outreach.

Families for Early Austism Treatment (FEAT)

P.O. Box 255722
Sacramento, CA 95865-5722
Phone: 916-843-1536
Website: www.feat.org
FEAT is a nonprofit that was founded in 1993 by a group of parents and professionals who wanted to improve the early intervention services that were offered in the Sacramento area. Currently, their mission is to provide world-class education, advocacy, and support for the Northern California autism community. Now other geographical areas in the United States have started chapters, and you can find links to them on the FEAT website.

National Alliance for Autism Research (NAAR)

99 Wall Street, Research Park
Princeton, NJ 08540
Phone: 888-777-NAAR (888-777-6227); fax 609-430-9163
Website: www.naar.org

Established by parents of children with autism concerned about the
limited amount of funding available for autism research, NAAR
is dedicated to funding and accelerating biomedical research fo-
cusing on autism spectrum disorders.

National Autism Organization (NAO)
P.O. Box 1547
Marion, SC 29571
Phone: 877-622-2884
Website: www.nationalautismassociation.org
The mission of NAO is to advocate, educate, and empower.

National Autistic Society (NAS)
393 City Road
London EC1V 1NG
England
Phone: 011-44-20-7833-2299; fax: 011-44-20-7833-9666
Website: www.nas.org.uk/
Great website with information for professionals, parents, and
adults with ASDs.

O.A.S.I.S. (Online Asperger Syndrome Information and Support)
Website: www.udel.edu/bkirby/asperger/
An excellent source of information about and for those with As-
perger's syndrome or those on the more able end of the spectrum.

Organization for Autism Research (OAR)
2111 Wilson Boulevard, Suite 600
Arlington, VA 22201
Phone: 703-351-5031
Website: www.researchautism.org/

Safe Minds
Website: www.safeminds.org

Gathers and shares information about the role of mercury in medicines.

Schafer Autism Report
9629 Old Placerville Road
Sacramento, CA 95827
E-mail: schafer@sprynet.com
Website: www.sarnet.org
Great online free daily newspaper published by Lenny Schafer about ASDs. Almost all the news appearing in print about ASDs anywhere in the English-speaking world ends up here.

Talk About Curing Autism (TACA)
Website: www.tacanow.com
This site has good information about therapies and treatments, great links to other websites and resources, and a special resource section for those who live in Southern California.

University Students with Autism and Asperger's Syndrome
Website: www.users.dircon.co.uk/~cns
This website is a great resource with useful information, including first-person accounts and links to other websites.

World Autism Organization (WAO)
Website: www.worldautism.org
Promotes a better quality of life for autistic people and their families throughout the world through public awareness, international conferences, and contact with organizations such as UNESCO, WHO, and the United Nations.

General Organizations

First Signs

P.O. Box 358

Merrimac, MA 01860

Phone: 978-346-4380; fax 978-346-4638

Website: www.firstsigns.org

Excellent website for parents and professionals who have concerns about a baby or child's development. Includes diagnostic guidelines and tools, as well as developmental milestones.

L.E.A.N. On Us: The Law Enforcement Awareness Campaign

P.O. Box 182338

Shelby Township, MI 48318-2338

Website: www.leanonus.org

This organization provides emergency (or first) responders with information and resources that will allow them to better serve individuals within their communities who are affected by hidden disabilities such as ASDs, Alzheimer's, Tourette's, epilepsy, deafness, and mental illness.

NICHCY (National Dissemination Center for Children with Disabilities)

Although the acronym NICHCY no longer fits this center's new name, it still has a great website with lists of every state's resources that might be of help, including: transition services, vocational education services, the Client Assistance Program, housing, and much more.

Website: www.nichcy.org

Government Agencies

Administration of Developmental Disabilities
Website: www.acf.dhhs.gov/programs/add

Federal Interagency Coordinating Council (FICC)
FICC Executive Director
330 C Street, S.W.
Room MES 3080
Washington, DC 20202-2570
Phone: 202-205-5507 ext. 3; fax: 202-206-0416
Website: www.fed-icc.org
Facilitates successful outcomes for young children with disabilities
and young children at risk for developing disabilities and their
families. Has good links to other resources and agencies.

Independent Living Research Utilization Project
The Institute for Rehabilitation and Research (TIRR)
2323 South Sheppard, Suite 1000
Houston, TX 77019
Phone: 713-520-0232 (voice) or 713-520-5136 (TTY)
E-mail: ilru@ilru.org
Website: www.ilru.org
At this website you can find the Statewide Independent Living
Council (SILC) in your state.

National Council on Independent Living (NCIL)
1916 Wilson Boulevard, Suite 209
Arlington, VA 22201
Phone: 703-525-3406 (voice) or 703-525-4153 (TTY)
E-mail: ncil@ncil.org
Website: www.ncil.org

This site has a nationwide directory of Centers for Independent Living (CILs), where you can find the ones in your state.

Social Security Administration (SSI)
Phone: 800-772-1213
Website: www.ssa.gov

State Council on Developmental Disabilities
Find the one in your state on the Administration of Developmental Disabilities website (www.acf.dhhs.gov/programs/add).

State protection and advocacy agencies
Know your rights. Every state has some sort of protection and advocacy agency. To find out your state's agency, look on the Autism Society of America website (www.autism-society.org).

U.S. Department of Education
Website: www.ed.gov

U.S. Department of Health and Human Services
Website: www.hhs.gov

Books

By People with ASDs

Aquamarine Blue 5: Personal Stories of College Students with Autism edited by Dawn Prince-Hughes
This is a collection of essays by different people on the spectrum. Most of the essays deal with college, the young adult years, and employment. The Aspie way of thinking comes through in these essays. Informative and gives a good idea of what they are going through.

Asperger Syndrome Employment Workbook by Roger N. Meyer

In this practical workbook, the author, who has Asperger's, encourages readers to explore their employment history and analyze their needs, talents, and strengths in order to identify the work they are best suited for.

Asperger Syndrome in the Family: Redefining Normal by Liane Holliday Willey

In this book, Liane shares with readers the perspective of an adult with Asperger's syndrome and what it means to be married and raise a family. Filled with wonderful explanations of the Aspie way of thinking in marriage and motherhood, this book gives good practical advice to couples where one spouse is neurotypical and the other has Asperger's.

Autism: An Inside-Out Approach by Donna Williams

In this book, Donna explains what it feels like to have autism, how her senses are affected, and what has been helpful to her in coping with some of the challenges. She describes useful strategies that may be helpful to others.

Autism-Asperger's and Sexuality: Puberty and Beyond by Jerry and Mary Newport

This book is a wonderful resource for the more able teenager and young adult, although parental guidance is recommended. The publishers suggest photocopying certain sections of the book to give to your child to read. In this way you can give him the information he is ready to handle. Jerry and Mary Newport are a married couple who both have Asperger's and share their experience and advice about puberty and sexuality.

Beyond the Wall: Personal Experiences with Autism and Asperger's Syndrome by Stephen Shore

Stephen shares much about himself now as an adult, and also as a child, talking about the bullying he was subjected to in school, sensory processing issues, dating, and marriage, among other subjects. He explains why college is heaven for him, and describes his experiences in working with children with autism and neurological impairments. He gives his thoughts on the world of work and university for people like him.

Developing Talents: Careers for Individuals with Asperger Syndrome and High Functioning Autism by Temple Grandin and Kate Duffy

This book explains how to prepare for an interview, how to prioritize work commitments, and how to deal with sensory overload. There is an informative and detailed section on the best jobs for people on the spectrum.

Freaks, Geeks and Asperger Syndrome by Luke Jackson

Here is a well-written account of an ASD teenager's experience and his recommendations to parents, professionals, and other teens with ASDs. If you only give your more able child with an ASD one book, this is the one you should get.

Martian in the Playground by Clare Sainsbury

This is very interesting reading for parents and professionals and will help them understand what many students with ASDs go through on a daily basis during their school years. Includes many helpful suggestions.

The Mind Tree by Tito Rajarshi Mukhopadhyay

In this book, Tito allows us a rare glimpse into the mind of someone with severe autism. He writes beautiful prose and poetry. His mother, Soma Mukhopadhyay, read to him constantly when he was little and developed a way to teach him to write and type by physically motoring him through the motions. Tito's descriptions of his feelings and what it is like to be trapped in a body that he cannot easily control help us to understand why some people with autism act as they do. Tito's book is a great reminder that you cannot assume what is going on inside the head of someone who is unable to communicate.

Nobody Nowhere by Donna Williams

This is Donna Williams's extraordinary first book, which takes you through her painful childhood and on to when she discovers that she has autism. This book is emotionally wrenching, so I would not recommend reading it when you are feeling overwhelmed. However, the last chapter, "An Outline of Language in My World," is a very helpful analysis of the meanings of some of her behaviors, which is interesting when trying to understand some of the behaviors of children with ASDs.

Pretending to Be Normal: Living with Asperger's Syndrome by Liane Holliday Willey

This is a wonderfully written account of how the world is perceived by someone growing up with Asperger's. Liane offers much insight into what she feels and what her senses tell her about the world. It is only when her daughter was diagnosed with Asperger's a few years ago that Liane recognized the traits in herself, although she had always known she was a bit different from others. Liane includes useful appendixes that cover such topics as explaining about yourself to others, survivor skills for college students, coping strategies, and employment options and responsibilities.

A Survival Guide for People with Asperger Syndrome by Marc Segar

Marc Segar passed away in 1997, but he left behind this wonderful guide, which covers many different areas including jobs and interviews, body language, boundaries, conversation, living with roommates, and finding the right friends. It is posted on this website: www.autismand-computing.org.uk/marc2.htm.

Thinking in Pictures: And Other Reports from My Life with Autism by Temple Grandin

In this book Temple shares with us how her thought processes work. A visual learner and thinker, she describes how that affected her growing up and even today. There is much valuable information about sensory processing, developing relationships, and empathy, which is useful in un-derstanding people with ASDs and how we can help them in their learn-ing. Temple includes an informative chapter on traditional medications and how they have been helpful.

Your Life Is Not a Label by Jerry Newport

Jerry has a wonderful sense of humor, and his positive outlook can only inspire us. This is a guide to help adults with ASDs handle the chal-lenge of living in a neurotypical world. Newport's can-do attitude is ap-parent in every aspect of his life. Diagnosed at age forty-seven, Jerry gives tips on everything from the small problems of everyday life to the big ones. This book has valuable information for all, including a great appendix section with resources and lists such as "Newport's Guide to Fast Money" and "The Newport 'Common Sense' Checklist for Autistic Personalities."

By Parents

Autistic Spectrum Disorders: Understanding the Diagnosis and Getting Help by Mitzi Waltz

This book written by a parent is very informative, with great appen-dixes in the back full of resources including information on medications and supplements. Mitzi's book covers education in all English-speaking countries.

The Boy Who Loved Windows by Patricia Stacey

This very good memoir tells the story of Patricia, her husband, Cliff, and their quest to find help for their son, which led them to Stanley Greenspan and his Floor Time approach.

Breaking Autism's Barriers: A Father's Story by Bill Davis

Bill does not take any prisoners in his fight to get an appropriate edu-cation for his son. Bill's philosophy and positive attitude come through clearly in this book. He and his wife organized a home program based on discrete trial teaching and left no stone unturned in their quest to get funding for it. Lessons can be learned from Bill's style and his questioning of professionals and authority figures, as well as his insistence on learning as much as he can about pertinent laws. This is the story of a couple who do all they can but are clearly accepting of who their son is. It is a very positive and uplifting read and highly recommended.

Facing Autism: Giving Parents Reasons for Hope and Guidance for Help by Lynn M. Hamilton

This book is highly recommended as a well-written account by a parent of her search for treatment, the options she chose for her son, and how she did it. More and more families and professionals are turning to a combination of treatments to help children with ASDs, and Lynn explains how and why. Applied behavior analysis, dietary and biomedical interventions, as well as education and communication needs are discussed. Her explanations about dietary and biomedical interventions are the easiest to read that I have seen anywhere. Lynn lists resources as well.

From the Heart: On Being the Mother of a Child with Special Needs edited by Jayne D. B. Marsh

Let Me Hear Your Voice: A Family's Triumph over Autism by Catherine Maurice

The first book written by a parent who used the Lovaas method with her two children and had great success, Catherine inspired many families to try ABA. Her description of all she endured on her search for help will come as no surprise to the parents who have been there. Her analysis of the treatments on offer at the time are very good.

The Oasis Guide to Asperger Syndrome: Advice, Support, Insight and Inspiration by Patricia Romanowski Bashe and Barbara L. Kirby

Barbara Kirby, who founded the award-winning O.A.S.I.S. (Online Asperger Syndrome Information and Support), wrote this excellent book on everything a parent who is bringing up a child with Asperger's should know, including informative chapters on medicines, the child in the social realm and in school, and the different options and interventions. There is a great section in the back entitled "54 Ways to Make the World a Better Place for Persons with Asperger Syndrome."

The Siege and **Exiting Nirvana** by Clara Claiborne Park

Clara has written two detailed books about raising her daughter with autism. *The Siege* covers the first eight years, and *Exiting Nirvana* talks about her daughter as an adult. Clara raised her child when knowledge about and help for autism were relatively unavailable.

Treating Autism: Parent Stories of Hope and Success edited by Stephen M. Edelson, Ph.D., and Bernard Rimland, Ph.D.

Uncommon Fathers: Reflections on Raising a Child with a Disability edited by Donald J. Meyer

For Educators and Parents

Activity Schedules for Children with Autism: Teaching Independent Behavior by Lynn E. McClannahan and Patricia J. Krantz

An Asperger Dictionary of Everyday Expressions by Ian Stuart-Hamilton

Asperger's Syndrome: A Guide for Parents and Professionals by Tony Attwood

This book outlines some of the strategies for communicating about emotions and learning about friendship.

Asperger Syndrome: A Practical Guide for Teachers by Val Cumine, Julia Leach, and Gil Stevenson

Autism: The Facts by Simon Baron-Cohen and Patrick Bolton

Autism: Preparing for Adulthood by Patricia Howlin

Children with Autism and Asperger Syndrome: A Guide for Practitioners and Carers by Patricia Howlin

Dangerous Encounters: Avoiding Perilous Situations with Autism by Bill Davis and Wendy Goldband Schunick
This excellent book is written with parents, shopkeepers, and emergency responders in mind. Davis, whose son has autism, gives good suggestions on how to teach your child about safety, a concept that is difficult for these children to learn. Explanations for people who work in the community about how to approach someone with autism are helpful.

A Mind of One's Own: A Guide to the Special Difficulties and Needs of the More Able Person with Autism or Asperger Syndrome by Digby Tantum

My Friend with Autism by Beverly Bishop

Overcoming Austism: Finding the Answers, Strategies, and Hope That Can Transform a Child's Life by Lynn Kern Koegel, Ph.D., and Claire LaZebnik

Primal Leadership: Realizing the Power of Emotional Intelligence by Daniel Goleman, Richard Boyatzis, and Annie McKee

Teaching Children with Autism to Mindread: A Practical Guide for Teachers and Parents by Patricia Howlin and Simon Baron-Cohen

For Families

Families: Applications of Social Learning to Family Life by Gerald R. Patterson

It Can Get Better . . . Dealing with Common Behavior Problems in Young Autistic Children by Paul Dickinson and Liz Hannah

Parents Are Teachers: A Child Management Program by Wesley C. Becker

Special Children, Challenged Parents: The Struggles and Rewards of Raising a Child with a Disability by Robert A. Naseef

For Adolescents

The Curious Incident of the Dog in the Nighttime by Mark Haddon
   A wonderful murder mystery appropriate for teenagers and adults. The detective and narrator of this book is fifteen and has Asperger's.

Talking Together about Growing Up: A Workbook for Parents of Children with Learning Disabilities by Lorna Scott and Lesley Kerr-Edwards
   This book takes a very practical approach by suggesting a range of activities parents can do with their children to help them understand the changes in their body during puberty.

What Is Asperger Syndrome, and How Will It Affect Me? A Guide for Young People by Martine Ives
   This is a very practical and useful booklet for adolescents, including more resources.

For Siblings

Everybody Is Different: A Book for Young People Who Have Brothers or Sisters with Autism by Fiona Bleach

Everything You Need to Know When a Brother or Sister is Autistic by Marsha Rosenberg

My Brother Is Different: A Book for Young Children Who Have Brothers and Sisters with Autism by Louise Gorrod

This book is aimed at younger siblings aged four to seven.

Siblings of Autism and Related Disorders

This website (www.siblingsofautism.com) was created by a sibling of a child with an ASD and is for siblings of autistic children. It has good information and lots of useful links.

Siblings of Children with Autism: A Guide for Families by Sandra L. Harris

Sibshops: Workshops for Siblings of Children with Special Needs by Donald J. Meyer and Patricia F. Vadasy

Sibshops

Information about Sibshops, a great support program for siblings of special needs children, is online at www.pyramidautismcenter.com/sibshop.

Views from Our Shoes: Growing Up with a Brother or Sister with Special Needs by Donald J. Meyer

For Partners

An Asperger Marriage by Gisela and Christopher Slater-Walker

Christopher has Asperger's and Gisela does not. In this book, each weighs in on the different areas that all couples grapple with but that are even further complicated by the fact that one of them has Asperger's. Understanding each other's viewpoints, conversation, romance, intimacy, and parenthood: all these are discussed. A great resource for "mixed" couples.

The Other Half of Asperger Syndrome: A Guide to Living in an Intimate Relationship with a Partner Who Has Asperger Syndrome by Maxine C. Aston

Maxine has worked as a couples counselor for "mixed" couples and who is married to someone who has Asperger's. She conducted research over two years for this book, which details in a somewhat clinical fashion her findings. An informative book.

Publishers/Distributors

The following publishers and distributors are a good place to investigate for more resources.

The Autism Asperger Publishing Company
P.O. Box 23173
Shawnee Mission, KS 66283-0173
Phone: 913-897-1004; fax: 913-681-9473
Website: www.asperger.net

Different Roads to Learning
12 West 18th Street, Suite 3E
New York, NY 10011

Phone: 800-853-1057
Website: www.difflearn.com

Future Horizons, Inc.
721 West Abram Street
Arlington, TX 76013
Phone: 800-489-0727; fax: 817-277-2270
E-mail: info@futurehorizons-autism.com
Website: www.futurehorizons-autism.com

Jessica Kingsley Publishers
116 Pentonville Road
London N1 9JB
England
Phone: 011-4420-7833-2307; fax: 011-4420-7837-2917
Website: www.jkp.com

Taylor & Francis/Routledge Books
Special Sales Department
29 West 35th Street, 10th floor
New York, NY 10001-2299
Phone: 800-797-3803, ext. 7856, or 212-216-7856;
    fax: 212-244-1563
E-mail: Brian.Roach@taylorandfrancis.com
Website: www.routledge-ny.com

The National Autistic Society (NAS)
NAS Publications
393 City Road
London EC1V 1NG
England
Phone: 011-4420-7833-2299; fax: 011-4420-7833-9666
Website: www.nas.org.uk

PRO-ED, Inc.
700 Shoal Creek Boulevard
Austin, TX 78757-6897
Phone: 800-897-3202; fax: 800-397-7633
Website: www.proedinc.com

Special Needs Project
324 State Street #H
Santa Barbara, CA 93101
Phone: 800-333-6867; fax 805-962-5087
Website: www.specialneeds.com

Woodbine House
6510 Bells Mill Road
Bethesda, MD 20817
Phone: 301-897-3570 or 800-843-7323; fax: 301-897-5838
Website: www.woodbinehouse.com

Bibliography

Aarons, M., and T. Gittens. *Autism: A Social Skills Approach for Children and Adolescents*. Winslow 1998

———. An Integrated Approach to Social Communication Problems.

Allen, A. (2002). "The Not So Crackpot Autism Theory." *New York Times,* November 8.

Allen, S. (2004). "Debate Grows on Vaccine-Autism Link." *Boston Globe,* http://www.boston.com/news/nation/articles (February 8).

All-Party Parliamentary Group on Primary Care and Public Health. (2000). *Conclusions on MMR Vaccine Safety.* UK: Heath Protection Agency.

American Psychiatric Association. (1994). "Disorders Diagnosed in Childhood: Autism Disorder—DSM-IV Criteria." *Psychologynet,* http://www.psychologynet.org/autism.html (January 28, 2002).

Anderson, W., S. Chitwood, and D. Hayden. (1997). *Negotiating the Special Education Maze: A Guide for Parents and Teachers.* Bethesda, MD: Woodbine House.

Aston, M. C. (2001). *The Other Half of Asperger Syndrome: A Guide to Living in an Intimate Relationship with a Partner Who Has Asperger Syndrome.* London: The National Autistic Society.

Attwood, T. (1998). *Asperger's Syndrome: A Guide for Parents and Professionals.* London: Jessica Kingsley Publishers.

———. (2002). *Why Does Chris Do That?* London: The National Autistic Society.

Ault, A. (2004). "Federal Panel Hears Testimony on Vaccinations and Autism." *New York Times,* February 10.

"Autism and Vaccines." (2004). *Wall Street Journal,* February 10. Schafer Autism Report, www.sarnet.org.

Autism Research Institute. *Autism Research Review International.* Vol. 14, No. 3. San Diego, CA: Autism Research Institute.

———. (2001). "Mercury Detoxification Consensus Group Position Paper." May. Autism Research Institute, http://www.autism.com/ari/mercury/consensus.html (January 14, 2003).

———. (2002). *Defeat Autism Now! 2002 Conference Presentations Book.* San Diego, CA: Autism Research Institute.

Autism Research Unit. "Autism and Vaccination." University of Sunderland Autism Research Unit, http://osiris/sunderland.ac.uk/autsim/vaccine.html (January 18, 2003).

———. "Descriptions of Common Vaccines Used." University of Sunderland Autism Research Unit, http://osiris.sunderland.ac.uk/autism/vaccine2.html (January 18, 2003).

Autism Society of America. (2004a). "Life after High School." Autism Society of America, http://www.autism-society.org.

———. (2004b). "Safety in the Home." Autism Society of America, http://www.autism-society.org.

Autism Treatment Center of America. "How Do the Son-Rise Program Profiles and Techniques Benefit Children with Special Needs?" Son-Rise Organization, http://www.son-rise.org/ (December 9, 2002).

Baker, B., and A. Brightman. (1997). *Steps to Independence: Teaching Everyday Skills to Children with Special Needs.* Baltimore, MD: Paul H. Brookes Publishing Co.

Baron-Cohen, S. (1995). *Mindblindness.* Cambridge, MA: MIT Press.

Bashe, P. R., and B. L. Kirby. (2001). *The Oasis Guide to Asperger Syndrome: Advice, Support, Insight and Inspiration.* New York: Crown Publishers.

Becker, W. C. (1971). *Parents Are Teachers: A Child Management Program.* Champaign, IL: Research Press.

Behavioral Intervention Association. "Exploring Treatment Options." Behavioral Intervention Association, http://bia4autism.org/ques3.php (December 7, 2002).

———. "Family Questions." Behavioral Intervention Association, http://www.bia4autism.org/ques2.php (December 7, 2002).

———. "Questions and Considerations Concerning Services for Young Children with Autism Spectrum Disorder." Behavioral Intervention Association, http://www.bia4autism.org/questions.php (December 7, 2002).

———. "Questions to Ask Providers." Behavioral Intervention Association, http://www.bia4autism.org/ques6.php (December 7, 2002).

———. (2002). *Fact File Two: Information on Subjects Including Benefits, Education, Leisure and Family Support.* Reading, UK: Berkshire Autistic Society.

Bernard, S., A. Enayati, L. Redwood, H. Roger, and T. Binstock. "Autism: A Novel Form of Mercury Poisoning." Autism Research Institute, http://www.autism.com/ari/mercury.html (January 22, 2003).

Bicknell, A. (1999). *Independent Living for Adults with Autism and Asperger Syndrome: A Guide for Families of People with Autistic Spectrum Disorders.* London: The National Autistic Society.

Bishop, B. (2003). *My Friend with Autism.* Arlington, TX: Future Horizons.

Billingsley, B. S. (2003). *Special Education Teacher Retention and Attrition: A Critical Analysis of the Literature.* Gainesville: University of Florida, Center on Personnel Studies in Special Education.

Bleach, F. (2001). *Everybody Is Different: A Book for Young People Who Have Brothers or Sisters with Autism.* London: The National Autistic Society.

Bobbitt, S. A., E. E. Boe, and L. H. Cook. (1997). "Whither Didst Thou Go? Retention, Reassignment, Migration, and Attrition of Special and General Education Teachers from a National Perspective." *Journal of Special Education.*

Bolton, P., M. McGuire, and S. Whitehead. (2001). *A Life in the Community... Supporting Adults with Autism and Other Developmental Disorders Whose Needs are Challenging.* Cambridge, UK: University of Cambridge.

Bondy, A., and L. Frost. (2002). *A Picture's Worth: PECS and Other Visual Communication Strategies in Autism.* Bethesda, MD: Woodbine House.

Boscardin, M. L., and C. Lashley. (2003). "Special Education Administration at a Crossroads: Availability, Licensure, and Preparation of Special Education Administrators." Gainesville: University of Florida, Center on Personnel Studies in Special Education.

Boyd, R. S. (2002). *The Epidemiology of Autism in California.* Davis, CA: UC Davis MIND Institute.

Boyles, S. (2004). "Study Suggests Vaccine, Autism Link: Thimerosal Can Disrupt Neurological Development, Researchers Say." February. WebMD Medical News.my .webmd.com.

Brownell, M. T., J. R. McNellis, M. D. Miller, and S. W. Smith. (2004). "Attrition in Special Education: Why Teachers Leave the Classroom and Where They Go." Questia, http://www.questia.com.

Bundy, J. (2004). "University Program Helps Autistic Students," Associated Press, February.

California Health and Human Services Agency. (1999). "Changes in the Population of Persons with Autism and Pervasive Developmental Disorders in California's Developmental Services System: 1987–1998." Department of Developmental Services: Report to the Legislature.

———. (2003). "Autistic Spectrum Disorders: Changes in the California Caseload: An Update: 1999 through 2002." April. Sacramento, CA: Department of Developmental Services.

Calman, K. "MMR Vaccine Is Not Linked to Crohn's Disease or Autism: Conclusion of an Expert Scientific Seminar: March 24, 1998." Autism Research Unit, http://osiris.sunderland.ac.uk/autism/vaccine.html (January 18, 2003).

CAN Consensus Group. "Autism Screening and Diagnostic Evaluation: CAN Consensus Statement by the CAN Consensus Group." Cure Autism Now, http://www.cure autismnow.org/aboutcan/consensu.cfm (October 30, 2002).

Carlson, E., L. Chen, K. Schroll, and S. Klein. (2003). "SPeNSE: Study of Personnel Needs in Special Education." U.S. Department of Education Office of Special Education, WESTAT.

Carter, J., C. Fore, and C. Martin. (2003). *Why Do Special Education Teachers Leave the Field? Possible Methods to Increase Retention.* Athens: University of Georgia.

Cave, S., and D. Mitchell. 2001. *What Your Doctor May Not Tell You about Children's Vaccinations.* New York: Warner Books.

Center on Personnel Studies in Special Education. (2003). "Teacher Education: What Difference Does It Make?" Center on Personnel Studies in Special Education, http://www.copsse.org.

Chambers, J., J. Shkolnik, and M. Perez. (2003). "Total Expenditures for Students with Disabilities, 1999–2000: Spending Variation by Disability." June. Washington, DC: American Institutes for Research, Special Education Expenditure Project.

Chassman, M. (1999). *One on One: Working with Low-Functioning Children with Autism and Other Developmental Disabilites.* Verona, WI: IEP Resources Publication.

Claiborne Park, C. (1967). *The Siege: A Family's Journey into the World of an Autistic Child.* New York: Little, Brown and Co.

———. (2001). *Exiting Nirvana: A Daughter's Life with Autism.* New York: Little, Brown and Co.

Collier, V. (2002). "Raising Teenagers with Autism." *Advocate* 35:18–24.

Communication (The Magazine of the National Autistic Society). Autumn 2002, 36:3.

Community Alliance for Special Education, and Protection and Advocacy, Inc. (2004). *Special Education Rights and Responsibilities.* Sacramento, CA: Author.

Community Services for Autistic Adults and Children. (2004). "CSAAC's Vocational Program." CSAAC, http://www.csaac.org/voc.htm.

Crook, W. (1986). *The Yeast Connection.* New York: Vintage Books.

Cure Autism Now Foundation. "Cure Autism Now Science Watch." Cure Autism Now Foundation, http://www.canfoundation.org/sciwatch/sciwatch.cfm (January 24, 2003).

Davis, B. (2001). *Breaking Autism's Barriers: A Father's Story.* London: Jessica Kingsley Publishers.

Davis, B., and W. Goldband Schunick. (2002). *Dangerous Encounters: Avoiding Perilous Situations with Autism.* London: Jessica Kingsley Publishers.

Defeat Autism Now! (DAN!). (2002). *Fall DAN! 2002 Conference: October 25–27.* San Diego, CA: Autism Research Institute.

Dental Amalgam Mercury Syndrome. (2004). "Virginia Introduces Mercury Amalgam Bill." Press release, February.

Department for Education and Skills: Autism Working Group. (2002). *Autism Spectrum Disabilities Newsletter.* (2001), "Supporting Adults with Autism in the Community." Paul Brookes Publishing Co. http://www.pbrookes.com.

"Diversity in Funding: Strategies Vary by State." *Education Week,* http://www.edweek.org (January 8, 2004).

Donaldson, L., J. Smith, and S. Mullally. (2001). *Current Vaccine and Immunization Issues.* October 15. Washington, DC: U.S. Department of Health.

Edelson, M. "Theory of Mind." Center for the Study of Autism, http://www
.autism.org/mind.html (March 23, 2003).

Edelson, S., and B. Rimland. *The Efficacy of Auditory Integration Training: Summaries and Critiques of 28 Reports (January 1993–May 2001)*. San Diego, CA: Autism Research Institute.

Edgar, J. (1999). *Love, Hope and Autism*. London: The National Autistic Society.

Editorial Projects in Education. (2004). "Count Me In: Special Education in an Era of Standards. January." *Education Week*, www.edweek.org.

The Council for Exceptional Children. (2004). "Finding Effective Intervention and Personnel Preparation Practices for Students with Autism Spectrum Disorders." Yellowbrix.com, http://infobrix.yellowbrix.com.

Falvey, M. A. (1989). *Community-Based Curriculum: Instructional Strategies for Students with Severe Handicaps*. Baltimore, MD: Paul H. Brookes Publishing Co.

"Famous People with Autistic Traits; Fictional, Real, Historical and Contemporary Celebrities." Geocities, http://www.geocities.com/WestHollywood/Stonewall/4502/famousac.html (March 20, 2002).

"Federal Funding for the IDEA." Alexandria, VA: National Association of State Directors of Special Education.

Feingold, B. (1975). *Why Your Child Is Hyperactive*. London: Random House.

First Coast News. (2003). "CDC Knew of Potential Link between Vaccines, Autism." First Coast News, http://www.firstcoastnews.com/news (February 13, 2004).

Fombonne, E. (2003). "The Prevalence of Autism." *Journal of the American Medical Association* 289:87–89.

Fowler, J., and E. Evans. (2002). *A Guide to the Education Act 2002*. London: Advisory Centre for Education and the Education Network.

Friend, M. (1997). "Educational Partnerships through Effective Communication: Workshop for North County CAC March 10."

Frith, U. (1989). "How Autism Was First Recognized." American Medical Association, http://www.ama.org.br/autism-history.html (January 17, 2002).

Georgia Institute of Technology Research News. "Vaccine Risk Acceptance Depends on What You Do and Don't Know." American Association for the advancement of Science (AAAS), http://www.eurekalert.org/pubnews.php (February 2004).

Goldblatt, E., and D. Mentink. (2004). *18 Tips for Getting Quality Special Education Services for Your Child*. Oakland, CA: Protection and Advocacy.

Goleman, D. (1998). "What Makes a Leader?" *Harvard Business Review*, Nov./Dec., 93–102.

Goleman, D., R. Boyatzis, and A. McKee. (2002). *Primal Leadership: Realizing the Power of Emotional Intelligence*. Boston MA: Harvard Business School Press.

Goode, E. (2004). "More and More Autism Cases, Yet Causes Are Much Disputed." *New York Times*, January 26.

———. (2004). "Lifting the Veils of Autism, One by One by One." *New York Times*, February 24.

Grandin, T. (1995). *Thinking in Pictures: And Other Reports from My Life with Autism.* New York: Bantam Doubleday Dell.

———. (1996). "Making the Transition from the World of School into the World of Work." Center for the Study of Autism, http://www.autism.org/temple/transition.html (February 10, 2003).

———. (1998). "An Inside View of Autism." Center for the Study of Autism, http://www.autism.org/temple/inside.html (November 14, 2002).

———. (1999). "Choosing the Right Job for People with Autism or Asperger's Syndrome." Center for the Study of Autism, http://www.autism.org/temple/jobs.html (November 14, 2002).

———. (2000). "My Experiences with Visual Thinking Sensory Problems and Communication Difficulties." Center for the Study of Autism, http://www.autism.org/temple/visual.html (November 14, 2002).

———. (2002). "Teaching Tips for Children and Adults with Autism." Center for the Study of Autism, http://www.autism.org/temple/tips.html (February 10, 2003).

———. "Evaluating the Effects of Medication." Center for the Study of Autism, http://www.autism.org/temple/meds.html (February 13, 2003).

Grandin, T., and M. M. Scariano. (1986). *Emergence: Labeled Autistic.* Novato, CA: Arena Press.

Gray, C. (1993). *The Original Social Story Book.* Arlington, TX: Future Horizons.

———. (1994a). *Comic Strip Conversations: Colorful Illustrated Interactions with Students with Autism and Related Disorders.* Arlington TX: Future Horizons.

———. (1994b). *The New Social Story Book: Illustrated Edition.* Jenison, MI: Jenison High School.

Greenspan, S. I., and S. Wieder. (1998). *The Child with Special Needs: Encouraging Intellectual and Emotional Growth.* Reading, MA: Perseus Books.

Gross, J. (2004). "As Autism Cases Rise, Parents Run Frenzied Race to Get Help." *New York Times,* http://www.nytimes.com/2004/02.30/nyregion/30AUTI.html.

Gutstein, S. E. (2001). *Autism/Asperger's: Solving the Relationship Puzzle.* Arlington, TX: Future Horizons.

Haines, G. "Vladimir Nabakov." Internet Obituary Network, http://obits.com/nabakov.html (March 20, 2002).

Hall, K. (1988). *Asperger Syndrome: The Universe and Everything.* London: Jessica Kingsley Publishers.

Hamilton, L. M. (2000). *Facing Autism: Giving Parents Reasons for Hope and Guidance for Help.* Colorado Springs, CO: Waterbrook Press.

Hammer, E. (1996). "Anticipatory Guidance for Parents of Children with Disabilities: What Happens to Families When a Child Has Chronic Problems?" Functional Skills Screening Inventory, http://www.winfssi.com/Anticipatory.html (September 8, 2002).

Harris, S. L. (1994). *Siblings of Children with Autism: A Guide for Families.* Bethesda, MD: Woodbine House.

Heath, S. (2004). "Wrightslaw: No Child Left Behind." Harbor House Law Press, http://www.harborhouselaw.com.

Heflin, J., and R. Simpson. (1998). "Interventions for Children and Youth with Autism: Prudent Choices in a World of Exaggerated Claims and Empty Promises. Part I: Intervention and Treatment Option Review." *Focus on Autism and Other Developmental Disabilities* 13:194–211.

Helps, S., I. C. Newsom-Davis, and M. Callias. (1999). *Autism: The Teacher's View.* London: The National Autistic Society.

Herlihy, W. C. (2004). *Phase 3 Study of Secretin for Autism Fails to Meet Dual Primary Endpoints Development of Secretin for Schizophrenia to Continue.* Waltham, MA: RepliGen.

Hersey, J. (1996). *Why Can't My Child Behave? Why Can't She Cope? Why Can't He Learn?* Orlando, FL: Pear Tree Press.

Hesmondhalgh, M., and C. Breakey. (2001). *Access and Inclusion for Children with Autistic Spectrum Disorders: Let Me In.* London: Jessica Kingsley Publishers.

Heywood, S. (2004). "Parents Push for Vaccine Options in British Columbia." *Parksville Qualicum News,* February.

High Performance/Organizational Effectiveness Unit. "Effective Meeting Guidelines." San Diego, CA: Office of the Deputy Superintendent San Diego City Schools.

Holmes, A. (2000). "Autism Treatment: Chelation of Mercury for the Treatment of Autism." Healing Arts, http://www.healing-arts.org/children/holmes/html (accessed January 22, 2003).

Holmes, D. L. (1998). *Autism through the Lifespan: The Eden Model.* Bethesda, MD: Woodbine House.

Hoopmann, K. (2001). *Of Mice and Aliens: An Asperger Adventure.* London: Jessica Kingsley Publishers.

Howlin, P. (1997). *Autism: Preparing for Adulthood.* London: Routledge.

Howlin, P., and S. Baron-Cohen. (1998). *Teaching Children with Autism to Mindread: A Practical Guide for Teachers and Parents.* London: John Wiley and Sons.

Immunization Safety Review Committee. (2001). "Measles-Mumps-Rubella Vaccine and Autism." Institute of Medicine Review. Washington, DC: The National Academy of Sciences, courtesy of the National Academies Press.

"Iowa State Senator Offers Bill to Ban Immunizations Containing Mercury-Based Preservatives." *Sioux City Journal,* http://siouxcityjournal.com/articles (February 12, 2004).

Ives, M. (1999). *What Is Asperger Syndrome, and How Will It Affect Me? A Guide for Young People.* London: The National Autistic Society.

Jackson, L. (2002). *Freaks, Geeks and Asperger Syndrome: A User Guide to Adolescence.* London: Jessica Kingsley Publishers.

Jackson, L., and M. Brenton. (2001). *A User Guide to the GF/CF Diet for Autism, Asperger Syndrome and AD/HD.* London: Jessica Kingsley Publishers.

Kaufman, B. N. (1979). *Son-Rise.* Novato, CA: HJ Kramer.

———. (1995). *Son-Rise: The Miracle Continues.* Novato, CA: HJ Kramer.

Kingsley, E. P. (1987). *Welcome to Holland.* Down's syndrome, http://www.nas.com/downsyn/holland.html.

Kirkey, S. (2004). "Vaccine Additive Linked to Brain Damage in Children." February. Vancouver, Canada: CanWest News Service.

Klein, F. (2001). "Autistic Advocacy." Frank Klein website, http://home.att.net/~ascaris1/index.html (September 8, 2002).

Kranowitz, C. S. (1998). *The Out-of-Sync Child*. New York: Perigee Books.

Kübler-Ross, E. (1997). *On Death and Dying: What the Dying Have to Teach Doctors, Nurses, Clergy and Their Own Families*. New York: Scribner.

Leaf, R., and J. McEachin. (1999). *A Work in Progress: Behavior Management Strategies and a curriculum for Intensive Behavioural Treatment of Autism*. New York: DRL Books.

Lewis, L. (1998). *Special Diets for Special Kids*. Arlington, TX: Future Horizons.

Lord, C., and J. P. McGee, eds. (2001). *Educating Children with Autism*. Washington, DC: National Academies Press.

Lovaas, O. I. (1981). *Teaching Developmentally Disabled Children: The ME Book*. Austin, TX: PRO-ED.

Malkin, M. (2004). "Beware of Vaccine Bullies." World Net Daily, http://www.worldnetdaily.com/news.

Manning, A. (2004). "Possible Role in Disorders Still Unclear." *USA Today*, February 10.

Markova, D., and A. Powell. (1992). *How Your Child Is Smart: A Life-Changing Approach to Learning*. York Beach, ME: Conari Press.

Marsh, D. B. (1995). *From the Heart: On Being the Mother of a Child with Special Needs*. Bethesda, MD: Woodbine House.

Maurice, C. (1993). *Let Me Hear Your Voice: A Family's Triumph Over Autism*. New York: Alfred A. Knopf.

Maurice, C., G. Green, and S. Luce. (1996). *Behavioral Intervention for Young Children with Autism. A Manual for Parents and Professionals*. Austin, TX: PRO-ED.

McCandless, J. (2003). *Children with Starving Brains: A Medical Treatment Guide for Autism Spectrum Disorder*. Bramble Co.

McClannahan, L., and P. Krantz. (1998). *Activity Schedules for Children with Autism: Teaching Independent Behavior*. Bethesda, MD: Woodbine House.

McGill-Smith, P. (1997). "You Are Not Alone: For Parents When They Learn That Their Child Has a Disability." *News Digest* 20:1–53.

McLesky, J., N. Tyler, and S. Flippin. (2003). "The Supply and Demand for Special Education Teachers: A Review of the Research Regarding the Nature of the Chronic Shortage of Special Education." October. Gainesville, FL: University of Florida, Center on Personnel Studies in Special Education.

Medical Research Council. (2001). "MRC Review of Autism Research: Epidemiology and Causes." December. London: Medical Research Council.

Mehl-Madrona, L. (2001). "Origins of the Mercury Controversy." Healing Arts, http://www.healing-arts.org/children/vaccines/vaccines-mercury.html (January 22, 2003).

Melberg Schwier, K., and D. Hingsburger. (2000). *Sexuality: Your Sons and Daughters with Intellectual Disabilities*. Baltimore, MD: Paul H. Brookes Publishing Co.

"Mercury Study Shows Permanent Damage to Kids." (2004). Reuters, February 10.

Mesibov, G. "What Is TEACCH?" TEACCH website, http://www.teacch.com/about us.html (November 14, 2002).

Meyer, D. (1995). *Uncommon Father: Reflections on Raising a Child with a Disability.* Bethesda, MD: Woodbine House.

———. (1997). *Views from Our Shoes: Growing Up with a Brother or Sister with Special Needs.* Bethesda, MD: Woodbine House.

Meyer, D. J., and P. F. Vadasy. (1994). *SibShops: Workshops for Siblings of Children with Special Needs.* Baltimore MD: Brookes.

Meyer, R. N. (2001). *Asperger Syndrome Employment Workbook: An Employment Workbook for Adults with Asperger Syndrome.* London: Jessica Kingsley Publishers.

Mockler Casper, C., K. Timmons, and B. Wagner Brust. (2001). *Emotional Intelligence Leader's Guide.* Carlsbad, CA: CRM Learning.

Moss, C. K. "Ludwig Van Beethoven: A Musical Titan." Classical Music website, http://classicalmus.hispeed.com/articles/beethoven.html (March 21, 2002).

Moyes R., and S. Moreno. (2001). *Incorporating Social Goals in the Classroom: A Guide for Teachers and Parents of Children with High-Functioning Autism and Asperger Syndrome.* London: Jessica Kingsley Publishers.

Mukhopadhyay, T. R. (2003). *The Mind Tree.* New York: Arcade Publishing.

Myles, B. S., and D. Adreon. (2001). *Asperger Syndrome and Adolescent: Practical Solutions for School Success.* Shawnee Mission, KS: Autism Asperger Publishing Company.

Nally, B. (1999). *Diagnosis: Reactions in Families.* London: The National Autistic Society.

———. (2000). *Experiences of the Whole Family.* London: The National Autistic Society.

Nally, B., and E. V. Bliss. (2000). *Recognizing and Coping with Stress.* London: The National Autistic Society.

Naseef, R. A. (2001). *Special Children, Challenged Parents: The Struggles and Rewards of Raising a Child with a Disability.* Baltimore, MD: Paul H. Brookes Publishing Co.

National Autism Association. (2004). "National Autism Group Urges CNN Coverage of Autism/Vaccine Hearing in D.C." National Autism Association, http://nationalautismassociation.org.

National Autistic Society. "The Special Educational Needs and Disability Act 2001 (SENDA)." National Autistic Society, http://www.nas.org.uk/policy/parl/westminster/SENDA.html.

———. (1991). *Approaches to Autism: An Easy-to-Use Guide to Many and Varied Approaches to Autism.* London: The National Autistic Society.

———. (1999). *Words Will Really Hurt Me: How to Protect Your Child from Bullying: A Guide for Parents and Carers.* London: The National Autistic Society.

———. (2001a). *The Autistic Spectrum: A Parent's Guide.* London: The National Autistic Society.

————. (2001b). "Briefing on Mercury and Autism." September. National Autistic Society fact sheet. London: The National Autistic Society.

————. (2002). *The Autism Handbook*. London: The National Autistic Society.

National Clearinghouse for Professions in Special Education. (1998). "Retention of Special Education Professionals: A Practical Guide of Strategies and Activities for Educators and Administrators." The Council for Exceptional Children.

National Institute of Mental Health. (2003). "Report to Congress on Autism." January. Washington, DC: U.S. Department of Health and Human Services.

National Research Council. (2001). *Educating Children with Autism*. Washington, DC: National Academies Press.

"Neal Halsey Reaffirms Vaccines Do Not Cause Autism." (2002). *New York Times*, November 14.

Newport, J. (2001) *Your Life Is Not a Label*. Arlington, TX: Future Horizons.

Newport, J., and M. Newport. (2002). *Autism-Asperger's and Sexuality: Puberty and Beyond*. Arlington, TX: Future Horizons.

Newport, M. (2002). *Education and Job Worthiness*. Arlington, TX: Future Horizons.

Nuehring, M.L., and P.L. Sitlington. (2003). "Transition as a Vehicle: Moving from High School to an Adult Vocational Service Provider." *Journal of Disability Policy Studies* 14 (1):23–25.

O.A.S.I.S. (2004). "Adult Issues, Resources and Contributions From and For Individuals with AS and Autism." O.A.S.I.S., www.udel.edu/bkirby/asperger/personswith .html.

Ogaz, N. (2002). *Buster and the Amazing Daisy: Adventures with Asperger Syndrome*. London: Jessica Kingsley Publishers.

O'Hare, A. (2002). "Severing the Link Between MMR and Autism." *Journal of the Royal College of Physicians of Edinburg* 32:167–69.

Olmo, F. (2004). "Powers That Be Should See the Needs of Frankie." *Los Angeles Times*, http://latimes.com (February 19, 2004).

O'Neill, J.L. (1999). *Through the Eyes of Aliens: A Book about Autistic People*. London: Jessica Kingsley Publishers.

O'Toole, M. "Boston Higashi School: Daily Life Therapy." Parents and Professionals Autism website, http: www.autismni.org/bostonhig.html (January 15, 2003).

Ott, J. (2000). *Health and Light*. Ariel Press.

Paige, R. (2003). "Principles in Reauthorizing IDEA." Wrightslaw, http://wrightslaw .com/news/2003.

Pangborn, J.B., and S. Baker. (2002). *Biomedical Assessment Options for Children with Autism and Related Problems: A Consensus Report of the Defeat Autism Now! (DAN!) Scientific Report*. San Diego, CA: Autism Research Institute.

Patterson, G.R. (1971). *Families: Applications of Social Learning to Family Life*. Champaign, IL: Research Press.

Perner, L. (2002). *Preparing to Be Nerdy Where Nerdy Can Be Cool: College Planning for the High Functioning Student with Autism*. Indianapolis, IN: Autism Society of America.

Pollack, A. (2004). "Trials End Parents' Hopes for Autism Drug Secretin." *New York Times,* http://www.nytimes.com/2004/01/06/heatlh/06AUTI.html?pagewanted=1.

Pollack, R. (1997). *The Creation of Dr. B: A Biography of Bruno Bettelheim.* New York: Simon and Schuster.

Pondrom, S. (2003). "UCSD Researchers Find Brain Overgrowth during First Year of Life in Autism." *Journal of the American Medical Association,* July 15.

Powell, A. (2002). *Taking Responsibility: Good Practice Guidelines for Services—Adults with Asperger Syndrome.* London: The National Autistic Society.

Powers, M. D. (1989). *Children with Autism: A Parent's Guide.* Bethesda, MD: Woodbine House.

Prince-Hughes, D. (2002). *Aquamarine Blue 5.* Athens: Ohio University Press and Swallow Press.

———. (2003). "Understanding College Students with Autism." Washington, DC: George Washington University HEATH Resource Center.

Rapp, D. (1996). *Is This Your Child's World? How You Can Fix the Schools and Homes That Are Making Your Child Sick.* New York: Bantam Books.

Rauscher, M. (2004). "Again, No Link Between MMR Vaccine and Autism." Reuters, February.

Rimland, B. (1964). *Infantile Autism: The Syndrome and Its Implications for a Neural Theory of Behavior.* Englewood Cliffs, NJ: Prentice Hall.

———. (1993). "Plain Talk about PDD and the Diagnosis of Autism." *Autism Research Review International* 7:3.

———. (2000). "The Autism Epidemic, Vaccinations, and Mercury." *Journal of Nutritional & Environmental Medicine.*

———. (2000). "The Most Airtight Study in Psychiatry? Vitamin B6 in Autism." *Autism Research Review International* 14:3–5.

———. (2003). "The MMR/Autism Controversy: Should We Believe the IOM?" January 24. Autism Research Institute, www.autism.com/ari/editorials/iom.html.

Robertson, A. (2004). "WSJ Covering Its Tracks?" February 24. Schafer Autism Report, www.sarnet.org.

Rollens, R. (2003). "Increases in Autism Diagnosis in California Keep Rising." FEAT-NEWS, http://www.feat.org (January 21, 2003).

Rosenberg, M. S. (2000). *Everything You Need to Know; When a Brother or Sister Is Autistic.* New York: Rosen Publishing Group.

Rzucidlo, S. *WELCOME TO BEIRUT (Beginner's Guide to Autism).* http://home.earthlink.net/~abaantonia/beirut.htm

Sacks, O. (1995). *An Anthropologist on Mars: Seven Paradoxical Tales.* New York: Alfred A. Knopf.

Sainsbury, C. (2000). *Martian in the Playground.* London: The Book Factory.

Satkiewicz-Gayhardt, V., B. Peerenboom, R. Campbell, and K. Belliveau. (1997). *Crossing Bridges: A Parent's Perspective on Coping after a Child Is Diagnosed with Autism/PDD.* Stratham, NH: Potential Unlimited Publishing.

Schafer, L. (2002). "Autism: A Hit and Run Epidemic." Schafer Autism Report, http://www.sarnet.org.

———. (2004). "When *Wall Street Journal* Goes Nuclear, Might Wall Street Be Nervous about Something?" Schafer Autism Report, http://www.sarnet.org.

The Scottish Parliament Health and Community Care Committee. (2001). "Report on Petition PE 145 calling for an Inquiry into Issues Surrounding the Alleged Relationship between the Combined Measles Mumps and Rubella Vaccine and Autism." Edinburgh, Scotland: Health and Community Care Committee, 8th Report. Scottish Parliamentary Copyright material is reproduced with the permission of the Queen's Printer for Scotland on behalf of the Scottish Parliamentary Corporate Body.

Segar, M. (1997). "A Survival Guide for People with Asperger Syndrome." Autism and Computing Organization, http://www.autismandcomputing.org.uk/marc2.html (January 18, 2003).

Semon, B., and L. Kornblum. (2002). *Feast without Yeast.* Madison: Wisconsin Institute of Nutrition.

Seroussi, K. (2002). *Unraveling the Mystery of Pervasive Developmental Disability.* New York: Broadway Books.

Shattock, P., P. Whiteley, and D. Savery. (2002). *Autism as a Metabolic Disorder: Guidelines for Gluten and Casein-Free Dietary Intervention.* Sunderland, UK: University of Sunderland Autism Research Unit.

Shaw, W. (2001). *Biological Treatment for Autism and PDD.* Lenexa, KS: Great Plains Laboratory.

Shellenberger, S., and M. Williams. (1992). *An Introduction to "How Does Your Engine Run": The Alert Program and Self-Regulation.* Albuquerque, NM: Therapy Works, Inc.

Sherman, D. "Autism: Your Child's Legal Rights to a Special Education." Autism Law website, http://www.aboutaustimlaw.com.

Shore, S. "Survival in the Workplace." www.autismtoday.com/survivalwork.htm.

———. (1961). *Beyond the Wall: Personal Experiences with Autism and Asperger's Syndrome.* Shawnee Mission, KS: Autism Asperger Publishing Co.

———. (2002). "Dating, Marriage and Autism." *Advocate* 35:24–28.

Siegel, B. (1996). *The World of the Autistic Child: Understanding and Treating Autistic Spectrum Disorder.* Oxford, UK: Oxford University Press.

Sinclair, J. (1993). "Don't Mourn for Us." *Our Voice* (Newsletter of Autism Network International) 1:3.

Slater-Walker, G., and C. Slater-Walker. (1988). *An Asperger Marriage.* London: Jessica Kingsley Publishers.

Small, T. (2004). "Letter to the Wall Street Journal." Schafer Autism Report, http://www.sarnet.org.

"Special Educational Needs and Disability Act." (2001). London: Queen's Printer of Acts of Parliament.

Stanberry, K. (2004). "The Individual Transition Plan: An Overview." Schwab Learning, http://www.SchwabLearning.org.

Stehli, A. (1991). *The Sound of a Miracle.* New York: Avon Books.

Stengle, L. J. (1996). *Laying Community Foundations for Your Child with a Disability: How to Establish Relationships That Will Support Your Child after You're Gone.* Bethesda, MD: Woodbine House.

Sullivan, R. (2001). "Position Paper on the National Crisis in Adult Services for Individuals with Autism: A Call to Action." San Diego, CA: Autism Society of America.

Sullivan, R. C. (2004). "Lifetime Services for Individuals with Autism: A Working, Community-Integrated Model." Trainland website: http://trainland.tripod.com/ruthchrist.htm.

Szatmari, P. (2003). "The Causes of Autism Spectrum Disorders: Multiple Factors Have Been Identified, but a Unifying Cascade of Events Is Still Elusive." *BMJ* 326:173–74.

Tantam, D., and S. Prestwood. (1999). *A Mind of One's Own: A Guide to the Special Difficulties and Needs of the More Able Person with Autism or Asperger Syndrome.* London: The National Autistic Society.

"Timetable for Autism: An Overview of Educating Children and Young People with Autistic Spectrum Disorders." (1999). London: The National Autistic Society.

UK Joint Committee for Vaccination and Immunization. "The British National Vaccination Schedule." Fit for Travel website, http://www.fitfortravel.scot.nhs.uk/General/british=_national=_vaccination.html (January 22, 2003).

U.S. Department of Education. (2002). "Executive Summary: Twenty-fourth Annual Report to Congress on the Implementation of the Individuals with Disabilities Education Act." U.S. Department of Education, http://www.ed.gov.

Vatter, G. "Group Homes and Other Alternatives." Autism Community for people w/autism, www.geocities.com/Heartland/Woods2869/alternatives.html.

Vermeulen, P. (2000). *I Am Special: Introducing Children and Young People to Their Autism Spectrum Disorder.* London: Jessica Kingsley Publishers.

Verstraeten, T. (2003). "Safety of Thimerosal-Containing Vaccines: A Two-Phased Study of Computerized Health Maintenance Organization Databases." *Pediatrics,* 112(5).

Wakefield, A. (1998). "Ileo-colonic Lymponodular Hyperplasia, Non-specific Colitis and Autistic Spectrum Disorder in Children: A New Syndrome?" University of Sunderland Autism Research Unit, http://osiris.sunderland.ac.uk/autism/vaccine.html (January 18, 2003).

Wallace, T. (2003). "Paraprofessionals." Gainesville: University of Florida, Center on Personnel Studies in Special Education.

Waller, E. (2001). "Gerontology 130: Working with the Frail: Lesson Twelve: Understanding Grief." Coastline Community College, http://www.cvc3.org/modelcvc3 courses/elliswaller/lesson12.htm (September 8, 2002).

Waltz, M. (2002). *Autistic Spectrum Disorders: Understanding the Diagnosis and Getting Help.* Sebastopol, CA: O'Reilly and Associates.

Wehman, P. (2001). *Life Beyond the Classroom: Transition Strategies for Young People with Disabilities.* Baltimore, MD: Paul H. Brookes Publishing Co.

Weldon, D. (2004). Speech given on the mercury-vaccine-autism controversy before the Institute of Medicine. February 9.

"What Is Autism? Genetic Conditions Associated with Autistic Disorder." Exploring Autism website, http://www.exploringautism.org/autism/evaluation/html (November 4, 2002).

Willey, L. H. (1999). *Pretending to Be Normal: Living with Asperger's Syndrome*. London: Jessica Kingsley Publishers.

———. (2001). *Asperger Syndrome in the Family: Redefining Normal*. London: Jessica Kingsley Publishers.

Williams, D. (1988). *Autism: An Inside-Out Approach*. London: Jessica Kingsley Publishers.

———. (1992). *Nobody Nowhere*. New York: Times Books.

———. (1994). *Somebody Somewhere*. London: Transworld Publishers Ltd.

Wing, L. *Asperger Syndrome: A Clinical Account*. London: The National Autistic Society.

———. (2001). *The Autistic Spectrum*. London: Ulysses Press.

Wright, P., and P. D. Wright. (2001). *Wrightslaw: From Emotions to Advocacy—The Special Education Survival Guide*. Hartfield, VA: Harbor House Law Press.

Wright, P. W. D., and P. D. Wright. (2002). *Wrightslaw: Special Education Law*. Hartfield, VA: Harbor House Law Press.

Yeargin-Allsopp, M., C. Rice, T. Karapurkan, N. Doernberg, C. Boyle, and C. Murphy. (2003). "Prevalence of Autism in a US Metropolitan Area." *Journal of the American Medical Association* 289:49–55.

INDEX

About the Author

Chantal Sicile-Kira has been involved with autism spectrum disorders (ASDs) for nearly twenty years, first as a professional and then as a parent. She worked for a California State Developmental Center, as well as a Regional Center for the Developmentally Disabled, and served for six years on the Community Advisory Committee to her Local Special Education Planning Area (SELPA). She is a frequent speaker to professional and parent organizations, as well as service providers on ASDs, special education, advocacy, and disability awareness. She develops training materials and regularly presents workshops on parenting strategies for empowerment. She worked for many years in film and video production in Europe.

The UK edition of Chantal's book, *Autism Spectrum Disorders: The Complete Guide*, was the recipient of the 2003 San Diego Book Award for Best Health Book.

Chantal is active in several nonprofit organizations, including the Cure Autism Now Foundation (CAN), Helping Autism through Learning and Outreach (HALO), and the Autism Society of America (ASA).

A regular visitor to the East Coast and France, Chantal lives in San Diego with her husband and two children. With the help of her son, she continues to train college students to be future autism professionals.

Visit her website at www.chantalsicile-kira.com.